ADVANCE PRAISE FOR PACKING INFERNO

Packing Inferno is a wonderfully written, deeply passionate account of one man's journey to the "Foyer to Hell," as Tyler Boudreau describes war. Tyler draws the reader into the subtleties of his "everyman" tale of conflict until it is too late, and we are trapped in a journey up the Euphrates River valley, a Mesopotamian *Heart of Darkness* which leads us straight into Dante's Ninth Circle of Hell, a place reserved for traitors.

It is here, in the unmaking of a Marine, that it becomes clear that Tyler Boudreau has jumped from the Foyer to Hell into Hell itself. Denied the brotherhood of the Corps which sustained him for so long, Boudreau must navigate his own way out of Hell, a journey upon which he is still embarked. This is what makes *Packing Inferno* so heartbreaking, because the reader knows that Tyler Boudreau has taken them on a journey which has no end. And while the reader in some way becomes trapped along with Tyler by reading *Packing Inferno*, we are traitors to humanity if we don't.

Scott Ritter
Former Major, United States Marine Corps,
and Chief Weapons Inspector in Iraq, 1991-1998

* * *

Eloquent, impassioned, written in the moments, written after, before, and around the moments, dripping with the blood of pain and seeking the blood of breathing, Boudreau has written from the zones of war under the guns and from the zones of war beyond the guns and from the zones of war in our hearts and minds — and in our memories and agendas — and he hasn't just written from those realms, about the culture, the training, the killing, the being killed, the coming home and not being home, he has displayed it all, dissected it all, unmercifully and mercifully relived and explored it all. Only a human ostrich can avoid these truths — don't be one. Read this.

Michael Albert
Co-editor of *ZNet* and co-founder of *Z Magazine* and *South End Press*

* * *

Tyler Boudreau has written a different war story which chronicles his journey of conscience. His feat is to survive the inferno of relentless anger to reach an understanding of what war entails. His is also an investigation into the morality of war, with all its quagmires and self-justifications. Soldiers must come to terms with their war to truly survive it, and Boudreau offers great insight into the hurdles facing returning veterans as well as advice for those who would help them.

Elise Tripp
Author of *Surviving Iraq: Soldiers' Stories*

* * *

What do you get when you combine *The Things They Carried* and *Dispatches* with the unblinking, crystalline style of Friedrich Nietzsche? You get *Packing Inferno*.

Boudreau has a gift for vivid scene and narrative pace, and brings those together with something very rare: an unblinking sight of what's right and what's not in this war, in his Marines, and in himself. There is a clarity in his words that will not leave you alone.

Jonathan Shay, MD, PhD
Author of *Achilles in Vietnam* and *Odysseus in America*, MacArthur Fellow

* * *

This book is angry and funny and insightful, about war and those whom war envelopes. It will bring knowing nods of recognition from veterans; it may shock others. To all of us, Tyler Boudreau offers a profound gift: the moral clarity we need to welcome the warriors back home.

David Bowne Wood
National Security Correspondent, *The Baltimore Sun*
Author of *A Sense of Values: American Marines in an Uncertain World*

* * *

Packing Inferno represents an extraordinary meditation on the lethal contradictions of war and a grunts-eye view of the debacle in Iraq. Tyler Boudreau is that rare creature: a literate observer of the absurdities and tragedies of modern combat (American-style), and a no-holds-barred participant in the carnage of Iraqi urban warfare. Forget the high-falutin' tomes on America's mission in Iraq; this book really explains why the U.S. strategy was doomed to failure.

Michael T. Klare
Author of *Rising Powers, Shrinking Planet: The New Geopolitics of Energy*

PACKING
INFERNO
THE UNMAKING OF A MARINE

PACKING INFERNO

THE UNMAKING OF A MARINE
TYLER E. BOUDREAU

FERAL HOUSE

ISBN: 978-1-932595

Feral House
1240 W. Sims Way Suite 124
Port Townsend, WA 98368

www.FeralHouse.com

10 9 8 7 6 5 4 3 2 1

AUTHOR'S NOTE

I would like to briefly address a few issues of terminology. The first has to do with how I refer to members of America's armed forces. In the Marine Corps, we always capitalized the word "Marines" whether we were referring to the whole organization or just a few individuals. It was a gesture of respect. I will pay the same respect in this book. I will also extend that courtesy to "Soldiers" any time I am specifically referring to members of the United States Army. In many cases, I describe the actions of members in my unit; when I do, I'll refer to those people as Marines. However, when I move into a more general discussion of war or when I am describing circumstances that affected all service members in Iraq, not just those in the Corps, I will use the generic term "soldier" with a lower-case "s".

The second issue of terminology involves the antiquated term, "Post-Traumatic Stress Disorder" (PTSD). While the Diagnostic and Statistical Manual (DSM) still uses this term, it is widely rejected by those who work in the field of mental health. I reject it too. I discuss this issue more fully in the book, but I felt it was necessary to declare my position on this from the outset. I do not consider the psychological struggle of returning veterans a "disorder" and so I will only refer to this *injury* as "combat stress" or "post-traumatic stress".

Finally, there is the issue of gender to consider. When my wife picked up this book for the first time, she said to me, "Your book is all about men. But there are women in Iraq too—women Soldiers and Marines, women commanders, women heroes, and women casualties. Where are they?" My wife is a veteran herself, so this is just the sort of thing that she would notice.

There are women in the military, I know, and there were women in Iraq when I was there. They were fighting, dying, and surviving, just like the men. They were courageous, they were decorated, and they were wounded and killed just like the men, too. Yet the reader will find that I use the masculine pronouns such as "he" almost exclusively when referring to soldiers. It's not because I'm unaware of women's service. I am aware. But in my twelve and a half years in the Corps, I never served with one of them. I was always in the infantry, where only men are permitted by law. Men I understand. My life has been spent almost entirely in that world, and so in this book that is who I talk about.

What I do not understand fully, is how women look upon the war in Iraq, or any other war, when they fight amongst so many men. Virginia Woolf described war as a male endeavor, observing that, "Scarcely a human being in history has fallen to a woman's rifle." That appears to be less true with every passing decade, and I'm not sure whether I should pay tribute to this step toward equality or simply mourn the entire human race.

PREFACE

PACKING INFERNO

Before I left for Iraq, I went to a bookcase in my house, pulled open my sea-bag, and started jamming books inside. I stuffed them wherever I could find a nook amongst all my combat gear. I had a list of titles that I wanted to bring along with me. There were a lot of them. Somehow I got it in my head I was going to have time to read. When I finished, my sea-bag weighed a ton like I was packing a corpse. When I finally arrived in Kuwait, I opened my sea-bag for the first time since I'd left home and discovered at the top of the heap a copy of Dante's *Inferno*. That was strange because I had no recollection of packing it. It wasn't on my list. I wasn't planning to read it. But there it was in my hands, on the outskirts of war. So I shrugged to myself, "They say war is hell," and I opened it up and began to read.

As I traveled with Dante and Virgil down through the circles of Hell, I noticed curious similarities emerging between the conditions of Dante's underworld and the battlefield which I was traversing. The heat grew more intense as summer approached, the danger more severe. There was death, and blood, and hypocrisy, and as much "sin" in one place as I'd ever witnessed. But it was more than all that. I saw the struggle in humanity, and in the heart; I saw the political strife, the regret, and the rage, and the hardship, even the characters—I saw them all in both the battlefield and the book. Our journeys were so similar, that I was compelled to take note physically. And so this story of *Packing Inferno* was conceived under fire, and I began writing it in Iraq with the war raging around me. When I got home, I found the war was still raging, but it was not outside me anymore, not to touch, or to see, or to hear, or to smell. It was within me. I was no longer packing Inferno in my sea-bag, but in my head.

I am still packing *Inferno*—in the day or the night, in my sleep, in my dreams, in my thoughts, in the midst of a sentence, in the blink of an eye, I am always packing *Inferno*. My wife will sometimes catch a shift in my eyes, while we're talking about groceries, or the kids' school, or the weather, and she'll ask me, "What are you thinking about?" She can see I've drifted off. But she doesn't need me to answer, because she knows, and because the answer is always the same. And the answer will remain forever the same, while I am alive, as long as I am packing *Inferno*.

Midway along the journey of our life
I woke to find myself in a dark wood,
For I had wandered off the straight path.

How hard it is to tell what it was like,
This wood of wilderness, savage and stubborn
(the thought of it brings back all my old fears),

A bitter place! Death could scarce be bitterer.
But if I would show the good that came of it
I must talk about things other than good.

All hope abandon ye who enter here.

—*Dante Alighieri*

FOYER TO HELL

They say war is hell. But I say it ain't. War is the foyer to hell. The journey home from war is the threshold between a killing order and a peaceful chaos, between the rational and the distorted. Those few hours on the plane are the last of a crystalline euphoria a soldier will know before he steps across the river for good. It was in the passage through Anchorage that I believed I was coming home. But just like war ain't hell, home ain't a point on the map—it's a point of view; it's an attitude, and the origin of all my points had broken from the mainland. I had no anchorage anymore. My attitude was like a cooked egg—permanently altered. My basis was adrift. I had completed the unmaking of myself. I just didn't know it yet. From the very instant my foot touched the American tarmac, I began my descent.

When all this talk of war was just academic back in 2003, I mulled it over with a friend of mine down on the Depot (The Marine Corps Recruit Depot—where I was stationed during 9/11 and the invasion of Iraq). I said to my friend, "What do you think about all this pre-emption business?"

And he said, "Man, don't sweat that shit. That's a question for the politicians. That's their show. You and me? We get paid to lead Marines and win battles. So when our time comes, that's what we'll do." Then he said, "Besides, Saddam Hussein was a bad egg. He needed to go."

Now I'm a natural cynic, not one to take anyone's word on anything. So I harbored some doubts, but then three things came to mind. The first was an old Gunny who used to work with me. I asked him one day how he felt about going to war.

He said to me, "My mama asked me that same question. She said, 'You been collecting a check from the man for sixteen years, and all that time you been telling him that if ever there's a war, you gonna go. Now what are you gonna do when a war finally does come along? You gonna make good on that word? Or are you gonna turn your back on him with that pocket full of jack you got?'" Gunny said, "I been paid. Now I gotta go." And I knew just what he meant because I'd been paid too.

The second thing that came to mind is something I always told myself. I always said that war was a reality. The politicians might be corrupt. The causes might be bullshit. But the wars aren't going away. And so long as there are wars, there are going to be young Marines sent off to die in them, and as long as that's the case, they're going to need someone to lead them home. So that's what I aimed to do. That was my cause.

The last thing wasn't really a thought. It wasn't a saying or a point of view. It was more like a condition or a state of mind. I called it lust—a lust for war.

It wasn't an interest in the political particulars of this war or that war, just a craving for the battle itself. I was a career Marine infantryman. I was out there training for combat, training for years, training to kill.

How long can you pretend to gouge eyeballs before you can't wait to do it for real—to see the thing dangling from its socket? How many times can you run the rounded edge of a bayonet across a man's throat before you crave the sound of a desperate gasp that comes only from the other side of that blade? How many shots down range can you send into dummies before you find yourself wishing the dummies would bleed? How many stories about fucking Nam can you hear before you go looking for your own war, before you start needing to live the stories that someone else can revere?

William James said, "Modern man inherits all the innate pugnacity and all the love of glory of his ancestors. Showing war's irrationality and horror is of no effect on him. The horrors make the fascination." And I know, if I am representative of the modern man, this is true. I have certainly owned my share of the fascination.

On the other hand, Douglas MacArthur asserted that, "The soldier above all others prays for peace, for it is the soldier who must suffer and bear the deepest wounds and scars of war." Well, I'm not so sure about that, because I find more resonance in the words of William James. For as long as I have been a soldier—that is, a man who might suffer and bear the deepest wounds and scars should my country enter war—I have always loved, really cherished, the novels, and the films, and the epics of war. The more brutal and tragic they have been, the more stark, the more realistic, the more heartbreaking, the more anti-war, the more I have loved them, and the more I prayed for my own war.

After a decade in the Corps, my prayers were finally answered. First it was 9/11, then al Qaeda, and then it was Saddam Hussein and Weapons of Mass Destruction. As far as I was concerned, that was enough. Nobody had to ask me twice. I saw the writing on the wall—the big letters H-E-L-L—just as clearly as I saw the letters spray-painted across that jersey barrier at the border, I-R-A-Q. The sign said, "Beware." I knew the deal, and I knew the way home. But when the beasts that lurk inside a warrior start to howl, there are no real choices. And there is only one path to take. We all knew that. Going to war wasn't an option, anymore than coming home was. I called them "orders" when the plan started to stray, but they never ordered me to do any damn thing my heart wasn't yearning for. So I strapped it on, locked and loaded, and I went.

The foyer was hot as hell, so I started thinking of it as hell. Then a couple of contractors—mercenaries really—were burned and dangled upside down from a bridge in Fallujah above a cheering crowd of Iraqis. That's when I knew this thing must be hell. And shit, that's what everybody'd always called it back home. But where was the misery? For a place called hell, we seemed to be in short supply. I'm not talking about discomfort here. There was plenty of that. We shed all the blood and sweat we could ever hope to and still survive. We had the hunger going on, and the filth, and the fatigue. We had the red spackled bodies, the severed limbs, the guts and the gore. We had all that.

And there was no dearth of longing for home either. The Internet cafés and phone centers brandished lines of troops three and four hours long. Guys bought contraband porn and crystal meth from Iraqi children and slipped into their private galaxies whenever a couple of extra minutes turned up. So yeah, it had kind of a hellish hue about it. But the misery—the kind of misery where a guy wants to peel back the skin on his own face just so he doesn't have to look at it in the mirror anymore, the kind of misery where a bullet hole in the head seems like a logical means of egress from all those hairy dreams—that kind of misery was nowhere to be found. War wasn't that bad.

In fact, the ironies of war so humorously recalled, like Marines surrendering their cuticle scissors while boarding the plane for Iraq with rifles and machine-guns slung over their shoulders, seem mostly to originate from *outside* the boundaries of the battle itself. Irony tends to plague those wars especially rife with political ambiguity. That set the stage in Iraq for some pretty ironic situations.

One month in theater (April of '04), and we were asked to leave our area of operations where we'd been getting shelled and IED'd like beetles in a jar to participate in the attack on Fallujah. The operation would be ten times more dangerous than the tedious missions we'd been doing. The casualties would be sky-high. Actually, when you're that close to a fight—a big fight, one where a lot of guys are going to get killed—the word "casualties" just doesn't work anymore. It doesn't sound right. Dead. Burned. Fragged. Ripped to fucking shreds. Those are words that better capture the moment. And yet, we were never happier. And when the siege was lifted and the attack called off, we were never more devastated.

Where in hell was the misery? When the aircraft that carried us from Iraq to the U.S. finally pulled to a stop at Cherry Point, NC, and the flight attendant mumbled over the PA, "Welcome home," I leaned back and smiled to myself. "No more of that fucking heat." But I was almost immediately stunned as I stepped out onto the flight line and felt that Carolina humidity slap me in my smug face.

Nobody was looking for misery. We were scanning the crowds of relieved parents, and cheering girlfriends, and crying wives with four and five screaming kids in tow. We were searching the mob for our own loved ones. I didn't anticipate that drop of sweat trickling into my eye. I didn't see the burn coming. But it came nevertheless. It was the first burn we'd feel as we traipsed blithely into the valley of the aftermath. Our bodies had been delivered from war, but our minds lingered on the battlefield. The intensity, the quick-release on our adrenaline, was hidden behind dull eyes and broad smiles. Nobody knew what was coming. Nobody wanted to know. The Marines and the civilians collided into a barrage of hugs and kisses. The civilians were the same as they always were, but the Marines they hugged and kissed were not the men they had once known. The consciousness of every man in that unit had been reconfigured. Our identities were altered.

I saw my wife and my boys waiting for me, and a few tears welled up and washed away the pain—for a while. The sight of her was asphyxiating. I can't put words to it without some damned cliché. I was choking on relief, but all the while lacking any true understanding of where or who I was. For the moment, all that meant nothing to me. For the moment, I felt good. I thought I'd finally reached normal. But normal, I would soon discover, was out of reach indefinitely. Normal is war, and war ain't hell. War is the foyer to hell.

PAIN JUNKIE

"What do you think about this war?" people always ask me, almost as often as I ask myself. And I've stewed it in a crock pot of sleepless nights a thousand times over, and it always comes out the same—a crock pot of shitty stew. What is the war to me, and who am I to the war? How do I talk about this thing? And who is going to listen?

When I was a kid, I watched an ad for a set of Vietnam history books. A guy—a vet—came on and relayed his story about coming home. He said, "I got into a cab and told the driver, 'I just got back from Vietnam' and the driver said, 'So?'" After Iraq, I came home and got that same line, but instead of straight-up not giving a rat's ass, people would give me this glassy-eyed smile and say shit like, "Wow man."

So I got the picture real fast. If my story wasn't tragic, if it didn't make 'em cry, or if it didn't yank 'em to the edge of their seats, or get a big laugh, nobody wanted to hear it. They didn't want to hear the dry particulars. They wanted high-speed adventure and witty heroes who escaped death by the skins of their teeth and saved the day in the end.

Well, I'm not a hero and I don't have that kind of story to tell. But I thought: *I'm a writer goddamn it!* (I call myself a writer like a guy who drinks too much calls himself an alcoholic. It's more of a habit than a profession.) So I said to myself, I can come up with something. I mean shit, I just went through a war. There's got to be a tale to tell somewhere in all that carnage.

Men slaying men in war is nothing new. So what's my angle going to be? It's got to be sexy. It's got to have a hook. Otherwise it's not going to be worth jack-shit. If only I was a poet and I had that gift. But I don't. I'm just a grunt who made a few observations that might be of some use to the folks back home.

My trouble was, when I got back home I couldn't get past the headlines. I was soaking up all the bad news like a pressure dressing. I wasn't sleeping, so I'd drive into the office at one or two in the morning and read articles until dawn. I had an addiction to the bad news. I craved all the death. I took hits of the bullshit that gushed from every pore in the media. But I didn't do it because it made me feel good, or even better. I did it because it deepened my pain, and I found that, ultimately, I liked the pain. I was a junkie. I studied the doctrine, the history, the tactics—all of it to keep my mind in Iraq. The night watch would duck in with a curious look on his face and ask me, "What are you doing here at this hour?" And I'd answer casually, "Just reading up on the war." I was a rifle company commander, preparing a hundred and fifty Marines to go back to Iraq and fight, so getting ahead on my reading wasn't all that strange. It was normal, to him…and to me. Normal.

I was writing at the time, too. I was writing constantly, and I'd look over what I'd done and I'd congratulate myself, "This is some powerful shit." The trouble was, it was only powerful to me. To everyone else, it was just a downer. I was pissed because I didn't have any of those death-defying war stories. I got into a few scrapes, but not the cliffhanger stuff. Not the shit that sells. On the other hand, I got a pretty good look at the war in my job. In Iraq, I was the assistant operations officer for an infantry battalion, which meant I was there for the planning, and then I watched the plan unfold on the ground from above. It wasn't glamorous by military standards, but it was a good place to be to understand how we were fighting the war.

DIAGNOSIS: NORMAL

I'm hemmed into the night. My brain has come to prefer the darkness. I can't say with any certainty if this is a product of never sleeping—that is, if it's just a bad habit I've got to break—or if there's something else going on, like the systematic avoidance of those bloody dreams. I told the doc I wasn't sleeping when I got home, and he glanced casually from his desk and said, "That's normal. It'll pass."

Normal, he said. When I told him I was just about jumping out of my skin every time I heard a loud noise, he said that was normal, too. Normal, as in commonplace, as opposed to, say, pathological, like it would have been abnormal not to jump out of my skin. It's what they expected from me. They figured I was in good working order, I guess.

Then they blew off my rage with the same line. "Everybody's got that," they said. I wonder if they'd call me normal now, with all that I've got to say. Three years later, my heart was still pounding, I was still raging, and I still wasn't sleeping. I was up, thinking about the war. I finally told myself it's like a bad back or a trick knee; you just learn to live with it and you walk on. So as I'm walking on, night after night, when the darkness has fallen, and the rest of the world is silent, I go looking for my narrative.

The Marine Corps made a schizophrenic out of me, figuratively speaking. I used to have only one voice, one point of view. All right, so I've got a new perspective now. It happens. But it's not like I just changed my mind. My mind changed. It split, two, and three, and four ways over. Now there are voices coming at me from all sides. There's no coherence to them, and no clear distinction either. There's the angry voice, and there's the broken-hearted one. There is the tender me and the savage. And of course, there is the Marine. There will always be the Marine, standing tall inside me, speaking smartly about values and patriotism. Then there's all the rest of me, the part of me that was left over when I left the Corps. He has no name, no identity, or credentials, or skills. He has no title or rank. He has no cause. He is just me in the wake of battle.

How could I have gotten it so wrong? How did I manage to evade those tough questions for so long? I signed an enlistment contract when I was seventeen years old. I went to war when I was thirty-three. That gave me sixteen years to think this shit over. I'd read a few books. It's not like I didn't know the deal. It's not like I hadn't heard about the grotesque deterioration of humanity on the battlefield. It's not like I didn't know that soldiers would be spent in war like loose change by powerful men. I knew. From the beginning, I knew.

My high school mandated that every student watch the movie *Gallipoli*, which might be among the more tragic of the tragic war movies. No doubt, they were trying to steer us away from the glamorous call to arms that lurked in our hallways donning dress blues and blazing medals. I loved that movie. I went back and watched it a dozen more times. I even bought it. I remember in the movie the makeshift sign at the deadly opening to the trench which read: "Abandon hope, beyond this point." But I didn't abandon hope, and I wasn't repelled by war. I became infatuated with it. I had a love affair with tragedy.

And then I fell in love with the Corps. *Semper Fidelis*—that's their motto—*Always Faithful*. For a kid coming from a broken home, that meant a hell of a lot. They could have said, "Always the first to go," or "Always in the shit," or "Always kicking ass" —though I'm not sure what that would have looked like in Latin. They could have come up with something like that, something bad-ass, something potent and for the ages.

But no. They chose, as the most crucial element of being a United States Marine: *Loyalty*. They said, above all, we're never, never going to leave your ass behind. I was hooked…by that, and by their reputation for being the meanest, roughest, toughest, hardest motherfuckers in the world. That's what I wanted. I wanted to be among those who said, "My loyalty dies only when I die." And I wanted to be a hard motherfucker. The Marine Corps promised me both.

BRAIN DAMAGE

I grew up working at a truck tire joint in Boston. It was a tough spot, in the tough part of town. The guys used to say you didn't work there—you served. And when you quit, or were fired, or hauled off to jail, deported, overdosed, or shot, your name would be commemorated on "The Wall." There was no real wall. The Wall was made up in our minds, kind of a joke, but it was real in the sense that we'd experienced something that struck all of us as surreal.

It wasn't war, but there were some commonalities beneath the surface. There was hierarchy, and exploitation, and manipulation. No question, there was all that. And there was desperation. There was suffering—especially when the cold months came around. There was racism. There was the clash of morality and immorality that left the shop ever-imbued with strife. There was the constant awareness of survival, and how close a man was to the edge of it when he worked there.

There was a lot of dark humor going around, the dark humor one picks up in dark places. And there was a bond too, like we were all in this shit together. There was a visceral feeling that life didn't get any better than this, which is why we used to say, "Nobody ever works here just once." We all tried our hand at quitting. But sooner or later, we all came crawling back. So above all, there was the dream of getting out. Everyone shared in that.

Sometimes I rode with a guy who called himself "Brain Damage" or "B.D." for short. He got hit in the head with a piece of flying steel. The doctor told him the blow should have left him with brain damage, hence his new name. He drove an old, beat-up Ranchero, which he called his "Lincoln with a flatbed." He stenciled onto his jacket BMFIC: Bad Mother Fucker in Charge. He shaved off the left side of his beard, and said to anyone in life who tried to tell him what to do, "You don't sign my God damn paycheck!" Brain Damage would do hits of heroin before we'd go out on road jobs, and then he'd pull over on the way and ask passersby what time the ten o'clock train was leaving—just for laughs.

I don't know. I think maybe the doctor got it wrong. Maybe he really did have brain damage. But I rode with him, and we had to talk about something. So I asked him one day, "How do you become a Marine?" I was fifteen or sixteen at the time. He said, "They only take football players—corn fed fuckers with twenty inch necks. They'd never take you." That did it. If Brain Damage, of all people, said I couldn't make it, then I was damn sure going to make it. I was determined.

BUSTED INTO THE GRUNTS

It took some looking, but I finally found a recruiter's office and wandered in.

"How old are you, kid?" the recruiter asked me.

"Sixteen," I admitted.

He laughed me out the door and roared after me, "Come back in a year."

I did go back in a year—to the day. I reserved a deep suspicion for recruiters when I was in high school. I'm not sure who taught me to feel that way, but it stuck. So when I went back to the recruiter's office to sign up, I watched his every move with narrowed eyes, like he was playing a shell game.

I marched in and announced, "I wanna be a grunt, that's it."

And he said, "No problem."

But still my suspicion lingered. When I went down to the processing building in Boston to sign my enlistment contract, I packed my suspicion right along with me. The enlistment contract is similar in many ways to a mortgage agreement: a lot of pages, a lot of fine print, most of it describing the consequences should the undersigned default on his or her end of the bargain. These are the sections most people tended to gloss over. I didn't gloss. I scrutinized every line with my eyes two inches from the page, unconcerned by the long line of recruits behind me, all waiting impatiently for their turns to sign their lives away, or by the irritable Gunnery Sergeant sitting in front of me, growing more irritable every minute.

The Gunny finally blurted at me, "Just sign the fucking thing!"

But I was stubborn and determined, so I shook my head and kept right on reading. Then something caught my eye. It's been a few years now, but the words went something like this: A Marine may lose his guaranteed Military Occupational Specialty (MOS) if he becomes the subject of disciplinary action.

"What's this?" I tapped the page dubiously.

The Gunny pulled the contract toward him, looked at it for a second, and then looked back up at me. "What's your MOS?"

"Oh-three" I said with pride. 0300 is the numerical designation in the Marine Corps for infantry. I hadn't even gone to bootcamp yet, and already I was basking in the glamour of being a grunt.

The Gunny laughed, "You idiot!" He shoved the contract back at me. "Nobody gets busted out of the grunts. They get busted *into* the grunts. Now sign the goddamn contract!" Contented by his answer, I signed.

When I was in the School of Infantry, I met just such an individual who got busted *into* the grunts. His name was Lorne and he was a former college football player. Lorne had a real proclivity for the beach—or maybe it was an addiction—which seemed to flare up every time he was supposed to be on duty. He was a guard at the Naval Academy in Annapolis (a desirable duty), but he went to the beach one too many times. So they busted him out, and sent him to be an Amphibious Assault Vehicle (AAV) driver. He did okay there for a while...but then he started going to the beach again.

So they busted him to us, the grunts, the bottom of the barrel, the end of the line. I liked Lorne a lot. He enjoyed working out and so did I, so we used to skip out of our clean-up duties to go to the gym. Lorne probably wasn't the best of influences, but I felt secure in the notion that no matter what happened, no matter how much trouble I might get in, nobody ever gets busted *out* of the grunts.

PURPLE HEART

Crossing over to war, or crossing back—I'm not sure which was more thrilling. To make that plane ride home is to have overcome war. It is to have made it through alive. And for that you get the solemn distinction, that enviable title of "combat veteran." There are men who seek the Combat Action Ribbon (CAR) more fervently than any other personal decoration.

It's true, because it means you've been in the shit—at least that's what it's supposed to mean. The intent was clear enough. A Marine was supposed to have been in a fight, a direct fire fight, with bullets whizzing by, some guys getting shot at, and others shooting back. But then people started scratching their heads as Marines were getting shelled and IED'd, day in and out, without ever having fired their rifles. Could you really tell them they weren't in combat? A guy could have his legs blown off from an IED, but no Combat Action Ribbon. It didn't seem right.

Suddenly the meticulous criteria for a CAR became hazy. Suddenly it was a matter of dispute. So they loosened the regs. And then they loosened them a little more. The next thing we knew, CARs were getting doled out to anybody with the loosest affiliation to combat. To us grunts, that didn't seem right either. Purple Hearts, as a result, took on an interesting new importance. It let people know that you were in a *real* fight, a fight close enough to feel the heat, close enough to catch some lead. But then the credibility of the Purple Hearts started taking hits too.

There was a corpsman—a medic—in my company who was hit in the face with a piece of shrapnel from an IED. But not to worry, it was no bigger than a staple. He didn't even realize he'd been hit. I had to point it out to him. He pulled the tiny piece of steel out of his cheek, tossed it in the trash, and went back to work. For that, they gave him the Purple Heart.

I remember saying to the Colonel, "What's up with that?"

And the Colonel said, "You know something? A combat wound is a combat wound, no matter how small. So he gets the medal."

Ironically, at the very same time the '04 Presidential elections were in progress. I remember watching Bob Dole on television commenting that John Kerry was a fraud because Kerry's Purple Hearts weren't for any real wounds—not the life-threatening wounds that Dole had suffered. Then, at the Republican convention, to further ridicule Kerry, they handed out little purple band-aids and called them "Purple Owies."

As I watched all this unfolding from Iraq, I couldn't help but wonder if these people would have had the audacity to put a picture up on the screen of our corpsman—serving in Iraq—and, in front of America, call him a fraud. I suspected not. But of course you can't have it both ways. Either both men were frauds, or neither of them were.

It was all politics and cheap shots. I knew that. But at the same time, I think it was more. Those cheap shots came at a price. Suddenly people were cornered into having to decide which wounded were worth caring for, and which were not. Suddenly every veteran with a Purple Heart was judged by his or her wounds, instead of being unhesitatingly treated for them. What I learned in Iraq from my own reaction and from the reaction I witnessed on television is that the act of privileging one wound over another, the mere distinction, creates a fissure in the consciousness, through which our humanity begins to slip away. That was the price we paid for those cheap shots. They were not so cheap, I think.

THE INVISIBLE WOUNDED

When I got home I heard people talking about post-traumatic stress. "There's going to be a lot of it," a Vietnam vet said to me one day.

And I said, "I don't know. The guys seem to be holding up okay."

And he said, "Wait a while."

To be honest, I didn't believe him at first. I figured I knew better than him. I was a rifle company commander. I didn't want to believe. No, it was more than that. I didn't have the capacity to believe—not in that role. To believe that there could be psychological injuries sustained from the violence we inflicted would be to acknowledge its inherent immorality. A commander must never go walking into that moral field of fire, for he will surely fall. So I traversed around my own conscience and denied the existence of remorse.

I guess I took a wrong turn. Because I found myself smack-dab in the middle of that damned field, where I'd explicitly tried not to go, and just as I suspected, I fell flat on my face. I saw all the Marines around me who were distraught by the things they'd done and taken part in. I read in the newspapers about incident after incident of veterans around the country who had come home and committed suicide, for what I can only assume was an inability to further reconcile their deeds in war with their sense of morality. There were thousands of them.

They were wounded, deeply, but their wounds were invisible, and therefore easily missed. I saw all the officers around me nod sympathetically. They shed tears, just as I did. They cared, just as I did. But in the end, they all went back to work, and I couldn't. I had to give up my company and resign my commission.

What gives? I thought. How do they go back to work, back to war, knowing of the wounds to a man's soul that war inflicts? But they did, nonetheless, and the denial of remorse went on and on. It goes on still. And consequently these veterans with invisible wounds became, by default, antagonists to their own country. They were swiftly cut loose and left to fester in isolation. Small wonder so many suicides occurred.

They said a combat wound is a combat wound, no matter how small, and that every last one rates the Purple Heart. Yet never once has a veteran been awarded the Purple Heart for combat stress. Never once. Perhaps that small token of recognition might have prevented a few of them from taking their own lives. Only through genuine acknowledgment that combat stress is an injury, not a disorder, can we ever give uninhibited affection to our wounded.

THE JOURNEY FROM CHERRY POINT (MARCH 1, 2004)

We almost didn't fly out that day. We had a great big jumbo jet waiting for us, the airborne equivalent of a luxury liner, and the damned thing was broken down. They toiled with it for half a day, while we waited and waited for "the word." The Marines, as they are so prone to do, curled and stretched their bodies across every surface of the hangar floor and slept. When even that did not kill enough time for the struggling mechanics to get our plane running, the Marines woke up and started thinking about chow.

Nobody expected to be around long enough to worry about dinner, so nobody brought anything to eat. And now we had a few hundred hungry, well-rested Marines on our hands (never a good thing), so a creative remedy had to be thought up fast. The remedy, it turned out, was right in front of our faces, and it was as obvious as a jumbo jet. We filed onto the disabled 747 and sat down to dinner. We got hot towels and meals brought to us by a conspicuously irritable flight crew, who clearly would rather have been on their way to a motel for the night than serving us our in-flight beverages, while we sat idly on the tarmac.

When we were finished eating, we got back off the plane. Now, I've noticed in my life that, as one climbs into an elevator, there comes a particular expectation to emerge into a new place when the doors open again. I realized that night, that a very similar phenomenon occurs when exiting a plane. You expect to be somewhere new. So it was a little strange filing off the aircraft and finding the same old place waiting for us at the bottom of the steps. A back-up plane eventually arrived, and we gutted the old plane's belly of all our luggage and weaponry and fed it to the new one. Finally, some thirteen hours from our arrival to the air station that morning, we took off.

On our way to Kuwait, we touched down in Ireland for a beer. It was eight in the morning and I ordered a pint of Beamish, the last beer before war. That was the best damned stout I ever tasted. Then we flew through the night over the Alps. The sky was clear and I could see all the way down to the little clusters of yellow lights nestled low in the deep blue valleys between vast ranges of snow-covered mountains.

They really were breathtakingly immense. It was a marvelous sight. The lights were so small. The people were not even specks. They were only an idea from my vantage point. There was no way in, so far as I could tell, and there was no way out. It struck me as a magical and mysterious and wonderful place. That was their life, hidden out there in the mountains, and isolated, where they could only be seen from afar, as little glowing lights in the night, where their existence was but a cursory notion. And then we flew on.

I thought about that dark valley and suddenly the twinkle in my eye flickered out. That's us, I thought, the warriors. Down there. Isolated. Mysterious. That's war. We are indeed viewed only from above, from afar, as cursory notions. Our families, our dreams, our futures, our humanity, our lives are all but cursory notions to the people who click by us on their television sets back home and peer down upon us like little glowing lights, marveling at our beauty.

There would come a time when I would no longer relish the battle. But the isolation I grew to really love and to desperately need. I sometimes wish to be seen as those tiny people in the Alps, as only a glowing light in the distance. I sometimes wish to follow in the footsteps of the movie protagonist *Jeremiah Johnson*, the soldier who'd seen enough of "civilized" life and headed for the mountains. The cold is a good place to be when you want those kinds of things. It's a good excuse not to come out and look at the world. But the mountains and the cold were a long way off from where we were heading that night. It was the flat hot lands we were after.

The Kuwaiti floor was littered with dozens of inexplicable fires as we approached the airstrip, giving me the immediate impression that we were touching down on the outskirts of hell. By contrast, I never saw the world coming when I flew home. The windows were all closed. So were my eyes. Once we were in Kuwait, we filed into a dusty hangar and checked into theater. They sat us down for an after-school special styled instructional video on the hazards of combat life. It was a joke to us mostly, that anyone could show up to war so utterly ignorant that he might actually find this video informative. But then again, it really wasn't a joke.

The legend of the Marine Corps as a "force in readiness" has merit, but the myth comes at a price, and it's paid for in the lives of its own. Four months before my unit was in Iraq, we didn't even know we were going. Two-thirds of the Marines in the battalion were brand new to the Corps. They'd trained with us for less than two months, been in the military less than six. Every rifle company commander and most of the platoon commanders were new to the unit, and so was the Battalion Commander and his Executive Officer. I was new, too. But being new or inexperienced has never in history been a good enough excuse not to cross the line of departure. We always go, ready or not. And we go on time.

At the Marine Corps Recruit Depot, I used to remind every recruit I trained of the acronym GRUNT. Now it's a term of endearment for an infantryman. It's a title of distinction. But it wasn't always. It once stood for "Ground Replacements, UNTrained." That was in WWII, when the troops were dying so fast that whole units were wiped out at once. The GRUNTs were bundles of bodies that had received just enough training to obey orders. Many Marines who landed at Guadalcanal, for example, had never fired their weapons before they went into the attack. Their sergeants let them take one practice shot into the air before they went in. Those were the first "Grunts."

I warned my recruits that nobody would care if they trained hard or they didn't. Nobody cared if they knew their jobs well, if they studied, if they worked out, or if they just sat on their asses and didn't do shit. Nobody cared. "When the time comes to go," I told them, "your ass is going. Don't you ever forget that. And don't you ever believe that any politician, no matter what he or she says on TV, gives two hoots about your life. When they need the Marines, they're going to call us, and they sure ain't going to ask if we're ready." Watching that little video reminded me that little had changed.

After my tour in Iraq, on the bus ride from the air station to our base in North Carolina, I spent most of that time thinking about what it was going to be like to finally be home from war. There was a strange mix of melancholy and joy brewing inside me. I'd spent weeks in Iraq thinking about nothing but this day. It was going to be all about the sex, and the booze, and the big steak dinner. My wife sent me an electronic picture of our fridge stocked with beer. We made that picture our wallpaper on the computer monitors in Iraq, and we stared at it for weeks with watering mouths. But when I got home, I couldn't stomach half a bottle. I had no appetite for steak, or any damn thing else. I collapsed in bed after scarcely a kiss. And when I woke up, I thought about being back in Iraq.

On the bus ride out of Kuwaiti International Airport, when we first got in theater, war was all I wanted to think about. I tried to make sense of the massive craters scattered all over the sides of the roads among the carcasses of dead camels. I tried to figure out why our convoy guides had zipped ahead in their pickup trucks and disappeared into the horizon without a trace, leaving a half-dozen buses full of tenderfoot Marines to find their own way through the desert. It all seemed so inexplicable, but all I could think about was how badly I had to go to the bathroom.

It was a three-hour ride. So before we launched, everyone went off to the head to drain his bladder. Meanwhile, I was filling mine up with a two-liter bottle of Saudi Arabian spring water. My mind was elsewhere. Bottled water in war? I'd never heard of anything like it. That must be some kind of oasis, I thought dreamily, as I stared down the long rows of palletized bottles. A salty First Sergeant grumbled at me, "In my day, we used fucking canteens." These were the vital contemplations that edged out my memory to urinate before we left.

That was a costly mistake. After an hour riding over the bumpy highways, the pain began to really swell. My teeth were chattering. My fists were clenched. My eyes batted nervously. I thought my bladder was going to rupture right there in my seat. It was a brutal ride. Under normal circumstances, I would have just jumped off the bus and taken a leak on the side of the road. The opportunity did actually present itself. Our convoy pulled over at a lonely intersection and the Kuwaiti drivers gathered to confer. As they pointed their arms in various directions across the open desert, it became apparent we were lost. There were only two options: turn left or go straight. By the infinite look of both roads, it was clear that to choose either one represented a major commitment.

A few of us officers stepped off the bus to help them out. "Udari," we said with commanding tones (Udari was the name of our camp). The drivers shot a few perplexed glances at us and continued their discussion. "Udari," we persisted. "Udari, Udari, Udari!" We kept repeating ourselves, and raising our voices, and slowing our words the way Americans tend to do with foreigners who don't understand us.

"Udaaaaari," we mouthed dramatically as if caught in slow motion. One of the drivers repeated, "Udari?" and we burst into chant again. "Udari, Udari, Udari." It sounded like a sort of primitive invocation. Of course, we had no better idea how to get to Udari than they did, but repeating the destination seemed like a good idea at the time. Personally, I felt no tactical urgency to get to Udari quickly. My interest in getting them on track was entirely selfish. I just wanted to find a toilet.

While all this was going on, I certainly could have stepped behind the bus and relieved myself, and I wouldn't have been embarrassed to do so, except that I found myself inordinately worried about what the locals might think. It's true, there wasn't a house or a soul as far as they eye could see. But then again, we would, along our days in Iraq, find people emerging from some pretty remote spots. I didn't know that yet, but the possibility seemed to occur to me. My great concern about urinating was the direct result of a brief we'd been given before we deployed, where they thoroughly beat into us all the idiosyncrasies of Middle Eastern culture.

Don't show the soles of your feet, they warned us. *Don't touch them with your left hand. Don't refuse a cup of tea, but then don't accept a second one. Don't mention their women in conversation, don't look at the women, and for God's sake, don't put your hands on them. Don't wear sunglasses when you talk to them. Don't wear shoes in their houses. Don't beat them with sticks (they'd rather be shot).* These were the kinds of admonishments that flashed to mind and got me thinking that urinating on the side of the road might just fall into that long list of things that one can do to inadvertently insult a Muslim. So, in the interest of preserving America's good standing in the Middle East, I decided I'd better wait until we got to Camp Udari.

ABANDON ALL HOPE—YOU WHO ENTER HERE

Camp Udari, Kuwait. It was one of many American bases in the country that functioned as a waypoint for arriving troops. They would wait there over a number of days while their units trickled into the country on staggered flights from the United States. Once a unit was assembled, they would calibrate their weapons, draft their orders, and prepare for the journey north into Iraq. I squirmed in my seat as we pulled to a stop, and then staggered from the bus to the porta-johns. I moved like a man with cerebral palsy. They were scarcely fifty feet away. I almost didn't make it that far.

The porta-johns were lashed down with heavy cables so the high desert winds wouldn't sweep them away, but the doors slammed open and shut incessantly, like the beating of a requiem march played for the arrival of war's newest fodder. Finally, I made it to the porta-john. *Finally.* That short walk felt like an eternity. I threw open the door and leapt inside. The intense chemical stench and blistering heat that gathers inside those blue boxes hardly made an impression on me.

Taking a piss never felt so good. But then that's what war is—the domain of extremes. The best beer. The greatest piss. The highest high and the lowest low, the deepest joy, and the hottest rage, and the coldest hate, and the meanest fear, and the blackest blood, and the sickest shit, and the longest hours, and the most fucked up things a man could ever fathom. That was war.

When I finished, I burst from the porta-john like a new man. I had my chest out; I was ready for battle. It was at that moment, at Camp Udari, that I got my first taste of the violence of war. A muffled shot rang out, right there in Kuwait, right there at the porta-johns. Where? Why? How? I was already spinning in confusion. Suddenly, Marines from every direction swung around and started running toward me.

Actually, they were running toward the porta-john three doors down. A Marine in our battalion had locked himself inside and shot himself in the abdomen with his pistol. As they jimmied open the door and the wounded Marine spilled out onto the sand, I remember feeling distinctly unsympathetic. I looked around me, and it didn't appear that anybody else was too broken up about it either. They looked stoic, or annoyed, or they just smiled. I shook my head and said, "Why the fuck would a guy do that?"

The Marine next to me muttered back, "Fuckin' scared."

"Scared?" I said. "What the hell could he be scared about? What'd be scarier than getting shot in the stomach?"

And the Marine shrugged. "The unknown."

When I think about that young Marine now, turning a pistol on himself on the doorstep of war, I feel pity. But I surely didn't feel it then. I felt disgust. For the life of me, I can't figure out why. I've heard vets talk about this—this apathy toward death and violence. I've heard all kinds of explanations. But I'm not buying most of them. Because nobody put a gun to my head, or twisted my arm. I wasn't coerced. And I wasn't worried about what anybody thought about me. I wasn't trying to conform, or fit in. And I wasn't there for a lack of options. When I looked down at that bloody Marine, I genuinely didn't give a rat's ass. He was a traitor, or he was weak. Either way, he could rot in hell, as far as I was concerned. But that was then. Now I think he was just hopeless.

The Marine survived. Apparently, that had been his plan all along—he'd shot into his flank deliberately to avoid hitting his stomach. He didn't want to die, but evidently he couldn't live with himself in war. He was released from the battlefield, but he'd never be completely free from its wrath. His colon was obliterated, a wound the doctor promised would haunt him for the rest of his life.

A NEW DAMNED FLAG

Hopelessness. There's a lot of that going around among combat veterans after war, particularly the disabled ones. "What am I going to do without my arm?" a guy might say to himself. Or, "How am I going to live with these stumps

I've got for legs?" Or even, "How am I going to get out of this fucking head of mine? How am I going to crawl out of this skin?" At first, there's a lot of talk of overcoming—and some do—but after the story's been done in the local paper, after the popular interest in him starts to fade, the veteran finds the interest in himself starts to fade too. Hopelessness sets in.

When I first arrived to our base in Iraq, I met a Soldier whose head was covered with burn scars. His face was melted and warped. He'd been inside a humvee when it was hit by an RPG and engulfed in flames. It was a miracle he'd survived. But he was tough to look at. I was surprised to see him still in country.

Some of the other Soldiers said, with a real sense of pride, "He could have gone home, but he wanted to stay with us." I remember looking at the Soldier with furtive admiration after they told me that. I thought to myself, "Man, I wouldn't stick around after that." But a long time afterward, I looked back on that Soldier, after I'd come home and I gave some real thought to the place where veterans return, and I realized that there was more to that Soldier's decision to stay in Iraq than unit pride.

Sooner or later he'd have to come home, and when he did, that face of his would make him an outsider, no matter how heroic his actions, no matter how selfless. He could never just blend in and be left alone, like I've been so inclined to do. He would always stick out. He would be judged by his ugly face. His face would become a symbol of the ugliness of war, and people, however sympathetic, would be inclined to look away. In Iraq, that wouldn't be the case. There he was accepted—more than that—he was admired. He was a hero. He was loved.

From the Vietnam era, we were given the POW-MIA flag that flies on the flagpole of government facilities—in many cases by law—and a lot of other places, too. There's a white silhouette of a soldier depicted on the black flag. His head hangs low. Maybe he's hopeless, too. And the words below him are most powerful. They read: "You are not forgotten."

The POW camps were a staple of the Vietnam War. Everybody knew about them, and that black and white flag made sure nobody forgot. But Vietnam is over and those camps are long gone. We have a new war now with a new problem. The problem is our body armor—it's too damned good. It actually saves lives. Unfortunately, it doesn't save limbs and it doesn't save souls. So we get a hell of a lot more wounded than any other war has ever seen. That means there are a hell of a lot more disabled vets trudging through the blackness, hopeless and forgotten.

I say we need a new damned flag. We need a flag with that same downcast soldier and the same bold white letters reminding him and everyone else, "YOU ARE NOT FORGOTTEN!" I say, it's time to run the down the old

POW-MIA flag, and run up a new one. We will call it the WIA-KIA flag. We will let it fly and we will think of them. And we will say quietly and loudly, and until our hearts burst, "You are not forgotten. You are not forgotten."

VESTIBULE

Udari was loaded with reservists who never left. To us, the active-duty members, reservists were the uncommitted. They were the weekend warriors, the guys who didn't want to *man-up* and do the warrior thing full-time. And for their indecisiveness, they were activated and sent to places like Udari to rot and to be bitten by pestering Kuwaiti flies, and to linger outside the boundaries of war, never dumped into the hot core of it, but not allowed to go home either. They were doomed to be exiled from both. (I realize, of course, that since my time there, reservists took a much heartier role in the war, but these were my impressions at the time.)

I wandered outside my tent one night toward the sound of gathered laughter and acoustic guitars. There was a cookout, a bevy of reservists celebrating one year in country.

"What, this country?" I asked one of them, surprised. "Kuwait?"

"Yep," he smiled like it was something to be proud of. "Three hundred and sixty-five days today."

"You never went up north?"

"Nope," he confirmed nonchalantly. "Been stuck in this shithole the entire time."

I didn't know whether to pity him or be jealous. "I guess that's pretty cool. Pretty relaxed eh?"

"Ha!" he scoffed. "Try doing it for a year."

I shrugged, "At least you don't have to worry too much about getting shot at here."

"I don't know," he muttered dubiously looking up into the sky, "There's always them SCUD missiles to worry about. Anything can happen, ya know? This *is* war."

I looked past him at the blazing fire, and singing reservists in their shorts, and flip-flops, playing guitars and drinking non-alcoholic beer. "Yeah right," I said to myself. "This is war."

I noticed little pockets of Marines huddled together, smoking cigarettes, and peering suspiciously at the hoedown from patches of darkness. The reservists had offered us chicken and sausages from the grill. But there were no takers. We just looked on sullenly and cursed their existence. As I gazed into the revelry, I couldn't, for the life of me, figure out how the hell they'd fit all those guitars into their sea bags.

PREP FOR COMBAT

Preparation for combat in Kuwait amounted primarily to a lot of meetings. As a member of the Battalion staff, I attended the daily operations and intelligence briefs given at the Regimental headquarters tent. The particulars of the briefs were mundane, but there was one issue that had the Colonel's bitterest attention. It was the Kuwaiti Army. They'd been training in the impact area of our firing range. That meant we couldn't shoot our rifles, which meant we couldn't calibrate them before we stepped off. That was a bad thing, and it had been dragging on for days.

The old Gunner (an infantry Chief Warrant Officer, and well-known for his vociferations), got up to brief the situation. "Sir," he said in his southern drawl, "the Kuwaitis are still in the impact area." The Colonel's face was long and exasperated. The mood in the room was grave. The Gunner went on, "But I got some great news sir." The Colonel's head rose hopefully to hear it. The room was silent. Everybody sucked in his breath with anticipation. The Gunner grinned, "I just saved a bunch of money switching to Geico." There were a few hearty laughs from the back, including mine, but otherwise resounding disapproval swept the room. Beyond those minor episodes of comic relief, the focus of the meetings remained ever the same: logistics and the enemy.

It was subtle, but it was a clue nonetheless to how we were going to fight this war. We weren't busting our asses trying to figure out how to establish rapport with the people of the Sunni Triangle. We weren't staying up long nights talking about out how the hell we were going to actually win their hearts and minds, the very thing we were sent in to do. Sure, the issue came up, but it was always a sidebar, an afterthought. This was the Marine Corps after all, the grunts, and grunts see the world in threats and responses, attacks and counter-attacks, offense and defense, allies and enemies, winning and losing. We weren't losing sleep thinking about Iraqi hearts and minds.

But I wasn't looking for clues either, not then. I was focused on exactly what everyone else was focused on—victory and survival. When a man straps a fifty-cal machinegun on his truck and tears up into a foreign country, I don't suppose he can afford to think about much else. So we talked to our boys constantly about fighting, and dying, and getting wounded. We talked to them like they were our own sons.

There's an age-old rift between officers and enlisted, but I never knew a commander who didn't love his Marines like they were blood. So when it came to getting more weapons, more armor, and more protective gear, they fought the chain of command tooth and nail. They fought for the things that were going to keep their Marines alive in a fight.

BID FOR VICTORY

Even in training, the focus was always on the fight, on winning and surviving. The military is called when a violent extension of policy is desired. They're called when there's killing to be done. And when they're called, they train for exactly that. We had two—three months tops—to get ready for war. Not much time. We had to prioritize. They came around and told us that Iraq had become a counterinsurgency situation, and they handed us a manual and said, "Learn it."

The manual said, you've got offensive operations, defensive operations, and you've got what's known as *stability operations*, or what was more commonly referred to as, *"SASO"* (the acronym for Stability and Support Operations). We knew we'd be doing all three in different proportions at different times, but stability operations was advertised loud and clear as the key to success. SASO was our *bid for victory*.

I'd been in the Marine Corps for over ten years by then, and I'd never heard the word "SASO" before. "What the hell is SASO?" I asked. SASO was essentially every decent thing we could do to keep the country from plummeting into a massive civil war. It was the meeting and the greeting, the gladhanding, the relating with the Iraqi people, even the embittered Iraqi people, and working with them to improve life in their neighborhoods. It was the winning of their hearts and minds, the gaining of their trust, the getting them to believe in the possibilities of democracy, getting them to believe in us over the insurgents. That's what SASO was supposed to mean.

We stood up in front of our Marines, our grunts, our young killing machines, and we held up our manuals and said, "Gents, we got an insurgency on our hands. That means there's a bunch of no-good terrorists running around Iraq, ruining things for the rest of the folks over there. We've got to stop them. And to stop insurgents, you've got to go after their center of gravity. You've got to take away that which gives them power. In an insurgency, the power is in the people. So that's what we've got to go after. We've got to get the people on our side. We've got to get their hearts and minds. We've got to get their support. When we get their support, the insurgency will crumble. That's what SASO is all about."

But for all our talk of gaining popular support, for all our long speeches, we didn't train like we meant it. We didn't focus on establishing rapport or helping a languished people left with no government or infrastructure. We didn't focus on demonstrating our good will or earning the trust of the Iraqi people. Those things certainly came up; they were understood and addressed often enough by the commanders, but when it came down to training hours, SASO took a back seat. Combat came first.

We focused on killing, on bringing violence to bear, and on surviving. That's what we were designed to do. So that's what we thought about doing all the time—*all the time*—even when SASO was the order of the day. I think it was exactly this obsession with the fight that squeezed us into a state of mind that guaranteed our inability to accomplish the mission.

MATILDA VILLAGE

The Marine Corps had a formalized SASO training center at the March Reserve Air Force Base in California, which, at the time, all units were required to visit for approximately nine days prior to deployment. It was a simulation of managing an Area of Operations in Iraq. It allowed the unit to function cohesively, as a whole, while other Marines outside the unit facilitated the training environment and provided evaluation.

The scenario was a small Iraqi town called Matilda Village, where any number of events could be experienced, ranging from a family seeking compensation for a child killed at a Coalition checkpoint, to a man claiming information about insurgent activity in his neighborhood, to a disgruntled sheikh seeking concessions from the American commander, to an Iraqi demonstration, to IED attacks, to a full blown chain of assaults on the Marines. These were scenarios drawn directly from the experiences of those who had already been to Iraq, so they were realistic, and they were played out by Marines dressed in their best attempts at Iraqi garb.

Initially, the village appeared to be relatively peaceful, but it had a distinct undercurrent of hostility. From there, the situation deteriorated. No matter how skilled the commanders or their Marines were at relating to "the locals" they would always ultimately face attacks. And that sent a subtle message in itself. The culmination of events, the most difficult stage of the training, was always the time when the fighting became most intense. That was the climax. And that too sent a message. It said to Marines, the fighting will be the most difficult challenge you will face. Relating to the people will be easy.

We had to push hard on the SASO and avoid offending the locals of Matilda Village. If we failed at SASO, the trainers would intensify the attacks against us. And that's just how the situation devolved. The syllabus required that we fail. As the training progressed, and the attacks grew in frequency, and the casualties grew more severe, we grew more frustrated.

Despite our best efforts to do it right, the trainers still escalated the violence. We knew this would be the case, of course, but as instinctively strong competitors we tried, almost irrationally, to overcome that inevitable outcome. As the intensity of the fighting continued to grow, we started feeling a conspicuous distaste for the people of Matilda Village, even though it was all just make-believe. We sneered humorously at each other, "Fuck Matilda Village." And that in itself demonstrated just how realistic the training was. They had created an environment that predicted exactly the kind of frustration and growing animosity we'd soon feel in Iraq.

THE BOX

Back at Udari, our turn finally came to cross the highway and get into a staging area we called "The Box." Once we left the camp, there would be no coming back—not for anything. It was prohibited. We had three days to rehearse our convoy before we journeyed up into Iraq. Three days—a "hell and calling" week. We put our vehicles into long lines and drove around and around in giant figure eights practicing convoy procedures. This went on through the days and nights. The training was not always smooth or productive, but the intensity was high, even volatile at times.

We stopped the convoy one afternoon for what appeared to be a roadside bomb, though oddly placed nowhere near any road. This was not a drill. It was the real deal. The war had come early. Hearts were pounding. Eyes grew keen. Voices stern. Three or four of the officers, including me, stood together for fifteen minutes or so pointing at it and discussing gravely our options until somebody else strolled out and picked the thing up. It turned out to be just a plastic bag from the Post Exchange making its own pilgrimage across the desert. Relieved though we were, a certain disappointment could be felt among us. Everyone seemed anxious for the war to get going. We'd all had enough practice by then.

At night we ran into other troubles. Keeping sixty vehicles together while trailing around off-road through the darkness with the lights out proved more challenging than we'd expected. There was always somebody meandering off the course and taking everybody else behind with him. Pulling ourselves together was no easy task, either. Not every vehicle had a radio, and not every Marine had a clue. We'd flag down passing trucks and yell, "Hey! Which convoy are you with?" And somebody would lean out the window, shrug, and yell back with a grin, "Shit, I don't know. I'm just following the guy in front of me." There were a lot of us out there. It's not as if we all recognized each other, especially in the dark. So the nights became something of a three-ring circus.

Finally the ammunition came, and boy did it come. Rockets, and bullets, and grenades—I'd never seen so much of it at once, and I'd been in a while by then. The crates and the cans were busted open and the bandoliers of ammo came spilling out at our feet. We stared down at it all as if we'd stumbled upon the cornucopia of war. The brass glistened in our beaming faces like a pirate's booty, and it was guarded fiercely at first. The logisticians tried to dole strict portions of the ammo to each man until it became perfectly obvious that there was far more than we needed or could carry. Then they began tossing boxes of it into our outreached arms like loaves of bread. "Take as much as you want!" they roared cheerfully. And we did. I was as enthusiastic as the next man, no doubt, though it was admittedly hard not to suspect, with all this superfluous ammunition in our hands, that someone, somewhere, knew something we didn't.

When our hell and calling week was up, so was our time, and we had to go. We may have looked good at a distance to our inspectors, and maybe we actually were good at some things, but up close it would be fair to say that we were not so good at many other things. We were good at putting on the dog. We might have been running around like chickens with our heads cut off, but evidently we looked sharp doing it. The Division inspectors put their stamp of approval on our movement plan, and we prepared to cross the line of departure on schedule. It was time to go. "Ready" didn't make a difference anymore.

That night, I couldn't sleep. Nobody could, as far as I could tell. We sat on our trucks waiting to go as attack helicopters roared by every few minutes, flying low, with spotlights shining down on us looking for bad guys. It felt surreal, like a futuristic movie. Yet, strangely, I never tired of watching them pass, so hypnotic they were, so mesmerizing.

I noticed a Staff Sergeant standing near me and greeted him casually, "Hot as hell today wasn't it?" It was still Spring and the Staff Sergeant shook his head and said knowingly, "This ain't shit. Just wait till Summer." He'd been in Iraq for the invasion and had a real *been there, done that* way about him. With him, the worst was always yet to come. We stared together out to the north, to the black sky that hung silently over Baghdad, over all the violence that raged beneath it, and we knew we'd soon be there. The worst was indeed yet to come.

ONE

THE GLORY OF COMMAND

So you make a commitment—and you live by it. You see your friends wasted, shot or fragged, quivering on the gurney, or limp in a bag. You take human life and you give it a back seat to mission accomplishment. You do all this when you journey through war. Can you have second thoughts? Are you allowed? From a commander's perspective, it comes down to effectiveness in battle. Good fighters don't waste a lot of time thinking shit over. They just fight until they can't fight anymore. That's what we call *morale*. Morale isn't food and water. It isn't sleep, or R&R. It's feeling good about the fight. That's how you win a battle. Commanders have to plug the holes in morale constantly to maintain their units' edge.

When a soldier is on the battlefield, he's containable. He's always within reach, and keeping him focused is much easier. But when the soldier comes home, his body and mind are free to roam the plains of doubt. And those are some pretty vast plains. If he's young, maybe on his first tour, the institution hasn't sunk its hooks in too deep yet. For me, with over a decade of active service under my skin, straying was a lot more difficult. I was in limbo. All I knew was the Corps. It was like being a cyborg, part human, part Marine. The longer I stayed, the less of me remained, and the more of me became "Marine," programmed through regulations, technical manuals and doctrinal publications. Exactly what stage of metastasis I'd reached, I don't know. But there was a part of me fighting back, screaming out, "This shit ain't right. Stop now, while you still got some of you left!"

Should I stay, or should I go? Turn my back on the Corps and my brothers in arms, or turn my back on myself? The answer seems obvious now, when I put it that way. But it wasn't obvious then. I could feel—physically feel—the struggle ensuing within me. I wanted to become two men, and settle it that way, make everyone happy. I wanted to be the Commanding Officer (CO) of a rifle company. I'd been clawing toward that day for as long as I could remember. It's stunning, what a person becomes willing to sacrifice for that title—*Commander*. My day came as soon as we got home from Iraq. As I assumed command of Fox Company 2/2, I was happy and proud, but I was gloomy at the same time. I felt an unexpected disappointment come over me. It wasn't the men whom I'd assumed custody for, in that moment, who disappointed me. It was I. And it wasn't the act of taking command that consumed me. It was the surrendering of my judgment for the sake of a title. Right or wrong, I gave in for the glory of command.

CROSSING THE BORDER

All people have a few pivotal moments in their lives that remain permanently engraved in their memories. For me, crossing the border into Iraq was one of them. I locked and loaded my M-16, not to shoot a target, but for the first time, to shoot a human being. This new experience came bundled with a melee of emotions. I thought for sure we'd be ambushed the moment we hit Iraqi soil. But we weren't. The night was utterly black and seemed to get only blacker the further we drifted from Kuwait. I could see nothing of the world we'd entered, except the occasional mud houses in the distance, faintly illuminated by dull yellow lights that flickered over their crooked doorways. They were eerie little shanties, all brimming, I was sure, with hateful Muslims peering from their windows, counting off our vehicles, and calculating kill zones. But despite my agitation, there was not a shot fired that night—not at us anyway.

MISSION STATEMENT

Before we deployed, they handed out audio CDs with useful Iraqi phrases to learn. I played them in my truck every night on the way home from work. A woman would utter a phrase in Arabic, and then an American male would come on and repeat it in English. First, *"Hello"* and *"God be with you"* and *"How are you?"* Then, *"Where are the weapons?"* and *"Lie down on your face"* and *"Where do the insurgents live?"* And finally, *"We come as liberators, not as occupiers."* That was the mission in a nutshell. To liberate the Iraqi people from an oppressive regime and give them a taste of the American way—freedom and democracy. "Win the hearts and minds" may have been just a slogan, but it captured our purpose well. That's what our leaders said they wanted. They said, whatever it is you're doing in Iraq, the bottom line is it had better make the Iraqi people happy.

I'm always going on about "the mission" when I talk about Iraq, and people say to me, "Why are you always going on about the mission when you talk about Iraq? It was a whole war and you keep harping about a couple of sentences, on some meaningless document, written years ago, by a handful of people in the Defense Department. Why?"

This is what civilians often don't get about the military. The mission statement is our life blood. It is the impetus for all action. It's that important. Everyone knows the old phrase, "mission accomplished," because it's deep in our popular culture, because mission accomplishment is everything to a soldier—everything. It's not, "Oh well, better luck next time," or "you gave it your best shot." There is no next time. There is no best shot. There is success or there is failure. In the military, failure is equated with death. Success is survival—in life and in one's career. The mission statement isn't merely some abstract idea ginned up by a few bureaucrats stuffed in a Pentagon cubicle. It is the soldier's reason for being. It is his purpose. It is why he's been sent to war.

In modern warfare—the kind of warfare where small patrols are scattered across the battlefield working and fighting independently from their superiors all the time, and young non-commissioned officers (NCOs) are making tactical decisions that can have strategic, even political level implications—there's a new style of leadership out there, a new way of doing business. We don't have generals on horseback leading the charge anymore. We don't have commanders pushing waves of assaulting troops across trenches onto enemy strongpoints.

Everything is decentralized. The method of issuing orders had to change to suit the times. You can't tell a guy when to zig and when to zag. He's out there alone, making his own choices. He's zigging and zagging according to his own interpretations of the events in front of him. So we give him what we call "mission-type orders," which means we don't tell him how to do his job. We just tell him how we want things to look when he's done. We call it the "end-state."

A commander can drop dead in the midst of a fight, but his unit will persist. They will press on without him because they don't fight for him. They fight for the mission, for the end-state. In the absence of his direction, they will recall what he said before he died. They'll remember the "commander's intent" and they will continue to operate on that basis. That's mission-type orders. And that is why the mission statement is so critical to know and understand. That's why it's not just a matter of semantics. The mission statement is why our troops fight.

WAVE TACTICS

An interesting thing happened in the summer of '03. This was after the invasion, after President Bush declared that the mission was accomplished and that the major hostilities were ended. An insurgency broke out. The signs were sparse at first, but the military experts knew what it was right off. The Marine Corps was long gone by then. Most of them had packed it up and gone home right after the fall of Baghdad. The Army was left to do clean-up.

By Fall, the Marine Corps was pointing its finger at the Army, saying, "You did this. You caused the insurgency." This went beyond the regular friendly inter-service rivalry. This was a no-kidding accusation. General Mattis, my Commanding General, gave us countless examples of methods the Army had used that brought Iraq into the turmoil it suddenly faced.

He said to us: You see this? This is what they're doing over there. They're cutting down Iraqis with 25mm chain guns. They're blowing away unarmed families at their checkpoints. They're laying their boots on men's heads. They're laying their hands on women's bodies. This, Marines, is why we've got an insurgency on our hands.

He vowed that we would do it better. We would do it right. We were going to help the Iraqi people rebuild their country. We were going to get to know the local leaders, establish rapport, fund new projects, bring back electricity and water, construct schools and medical clinics, build new soccer fields and hand out thousands of soccer balls to go with them. We were going to show them how to develop democracy in their own country and vote for their own leaders. We were going to win their hearts and minds, and every once in a while, we were going to get in a fight with the bad men who didn't want to see progress in their country and who couldn't fathom the peace.

General Mattis said to us: You've got to know their culture, so you don't inadvertently aggravate the people and invigorate the insurgents. That's what the Army is doing. Think about that, Marines, when you're out there on the streets in Iraq. We were so intent on setting ourselves apart from the Army that, when we went over to Iraq, we wore our green utilities (The Soldiers were all wearing the brown desert fatigues). We said we were going to show the Iraqis that the Marine Corps got the picture, that we gave a damn, and that we weren't going to do it like the Army.

General Mattis came up with a new strategy for success. He called it "Wave Tactics." He said, "Marines, every time you pass an Iraqi, I want you to wave at them." This was going to show them our humanity, show them that we wanted to be their friends. This was going to demonstrate our good will, and then the Iraqi people would know—they could see with their own eyes—that we'd truly come as liberators, not occupiers.

As dawn arrived that first morning on our convoy north into Iraq, and the tilted half moon disappeared, the horizon lit up blazing red across a sharp black horizon. The landscape slowly brightened, and as we approached the eminent Euphrates River, I found myself strangely awed by what I saw. It was not exquisite, but it wasn't terrible either. It held an ineffable beauty, like a scene from biblical times. The Euphrates brought an abundance of verdant pastures interspersed with a rich brown land. Clusters of clay huts surrounded herds of sheep, and goats, and chickens, and women dressed in black, strolling in the distance carrying comically large sacks on their heads. It was a simple world, breathtaking in a peculiar way, and it stole from me that nervous edge that had gripped me in the darkness.

As the hours rolled on and the sun rose above us, we moved very slowly north and left the bounty of the Euphrates behind, falling almost suddenly into the severity of a rugged and endless desert. This desert was not like the one in Kuwait, an infinite bed of soft white sand. It was a boundless expanse of short, jagged dunes of rock and dust that looked like the ferocious teeth of a land with an insatiable appetite for life.

The clay houses disappeared. The goats, the chickens, the women with their comical sacks, and the pastures all faded into the distant past. I felt as though we were traveling further and further back in time. This world appeared barren as far as the eye could see, forsaken and lifeless. But then, oddly, we began to see people emerging from its recesses to greet us on the road. We drove slowly by, waving to them with one hand, and pointing our rifles at them with the other. That must have looked a little strange to them, and I believe that might have been exactly the moment my inner struggle really began.

It was a struggle because I wanted to believe in the mission, and in SASO, and in the good, and in the liberation. I wanted it deeply. But then I also wanted to fight, deeply. And it was a struggle because one does not generally wave and smile without some notion of humanity. On the other hand, I don't think one can point a loaded weapon at a person without attaching some feelings of hostility. So it was a struggle from the start, a paradox that confounded me both emotionally and psychologically. I can only imagine how it must have looked from the point of view of the Iraqis. But to my astonishment, these desert folk, so utterly different from us, and staring down the barrels of our machine guns, returned the widest smiles and waved back. I was impressed. *So maybe this wave tactics thing makes sense,* I thought. Maybe the General knows what he's talking about.

If there was one feature most memorable about that initial trip north, at least from a mechanical perspective: it was all the break-downs we had to deal with. We'd strapped on as much armor as we could rummage to protect ourselves from IEDs, but because of the added weight, all the transmissions started letting go. So on one of the many stops we made to deal with these persistent snafus, I emerged from my vehicle and found myself face to face with an Iraqi man and three boys, who I presumed were his sons. Two of the boys were teenagers. The third was no more than eight. I was nervous. I hadn't interacted with any Iraqi people yet.

I'd practiced my phrases a bit over the past several months, but I felt embarrassed trying to actually speak the language with real people, particularly at gunpoint. I felt so embarrassed, in fact, that I left my rifle in the truck. I couldn't bear to carry it out in front of them. I'd heard so many stories about the indigenous people from other Marines who'd been there during the invasion. They said Iraqis were pushy, desperate to swarm around and take whatever scraps we had to throw at them. But these people didn't swarm. They stood still, watching us. I sensed their nervousness, even over my own. I knew they were scared. The boys huddled by their father and stared at me as I climbed out of my vehicle. I looked at them with a meek smile and I waved. They waved back and slowly approached. Their trepidation was subdued by curiosity. My wave was enough to let them know it was safe. The wave tactic was growing on me all the time.

Whenever our convoy stopped, each vehicle deployed a few Marines for security. So in accordance with protocol, I began scanning the ground for concealed explosives. We'd barely touched the war; we knew nothing of it for real. Our movements weren't real yet. Our emotions weren't real. It was all pretend. We pretended gravity. We pretended to take it all very seriously. But we didn't take it completely seriously—not yet. I paced aimlessly around for several moments looking for something I didn't know the shape of, until I glanced up and noticed that the father and his sons had fanned out and were all scanning the ground too, as if to help me find whatever it was that I'd lost.

The father spoke with a smile and pointed to the ground as if to ask, "What are you looking for?" Suddenly I felt ashamed of myself. I smiled and attempted "hello" in Arabic. They stared at me blankly with no response. Then I tried "shloeneck." That's *How are you?* They all smiled and repeated it several times cheerfully. The little boy was the most exuberant of all. He kept repeating "shloeneck, shloeneck" with an encouraging tone as if to say, *That's right, you've got it.*

They gathered close to me now, more comfortable with my presence, and began to inspect my equipment. One of the older boys showed me his watch and asked to see mine. He suggested, through gesticulation, that we exchange them. I waved my hand and said, "No." The father laughed quietly and repeated to his sons in English, "No, no, no." His nervousness overwhelmed me. The boys were pointing to pieces of my gear and asking to hold them. Their father kept smiling, saying, "No, no, no." He understood. Then they pointed at my sunglasses. I felt suddenly embarrassed.

"How many times?" I scolded myself, "How many times had they told us never to speak to the Iraqi people wearing sunglasses?" I snatched them off my face and cursed myself for the gaffe. The boys, apparently unfazed by my social blunder, thought I was going to give them my sunglasses. They put their hands out excitedly and their father laughed again, "No, no, no." Where were these people from? I wondered as I peered out across that sea of jagged teeth. Where in all this barren land did they live, and how?

How could people from this mean place, so empty, and so unforgiving, be so kind to me, a soldier of an occupying force? I cannot recall a place or a time, before or after, when I ever felt so keenly aware of my battle gear—my helmet, my flak jacket, my cartridge belt, and my pistol. I was never so conscious of my uniform. It all seemed very foolish suddenly. I wanted to strip it all away, peel it away like poison skin, throw my weapon, and ammunition, and my protective gear back into the truck, put my arm around this man and say to him, "Let's just forget about all this, all this war business. Let's have a cup of chai and settle this like men—just you and I—and I'll tell my friends here to put their guns away, too, until we've figured it all out." That's what I wanted to do. But of course I couldn't, so I didn't. I felt deeply ashamed as I climbed back into my gun truck and pressed further into his homeland…waving incessantly along the way.

Maybe they're not so bad, these Iraqis, I thought. Maybe we can learn to be friends. So I kept right on waving. But then a funny thing happened. As we were driving North toward Baghdad, there were convoys heading south toward Kuwait. They were filled with Soldiers who were going home. They'd already done their stretch in Iraq. And I noticed something. I noticed that in all those convoys, and of all those Soldiers, not one of them was waving. I wondered about that.

I thought to myself, "obviously they haven't been briefed on the merits of the wave tactics campaign. Obviously they don't know that this is how we're going to show the Iraqi people our humanity. This is how we're going to win the war. We're going to wave at them!" But then I thought again. I thought maybe it was not they who were so foolish, but we. Maybe it was we who did not understand the nature of this war as we waved blithely at our soon-to-be enemies. I wondered if we would be waving when it was our turn to drive south again. It hardly took that long for the waving to stop.

There was an interesting article written by an Army officer who expressed a certain skepticism about the Marine Corps' notion of winning hearts and minds. He was still in Iraq when the Marine Corps had packed up and gone home. The article was among the officers' required reading before the deployment. This Army officer said in a nutshell that the Marine Corps was full of shit. He wrote of us: They can talk all they want about being a friend to the Iraqi people, and they can wave at them all day long, but when the shooting starts, they're going to do it just like we do—they're going to shoot back.

I'm sure it would have been tough for us to admit, but the fact is, he was exactly right. One week into our tour in Iraq, we'd reached the dour limits of the Sunni Triangle and one of our Marines was caught by an IED. The shrapnel went through his shoulder, in through the sleeve of his flak jacket, and into his body, slicing open one of his lungs. I never saw another Marine wave after that.

LIMBO

But I'm getting ahead now. Let me take you back to a place called Convoy Support Center (CSC), Scania. It was the first major truck stop we hit between Kuwait and Baghdad, and also the first American outpost I'd seen in the country. It was an Army facility. The plan was to pull in, fuel up, eat, sleep, shit, and hit the road again before dawn. The first order of business at CSC Scania was an ass-chewing by the Colonel.

Too many negligent discharges was the issue. We used to call them "accidental" back in the day, but then someone, somewhere got to figuring that all these accidents were always the result of some damned fool mistake. So ever since, we called them negligent. Our most recent negligent discharge claimed the hand of a Marine who shot himself while driving a humvee. Don't ask me how, I didn't see it. I was about twenty vehicles ahead of him in the convoy at the time, which put me at least a quarter mile away.

What I do recall is a muffled call over the radio from someone saying a Marine had shot himself in the *head*. And this was right on the heels of the Marine who'd shot himself in the gut. So it caused a stir. The Colonel was raging. He burst out of his vehicle and sent the Air Officer back to call in a Medevac. Then a second call came in to clear things up. "No, no," the voice crackled. "He was shot in the *hand*, not the head. Hotel-Alpha-November-Delta. Hand!"

Hand or head, the Colonel was still hot. I'm sure he cared about that Marine's injury, but I'd guess he was also concerned about his job. The general had made clear that an overabundance of "NDs" (as we called them), would not be looked upon fondly. I don't know if we had an overabundance or not, but there were surely a lot of them. You just never knew when a stray round was going to come sailing by from the muzzle of some absent-minded Marine. It was enough to give the Colonel cause for concern. NDs that produced casualties just made matters worse.

The fact is that the Colonel's job could very well have been in jeopardy. And in the military, an officer, especially a commander, doesn't get to just pick up the pieces and find a new job. There are no second chances. If he blows it once, he's done. If he gets fired, his career is over. That little bit of reality can have an incredibly powerful, almost coercive effect on anyone, no matter how high or low he is in the chain. And if he could lose his job over a negligent discharge, he could lose it for a whole lot more. And that is worth bearing in mind.

At the close of our tongue-lashing, we assembled in the camp's headquarters and listened to the Army's latest intelligence update. Every mile closer to the Sunni Triangle we traveled, the more risky travel became. The Soldiers of Scania were there to tell us about all the ways that bad things could happen. "Watch out for erratic drivers," they told us. "Watch out for suspicious debris on the side of the road." They said it as though a stray trash bag would look out of place in Iraq. "Don't let them drive between your trucks, or come up from behind you," they warned. "Watch out for abandoned vehicles. And watch out for cars traveling on the wrong side of the road. Watch out for men driving alone in clean clothes—it means they're preparing to give their lives for Allah."

I tried to imagine the feasibility of inspecting the attire of every passerby on the highway.

The suggestions became only more ludicrous from there. The Army Sergeant spoke bitterly, and his eyes were constantly shifting left and right. "Watch out," he said over and over. "Watch out! Watch out! Watch out!" But we'd heard it all before. We listened because it was part of the program, and because it was their house, but there was a distinct feeling among us that we knew better than they about the things we'd soon face.

I met an Army Captain there who seemed to be particularly pissed off at life. We hit it right off. It turned out he was assigned to Scania indefinitely. We walked together for a while and he said, "Fuck this war." But he wasn't worried about Iraqis, or the troops, or politics, or anything else. He just didn't want to be there. "I got out of the Army, man," he told me. "I did my time. They want to start a war after I'm gone—fine by me, just leave me out." He'd gotten out almost two years before the war had even begun, but then the Army called him back. "I was making six figures man, living in Chicago," he ranted. "You think I can afford a place in Chicago on an Army salary? You think the Army gives a shit?"

Guys like this Captain had an unusual status. He'd been active duty, at one time, so he wasn't quite loathed the same way the reservists tended to be. But then he'd committed the cardinal sin—he'd gotten out. The one thing I learned well in the Corps is that you can serve your country for two years or twenty, but it will never ever be enough, because the decision to get out will always be looked upon with suspicion by all those who decided to stay. Scania was manned almost entirely by this particular breed. They were in Iraq, in the war, but they stayed permanently behind those twenty-foot walls in a fairly non-hostile part of the country, destined to watch as others passed them by and journeyed up into the fiery core of battle. It was their own little limbo.

"Watch out for bridges," he warned me. "They'll stand on top and drop grenades into your trucks as you pass under."

"You been out there much?" I knew he hadn't. I just couldn't help the dig.

"Nah," he answered. It didn't seem to faze him. "Not once." Then he dug back a little. "Marines have only been coming through here for a month or two. Been mostly Army till now." It was hard to avoid the rivalry.

"Yeah after we took Baghdad and killed all the bad guys, I guess we figured the Army could handle the rest." I smiled. It wasn't meant to be a serious point of view—not completely anyway.

But he didn't smile. He turned to me and I could tell he understood what I was getting at. He said gravely, "Believe me, all the bad guys weren't killed. There's plenty of them out there, and where you're going, you're damn sure going to meet 'em."

TWO

QUAGMIRE

Getting out of Dodge (Scania) turned out to be a more tedious proposition than we'd bargained for. They opened the King Kong gates at 0400 and let us file out, but before we were given the okay to push, they called us on the radio and told us to "stand fast." A report came in that an IED had been spotted and EOD (Explosive Ordinance Disposal) teams were called in. EOD teams were one of the most precious of the specialists in country—precious to us for their ability to defuse IEDs, and consequently precious to any Iraqi who was able to kill them. I'd once heard that the price on the head of any EOD tech had reached as high as fifty thousand dollars. In a country stricken by destitution, that was an enticing offer, even if it was exaggerated. As the number of IEDs climbed exponentially around the country, they were often boobytrapped by individuals seeking the bounty of an EOD tech, making the EOD techs consequently more cautious, and slow to boot.

All this made the wait for their services lengthy at best. Fortunately, this particular IED was on a Main Supply Route (MSR), which hindered not only our progress but the progress of some much-needed supplies heading north to the Green Zone and Fallujah, consequently making it a top priority. Even still, we had a little time to kill. While we waited, I thumbed casually through an intelligence summary, and along the way I spotted the word "Quagmire." That's what the authors of this report were calling the war. I'll be honest, I was stunned. "That's some word," I thought. "I haven't heard anything like that since Vietnam." To hear this brand of analysis in a military document was unheard of. At least it was back in 2004. Nobody was saying that back then—not in the circles I ran in anyway, and not in the newspapers I read. So I kept reading and found it astonishingly pessimistic about our chances for genuine success. This same report brought up a little history and suggested the interesting possibility that it might repeat itself. In the early part of the twentieth century, when the British were playing this same game in Iraq, the Sunni and the Shia had banded together to oust them—the invading infidels.

In essence it asked: Would they or could they do it again? Would they band together to fight us? Had we made the same mistakes as our esteemed forebears? Ultimately, the question became moot. The Sunni and the Shia would not be banding together. Over the course of my time in Iraq, the possibility seemed increasingly unlikely. Now, sitting on the low end of the totem pole, it was tough to know who made which decision and why, but we all saw the Shia out there in police uniforms, in the *Sunni* territories, employed by the United

States, enforcing our laws. Intentional or not, the effect was divisive, and it surely had its hand in the civil war that we all saw coming, even back then. The sectarian violence that would eventually take hold of Baghdad, while trying to our eyes, was not all that surprising.

Of course I'm no history buff, so I tended away from these types of debates, but one thing I did notice about Iraq was that it was still ruled by Iraqis. In all the years of conquests and all the occupations—and Iraq has had more than its share—nobody stayed the course. There are, no doubt, volumes devoted to explaining exactly why that is, but as I sat there outside Scania, sweating in my gun truck, watching the sun creep up over that baking land, I thought, "It's not the politics, or the battles, or the twists of fate that drove out the invaders; it's all this fucking heat."

Who would want to live in such a place but those who had lived there forever? It was too rough. It was too sandy. It was too damned hot. We westerners do have a taste for comfort. Even our military packed air-conditioning when it went there to war. There were thousands of those cumbersome machines littered across the country, pumping cool air into berthing spaces and offices. I say that with a scornful tone like I didn't like the cool air myself, and of course I did. But really, how long would we be able to endure the stifling heat before we said, "Fuck it" and went home? The Iraqis had been there since the dawn of civilization. How many years could we tolerate? I couldn't speak for anyone else, but I knew I was ready for a cooler climate almost from the moment I arrived.

Outside the gates of Scania, I looked across the silent countryside at farmers, meandering goat herders, and the battered compacts that drifted down dusty roads into the shimmering distance. I studied the idle men loitering around shabby straw kiosks filled with shabby produce. The morning was warm and intoxicatingly tranquil, so much so that it lulled me into passivity. It was in the midst of all this that my thoughts roamed freely through the heat and the history of Iraq.

It was not an unpleasant morning. But lingering about in one spot in a hostile country (or arriving hostilely in a defiant one) can become unsettling after a while. Even with all our guns, I started to feel uneasy as we waited for EOD to clear the highway. It was just too easy for a person to take a shot at us with an RPG or a mortar from behind a mud wall, or a herd of sheep. We found the Iraqis quite resourceful where it came to creating discreet firing positions.

So I, for one, was not disappointed when we finally got the word to roll on. This was our last leg of the journey. By day's end we would be into the Sunni Triangle. Our destination was the Forward Operating Base, Saint Michael, which was in a small urban town called Mahmudiyah within the Northern

Babil province, just south of Baghdad. It was where the urban people lived, with their urban skepticism, and their urban glowers. Never had I witnessed such latent aggression as in those urban eyes. But that was by day's end. There was still a lot of driving to do before we got there.

TO SHOOT OR NOT TO SHOOT

It was on that drive, on that very morning, that I faced a situation exactly like the Soldiers at Scania had described. A truck pulled out onto the road ahead of our vehicle and turned into traffic heading in the wrong direction. It rode on the shoulder and was moving toward us, fast. We were all new in country, so it got our attention. Pulses jumped and our voices grew sharp and edgy. I leaned out the window and aimed my rifle at the truck. We struggled to see inside it, to spot some kind of clue that might tell us with any certainty whether or not the driver was a suicide bomber.

My heart was racing. I was breathing hard as it drew closer and closer. Fire? Don't fire? It was so difficult to know what to do. Will we live? Will we die? This could be it. And the truck drew closer still. And still we couldn't seem to come up with a decision. There was no one to ask. There was no manual to reference. There was no time to think it over. There was only now, the moment, and we had to decide. In the end we resolved to hold our fires, and I was glad we did. The truck floated quietly past us without exploding into a million bits of fragmentation in our faces. We stared, agog, at the passengers, a family of four or maybe five crammed into the cab staring back at us, all agog as well.

To shoot or not to shoot—that was the question. That was always the question in Iraq. To preemptively fire on a person or a vehicle that looked like a threat was not only a tactical problem, it was the central question of the war. The debate always seemed to center on the consequences of guessing wrong. We didn't know who was in that truck. We couldn't tell if they had a bomb or not. If they did, we'd have all been dead. If they didn't and we fired, the insurgency would be strengthened. To guess wrong either way was to lose. There just weren't any good choices out there. Every approaching car was like the war on wheels. Every time we fired on them was like an invasion. The entire war was fought from beginning to end every day, again and again.

This time we were lucky. We had a hunch and our hunch was correct. I reasoned that, by not shooting, we risked our own lives for the sake of the relationship that America was hoping to build with Iraq. We held our fires for the mission. But then again, we were new to the war, and green, and probably still a bit entrenched in our moral ways. Maybe we didn't want to fire. Maybe we couldn't. Combat demands a degree of cold amorality from every soldier. We didn't have that…not yet.

THE FAST AND THE FURIOUS

Contrary to the opinion of those at Scania, driving on the wrong side of the road in Iraq turned out to be almost as common as driving on the right side of the road. In fact, there was virtually no discernible order to the traffic behavior in the country at all. There were no traffic lights, or signs anywhere to be seen, or lines on the road that anyone paid any attention to. There were no laws whatsoever governing the conduct of drivers. Even if there were, there were no police to enforce them. So using "erratic driving patterns" as criteria to blaze away into the windshield of a car seemed to me a questionable policy at best. Everyone in the whole damned country drove erratically, especially us.

We weaved through and around the most spectacular traffic jams I'd ever seen. We bounced over medians, hopped curbs, streaked through intersections, and roared through village markets. We cut off everyone—vehicle or pedestrian—it didn't matter. None of us wanted to slow down or stop even for a second, because we just didn't know what might happen if we did. We didn't want to make ourselves good targets. But every time we went hurtling through their neighborhoods at breakneck speeds, we evoked as much fear and contempt in the Iraqis for us as we possessed for them. And we were doing all that before we ever reached the walls of Forward Operating Base (FOB) Saint Michael.

SAINT MIKE

Saint Michael, the patron saint of warriors, according to Catholic lore, descended into Hell to combat the Devil, and that's how he's depicted on the talismans worn by so many soldiers. In Iraq, I was wearing one. I grew up Catholic, so it seemed like the thing to do. I guess someone thought it would be a good name for a base. Maybe they grew up Catholic too. We called it, affectionately, "Saint Mike." Actually, all the bases were named after saints when I arrived in country in early 2004. And the next thing I knew people everywhere, including the President, were describing the war as a struggle between good and evil. The answer to jihad, they called it. They said the word "righteous" in that righteous tone of voice that people use when they have God in mind. And the damn thing turned into a holy war before our eyes. Small wonder. Religion may not have been the genesis of the war in Iraq, but its fervor unquestionably stoked the flames of our fury.

Our bases weren't just posts; they were bastions of Christianity. Then finally someone came along and figured maybe the whole saint thing wasn't such a great idea after all. The names of the bases were officially changed to the geographic locations in which they were located. Problem solved. FOB Saint Michael became "Camp Mahmudiyah," but it would always be Saint Mike to us. You can't pry a man from his saints that easily, nor his notion of eminence when he stands among the most powerful military in the world bearing the cross. That's what the FOB was all about. It was our brand of attitude. We were the Provost Marshall, the new sheriff in town, and the FOBs were our precincts, and the towns were our jurisdictions. It was our way of declaring, *We're in charge, we're here to stay, and this is our ground. From now on we determine the law of the land.*

So we maintained the peace. But there was no peace. Our very presence drew violence where there had been a fair degree of tranquility. We arrived, and then insurgents sought us out and attacked. We couldn't stop that, though we did try in vain with patrols circling our FOBs twenty-four hours a day. But they'd always find a way to launch a couple of rounds down range and slip away undetected. They had the advantage of being maneuverable. We had the disadvantage of being fixed. The cards were stacked against us from the start, and we're the ones who stacked them.

We garrisoned ourselves in the center of the city to put our Marines in close proximity to the enemy, but we also put the enemy in close proximity to our Marines. In other words, as we patrolled and watched them, they patrolled too, and watched us, like hawks. They watched us burst from our gates in humvees, and they watched the times we did it. They watched the routes we frequented and the techniques we used for movement. They watched our reactions to indirect fire attacks, to IEDs, to ambushes, and they watched to see how fast we did it. They watched our patterns, and they could do it very easily from their windows or doorways or even out in broad daylight, in their civilian clothes, blending in with the scenery. That was their advantage. We were very apparently American, but the insurgents were not apparent at all.

But the FOB would never fall as long as we chose to remain. The insurgents could never organize a body large enough to penetrate even the smallest of our camps. We had too much firepower for them to ever absorb in a full-scale assault. They'd never overrun an American FOB, and so they'd stick to their harassing attacks with mortars and rockets and car bombs, but with nothing significant enough to drive us out physically.

And that is what would perpetuate the myth among us that our force was impregnable, that our resolve was unbreakable, and most critical, that our mission was achievable. But all the while it was the *attitude* that the garrisons represented that was diminishing our chances for success. The more we asserted ourselves, the stronger we made our FOBs, the tighter the grip we put on Iraq, the greater the contrast we drew between their religion and ours, the more we lost the very hearts and minds of the people we said we came to win.

WARLORDS

We called ourselves the Warlords. It was a name adopted by the unit years ago and approved officially by headquarters Marine Corps. *Warlord*—the word it-self summons powerful images, but exactly what does it mean? Did anyone ever ask? Meticulously attentive to every detail as Marines tend to be, I think they must have. Somewhere along the line, in that long approval process between the battalion commander and the Commandant, when the decision was being made whether or not to call a Marine Corps infantry battalion the "Warlords," someone must have flipped open a dictionary and looked up the word.

You'd have to scour long and hard to find a person or a reference that might have anything positive or noble to say about a "Warlord." It's just not generally considered a term for the good guys. And yet that was our handle. One wonders what sort of impression we were seeking to make. *Warlord* may have been just a name, just a word, but it contributed to a mentality, I think. Actually, on several accounts, it was a fairly accurate description of us. We were the new order, and our battalion commander was the despot. His words were the law of the land. And at every single commander's meeting, every single day of our deployment, he uttered the same words to his staff: "Be the hunter, not the hunted."

THE JACKSON PATROL

Frankly, we didn't have to be told. Most of the Marines, like me, were hungry for blood, really starving for that combat experience. As we rolled into Saint Mike for the first time, we were greeted by a dusty SUV sitting ominously on four flat tires. By the look of it we knew we'd be seeing all the blood we'd ever want to and more. Hundred of bulletholes were scattered in the black paint like constellations in the night. The windows were all shot to hell and shattered glass covered the seats and floors inside. We walked up to it, gawking like tyros. The upholstery was shredded and drenched with dried blood. I stared at all the little frayed holes. It had never occurred to me, however obvious, that bullets could pass so easily through car seats.

My eyes moved slowly through the fragments of bone left in the driver's seat. A large piece of skull sat prominently among them like a crude bowl with a small pool of blood turned brown and crusted within. I looked up from the piece of skull to a passing Soldier from the unit we'd come to relieve. I pointed at the vehicle and asked him, "What happened here?" He shrugged and said, "Route Jackson happened." A few clicks (kilometers) south of Mahmudiyah was the town of Lutifiyah, an area immediately characterized by its hostility toward American forces. Between these two towns was a road we called "Jack-son". We spent a lot of time on that road, and Jackson was littered with IEDs.

The Improvised Explosive Device. The ubiquitous, notorious, IED. It was the staple of the Iraq War, and the inflictor of more casualties than any other kind of enemy attack, bar none. It was the roadside bomb. It was what every soldier would remember about the war, what every soldier feared most about the war. In our Area of Operations, every drive down every road was a round of Russian Roulette. You never knew when the chamber was going to be loaded. You never knew when that IED was going to have *your* name on it. Some IEDs killed, some maimed, some misfired or hit nothing at all, but they were always present. It was really less a matter of *if* you got IED'd than *when, where,* and near *whose* vehicle. Those were the questions that nagged at Marines every night as they conducted their pre-combat checks. Those were the thoughts that weighed heavy in their minds.

For the unacquainted, an IED was simply an explosive boobytrap meant to kill Americans as they passed by. They were most often remote detonated, though periodically by some other trip device. In the beginning of the war, the IED was nothing more than a lone mortar round, wired crudely to an electronic receiver and tossed on the side of the road. But then our soldiers got better at spotting the IEDs as they traveled, so insurgents started burying them in the ground, or under rock piles, or in trash bags.

The remote detonator was usually some sort of short-range radio wave transmitter like a garage door opener. Its range would be scarcely fifty meters. But as we improved our reaction time and learned to quickly sweep out across both sides of the road, being a trigger man became more dangerous. That's when the remotes escalated to cellular phones, for their unlimited range. A trigger man could be anywhere. His only requirement was that he could see his target—us.

When mortars failed to produce the devastation the insurgents were look-ing for, they began using artillery shells, the mortar's big brother. Then stacks of artillery shells. Then there were the daisy chains—long rows of explosives all wired together along the sides of the road to engage not just one vehicle, but several simultaneously, and often placed hundreds of meters behind a more obvious decoy, to catch the convoy in a halt as they focused on the IED ahead. When the artillery shells proved still not powerful enough, the insurgents turned to anti-tank mines and empty bomb casings filled with plastique, and multiple artillery shells, and scraps of metal for added shrapnel. They were so big that they had to be tunneled under the pavement.

The techniques for hiding explosives were as prolific as the operations con-ducted to counter them. There were IEDs hidden everywhere. They were stuck in rotted logs and sent drifting down the river to eventually get snagged on bridges that Marines would have to drive across. There were IEDs tucked in the carcasses of animals and laid inconspicuously among all the other dead animals lying around the streets of Iraq. There were IEDs in our own sand-filled barricades that had been stuffed there when we weren't looking. There were IEDs attached to the backs of anti-Coalition posters that would detonate when we tore them down. There were IEDs molded into curbstones. There were IEDs stashed in broken-down cars. There were IEDs hidden in the wreckages of cars that had already been blown up by previous IEDs. There were IEDs buried in potholes, stashed in milk cartons, and soda cans, and cinder blocks. IEDs were everywhere.

The effort to stabilize route Jackson, and maintain its viability as a supply route for the Coalition proved to be much more difficult and lethal than we'd expected. The method by which we secured this route was nothing more complicated than running continual "presence" patrols. Of all the places we traveled, of all the operations we conducted, I doubt any was more notorious among us than the Jackson Patrol. Getting attacked with an IED on route Jackson wasn't merely a possibility; it was inevitable. So we decided that Jackson should be patrolled a minimum of two times per day, once in daylight hours and once at night. It was my job to assign units to this task each day and dispatch them out on patrol. It was a lousy job. As a result of the Jackson Patrol, two of our Marines were killed by IEDs and quite a few more were wounded.

After a while the Marines started coming around on the side asking me, "Why are we doing this? What's the point?" And I'd say to myself, "Yeah, what is the point?" The pat answer was always the same. First, because it was a supply route, and it had stay open. And second, because this was our ground. *OURS.* We owned it—The Warlords, The U.S. Marines—and we weren't about to let a few insurgents deny us our ground. That's what it boiled down to—turf—and it might have been articulated in just so many words.

While our arrogance may have been unproductive, our supply lines were surely vital, and arguably, that made the Jackson Patrol vital as well. From a strategic perspective, we had to keep the supply lines open or our military would cease to function. That's basic material, learned over a thousand years of warfare. On the other hand, if an army wants to control a piece of ground, it has to occupy it. It needs boots on the ground, all the time. That's also basic material. Every infantryman knows it; every historian, every military scholar, and every person who's ever survived the pummeling of indirect fire and air attacks knows it, too.

An army can't control ground with aerial bombs or artillery. It can't control ground by running occasional raids in the wee hours of the morning and slipping back to base before dawn. And it certainly can't control ground by racing from one end of town to the other as fast as possible in a few humvees. If they don't occupy it, they don't control it, period. So driving down to Lutifiyah a couple of times a day didn't make the area any more safe or stable. It didn't serve much purpose at all, as far as I could tell, other than giving the *impression* that the route was secure, and all the while providing insurgents with targets for their endless supply of IEDs.

The Marines would insist to me, "This is a suicide mission. The insurgents know where we're going to be and when we're going to be there because we're out there every night." And I'd tell them dutifully what I was told when I brought up the same concerns to my bosses. "You've got from six in the evening to six in the morning to run a four hour patrol. Nobody's telling you what time to go. Mix it up. Do the tough hours." I'd slap them on the shoulder and nod, "You'll be all right."

It was a bullshit answer, and I knew it when I heard it, and even more so when I said it myself. The Marines knew it, too. We all got the same classes on route planning. We all knew that switching patterns, routes, and times of travel was a standard tactic to avoid an ambush. But when the route was designated and couldn't be altered, and when the enemy knew we were coming every night, which particular hour we arrived became a moot point. That's how I looked at it.

Driving route Jackson wasn't any fun. There was no question about that, and I didn't do it nearly as often as a lot of the Marines. Unfortunately, the fun of a mission is seldom considered criteria for canceling it. The troubling part to me was that it was so painfully lacking value. The Marines would do a lot of tough things for us, a lot of brave things, just because we asked them to. That's the way they were. But what they didn't respond so well to was futility, and I think they got a good whiff of that from the Jackson Patrol.

The greater the futility of an operation, the more deeply a Marine must believe in his own immortality to participate. Death is rarely pre-empted with goodbyes. Of course, we could have all talked, and acted, and thought as though every minute were our last. But we didn't. We didn't because the mere idea of mortality would have been detrimental to our ability to fight. We couldn't fight if we were too busy thinking about dying. A Marine can't believe that he's going to die. He's got to fight believing that someone else will die. That's how he does it. That's how he stays focused. "Someone is going to get hit," he tells himself. "Someone is going to die I know, but it ain't gonna be me." And he's right every time until it happens to him.

When an IED blew a few meters from my truck on the way back to base from Lutifiyah, the concussion shook the ground so hard my teeth ached. I'm glad that's all it did because we didn't have any heavy armor to protect us. Dirt and debris flew in the windows and into our faces from the darkness. Luckily, no shrapnel came with it, and aside from swerving to a halt and being a bit shaken, nobody was hurt. With the IED exploding so close to us, we were surprised we'd survived. But that's the way it goes with explosives. Sometimes they get everybody. Sometimes they don't get anybody.

An anti-tank mine buried under the road ripped one of our humvees to shreds and all the passengers walked away without a scratch. But then another time, a single- shell IED blew up and a small piece of shrapnel flew through the air, well outside a mortar's effective casualty radius, and snagged a Marine in the neck. There was just no telling how these things were going to go. Either you were lucky, or you weren't. I was lucky. Not everyone was.

One late night at Saint Mike, I saw a platoon tearing through the front gate and up to the door of the Battalion Aid Station (the medical facility). They'd just gotten back from Jackson. I could hear their haste in the winding engines and the urgency in their voices as they scrambled to unload their cargo. It was one of their fellow Marines, hit by an IED. I could tell he was dead from ten feet away by the bag they carried him in. As I watched the Battalion Surgeon poke through the remains of the dead Marine's head, I felt a distinct hatred churning up inside me. And I think it would be fair to say that there wasn't a single Marine in that room, the Battalion Commander included, who wasn't feeling that same thing. To one extent or the other, we all wanted payback. We all wanted to see some Iraqi blood spilled for the blood of our Marine. And I think that played a significant role in the deterioration of our mission.

What was particularly disturbing about the IED was that when it deto-nated, when it killed someone, it really wasn't a random or detached instance of violence like a falling shell. It was personal. If a Marine looked out into the darkness, he might not see anyone, but he would know just the same that some-one—an Iraqi—was out there watching. He'd know because he understood the tactic. He'd know someone was out there watching at that very moment as he collected up the bloody remains of a mangled friend while his ears were still ringing from the blast.

He'd know someone was out there watching as he thought about the last time he saw his friend's face. He'd know someone was out there watching as he shook with rage for having no way to fight back. Someone was watching the frustration, the fear, and the fury all manifested in his frantic movements. Some insurgent, some Iraqi, was out there watching…and he was pleased. And I think knowing that fueled our hatred for them all that much more.

BAD FRIDAY

In Iraq, I spent most of my time in the Combat Operations Center—the COC. It was our headquarters, the place where we made decisions and sent orders out over the airwaves, and it had its own brand of battlefield chaos. Our fog of war was the walls around us, and the defective radios, and the half stories that came over them through the static, and all the phone calls from the brass wanting the rest of the stories.

On April 09, 2004, the fog was thick. It was Good Friday, but it turned out to be a pretty lousy day. I called it "Bad Friday" in my journal, and I wrote: You just can't see a shitty day coming. It creeps up on you like a war. One minute it's all talk and coffee, and the next minute you're neck deep in a fight and you don't know how the hell you got there, or how you're going to get out.

Somebody stuffed an IED in the carcass of a dog, and that got the morning going. That's the kind of news you wake up to in war. "Hey guys, there's a bomb inside a dead dog. I need you to go down there and dig the fucking thing out." We said it like we were sending them in to snake the toilet. The EOD techs had a remote-control robot with a monitor, so they could see its fingers as they worked. It must have looked like they were doing a canine kidney transplant. The bad news was that the IED-laden dog was just the lure. There was a lot of bad news that day.

First it was the ambush down in Lutifiyah. The radio kept sputtering fragmented words at us, and fragmented reports. I kept hearing bits like, "Been hit…ambush…under fire…split up…fuckin'…low on ammo…can't get out…" And then nothing. It was always the silence that killed us. I didn't know where they were anymore—not precisely enough to launch reinforcements. I didn't know if they had wounded or they didn't. I didn't know shit. That's the fog I'm talking about. But what I did know is that they were down in Lutifiyah, and I knew how much I was starting to hate everyone who lived there.

I called for some help from a rifle company in the area. But their CO, one of my fellow captains, told me he had some other things going on. There was a crowd of Iraqis gathering up in town with growing fervor. Maybe they were just going to protest, but then again, maybe they were looking for a fight. He couldn't say for sure until the rounds started flying. Then he knew. And that's about the last I heard from him for a while.

Just like I didn't have time to tell higher headquarters about all the things I was doing while I was in the middle of doing them, neither did he. So back in the COC, I had to just sit on my ass, and wait, and hope. Every once in a while, I'd check in and ask him how things were going. I could tell he wasn't interested in hearing from me or chatting on the phone. He'd tell me, "I've got about thirty insurgents moving toward me with small arms. I'll get back to you!" Then the company to our west reported fighting in Yousifiyah as well.

Then an Army refueling unit reported from the refinery in Lutifiyah that they were being surrounded by an angry mob, and the mob was shouting. They didn't know exactly what was being shouted, but it sounded hostile to them and they weren't feeling confident about their prospects of getting out alive. So we sent another rifle company down to help. This was about the moment we found out that one of our Marines had been shot in the face. He was dead. He was the first one to go in the battalion. Now we knew this thing was real. I didn't know him at all, but they said he was a good man. Honestly, that was all the reason I needed to get mad. His blood trickled down onto the seeds of our rage and made them flourish. By day's end we were in full bloom.

WAR FROM IN THE COC

The COC was like the stock exchange. Guys were shouting. Guys were swearing. Guys were on three phones at once. And everyone was hot, and mad, and watching the radios like the ticker-tape. Everyone wanted updates. Everyone wanted the details, the details that no one had. "What's their position?" someone with shiny collars would yell. "What's their situation?" "How many enemy?" "How many wounded?" "How many killed?" "What's their fucking position?!" Still nobody knew. Phones just kept ringing. Officers kept asking questions. Clerks and radio operators struggled to understand what the hell was going on with only a fraction of the tactical picture. They were young and inexperienced. They weren't in on the planning. They didn't get copies of the op-orders. They just didn't know. But in the COC, they were on point. They had the handsets pressed into their ears trying to decipher the garbled harangues. "What's their fucking position?!" someone would shout again.

Then the incoming would start. The low wumping outside would shake the building. "Duck and cover!" we'd blare over the loudspeaker. If we'd had open windows we would have seen that nobody was ducking for cover. Nobody ever seemed to duck for cover, except maybe the officers trying to set a good example. It was apathy or it was stupidity or it was cockiness. Whatever it was, it was reality. No one ever ducked.

We checked our counter-battery radar and our satellite imagery and we loosed off a couple of volleys of artillery at whoever was shooting at us. We didn't hit anybody. We never did. But it kept the enemy from hanging around and adjusting fire on us. So that was the process. If the area was deemed "thickly settled," we wouldn't fire high explosives (in the interest of safety). We'd just launch illumination—we called them "lume" rounds—up in the sky to let the insurgents know we were onto them, that we knew where they were hiding, and that we were coming to get them.

Funny thing about the lume rounds: Most people looked up at that flare floating in the sky under a little parachute, and they figured the damn things were harmless. But they often forgot about the eighty pound casings that got fired up there with them, which would then have to come plummeting to the ground somewhere—somewhere in that place we just deemed "thickly settled." There was an Iraqi man in Yousifiyah who learned this lesson most intimately when a casing crashed through the roof of his house. We shrugged it off as collateral damage and we paid him to go away.

Whenever the fighting got going, we in the COC would invariably find ourselves bombarded with a lot of extraneous business. Disgruntled locals rattling our gates, blood resupply helicopters arriving unannounced, pot shots whizzing in from the neighborhood, tactical vehicles plunging into canals, new units calling in under fire, old ones calling for more ammo, IEDs going off, and more IEDs, casualties, medevacs, detainees arriving and departing, generators failing, lights blinking out, people shouting, phones ringing, radios humming, computers crashing…all of it, all at the same time. And then from the corner of the room, the sat phone would ring….

ADC JUMP

The satellite phone was the latest addition to the military's repertoire of long range communication assets. It was pretty handy when we wanted to call home, but the damned things never seemed to work right when we needed them for incidental shit like combat. "COC!" I yelled into the phone over all the noise. The voice on the other end was young and buried in the static. I couldn't understand what the hell he was saying. "Who is this?" I shouted. I couldn't hear his answer. I caught "Lance Corporal" something or other, but I didn't catch the name. *I don't have time for this shit*, I was thinking to myself as I started to hang up the phone.

Then I heard the kid yell, "ADC Jump!"

I mashed that phone up to my ear and I listened real hard. "What did you say?" I shouted.

He shouted back, "We've been hit!"

ADC Jump was the name for the Assistant Division Commander's mobile entourage. It was Brigadier General Kelly. We'd gotten to know each other a little because he was from Boston—he grew up a few blocks from where I was living during my college years. *Son of a bitch*, I thought as my stomach started turning over. Suddenly the reception on the Sat Phone became crystal clear.

It turned out that the General and his crew had taken an alternate route back to our base rather than deal with Jackson. Frankly, I can't say that I blamed them. Unfortunately, they didn't tell us where they were going, and if they had we probably wouldn't have approved. (Not that we'd have been in a position to disapprove.) The road they were traveling on moved out into the desert and was utterly isolated from us, or any other unit that might reinforce them if an emergency arose. And of course an emergency arose. Once they crossed the

Euphrates, they were on their own. Evidently that was well-comprehended by a handful of Iraqis, who hastily ambushed them.

By the time they got us on the phone, one of their turret gunners had already taken a burst of machine gun fire in the face. He was gone.

"Anyone else hit?" I asked the Marine.

He said, "Yeah, a lot of guys." I asked him if the General was hit, too. He said, "No, the General is all right."

They were beyond our reach. There was really nothing we could do to help them. A ground force would have taken nearly an hour to get there, and most firefights don't last more than a couple of minutes. I put a call in for air support, though I was skeptical about our chances of getting it. I'd called up for air a million times before, always begging, pleading, and cajoling, and most times unsuccessfully. But not this time. I mentioned the ADC was under fire and I think they deployed the entire Wing.

Attack helicopters and fighter jets were buzzing overhead in minutes. By then the firing had subsided. The ambushers had disappeared into the desert. The danger was at bay. The aircraft escorted the General home from above. When he came up to the COC to tell us his story, I noticed his uniform was covered in blood. It was not his own. I remember thinking at that very instant that he looked too old to be among the bloody.

THE MISSING WAR STORIES

Shit. What did I care about a General anyway? Like I said, it wasn't his blood. And he's the one who'd taken that ridiculous route back to base. But I did feel sorry for him in the moment, and I don't know why. It was the first thought I'd had that day that wasn't about the fight itself. The COC was a pressure cooker, and the fight was our meat and potatoes. It was always either feast or famine. So when it was feast, we found ourselves ravished at first, starving for a fight, then suddenly we were engorged so that we couldn't take another bite.

Sooner or later, the bullets would stop flying and we'd catch a break. That's when we'd suck in a deep breath and think things over. I think most of us were pulling it all together into a story—a war story. It could be a sad story, or an exciting story, or maybe even a funny story, but they'd still just be stories. And no matter who we were, and how much we saw, the stories would always, *always* be incomplete.

The story of Bad Friday is broken and discombobulated from my perspective. There are a lot of gaps. But I'm the guy who wrote everything down in our operations log, and many of those little stories never made it to the log. So when the log turned into unit diary entries, and the diaries were turned into history, those little stories would be forgotten. Much of history is made from behind the walls of command posts, through the hazy channels on the radios. The world will only know what we wrote down, and so much is not written.

THE JOY OF KILLING

When the fighting to our west and south tapered off into an eerie tranquility, when the insurgents vanished into the woodwork, when everybody was good and beat through, and the bodies were all counted up, we eased back into the silence of the COC and waited for our next turn with the enemy. Our next turn came two days later.

I was outside the command post, plugged into the generator with my clippers, cutting my hair, when one of the majors in the battalion stopped over and said, "Hey, there's something going on down in Lutifiyah. We're going to check it out. You coming?"

I said, "Shit. You better believe I'm coming." I had a fresh haircut and my stomach was already growling for another fight. I grabbed a rifle, a pistol, and a bunch of ammo, and I loaded up with the Air Officer. We waited for the short-count, started up our engines, and headed down route Jackson.

The COC was all right, I guess. I learned a lot, saw a lot. But you weren't in the shit if you were in the COC. You were always just hearing about the shit secondhand from the guys who were. You missed out on the glory, and it made you kind of crazy sometimes. It was making me crazy. I wanted to get shot at. (The culture of war really is insane when I think of it now—literally insane— where you wake up in the morning, stretch out, and yawn to yourself, "Man I'd love to get shot at today." It's ludicrous, but it's the truth.)

We got within a mile of Lutifiyah and I could see a trail of black smoke rising into the distant sky. I said to myself: Here comes the fight. Then small arms fire started raging from both sides of the road. An RPG sailed a few feet over the truck in front of us like a bottle rocket. It didn't look real. It seemed like a movie, until it blew up on the other side of us in a huge ball of flame and shook the earth. Then another rocket sailed by. And another. I peered through the windshield from the back seat and watched all the Marines riding in the back of the truck in front of us. They were opened up, wide, with their machine guns, and still I didn't seem to fully appreciate the fact that we were being attacked.

Then the bullets started tearing over my own head, and I knew that sound. The fire was coming from all directions. Everybody was speeding up. We were moving fast, slouched down in our seats, and pulling our helmets low. I had my rifle out the window firing back, and I remember feeling angry because I couldn't get a clear field of view. I shot into the passing apartments as quickly as I could pull the trigger. This was the first time I'd ever fired my weapon at another human being.

The Air Officer up front had his head in his lap with his arm hanging out of the window blazing away with his pistol. God knows he wasn't hitting anything that way, but the enemy was far enough away that he probably wouldn't have hit anything even if he was aiming. Firing from a moving vehicle is no easy task, so chances were I probably wasn't hitting anything either. The driver had his pistol out the window, too, and was steering with one hand, which was a little scary, because he was a terrible driver, even with two hands.

Another RPG whizzed overhead and the bullets kept snapping on by. I threw out a couple of quick prayers (most people find a touch of religion in war). Being stuck inside a vehicle is not the most comforting spot to be in a firefight. The tacticians would have had us pull over and assault the ambushers on foot. In hindsight, maybe we should have. We certainly talked about that option afterwards. But this was the first real firefight many of us had been in, and it was a fairly heavy one at that. I know personally, I wasn't thinking about much other than getting through alive. I suppose that's what we all had in mind.

When it was over, I was happy to have survived. And as luck would have it, everyone did. That's one of the things that made that day especially exhilarating. We gathered in the middle of Lutifiyah next to a line of Coalition tractor-trailers. Eight out of eight of them were hit by RPGs in an ambush. All of them were burnt out with black smoke billowing out from their cabs and spreading into a dark haze across the sky.

Shots rang out sporadically in the distance, and muffled explosions shook the ground. A fuel tank exploded and a blazing inferno rose up into the air two stories high. The heat scorched our necks and faces. The roar was deafening. These were the sights and sounds of war that I'd been waiting all my life to experience. This is what it was supposed to be all about. We huddled together and exchanged accounts of the fight. Everyone was happy and excited. The Air Officer and I weren't even close until that moment. We barely spoke. Suddenly we were the best of friends.

For most of us, this was our baptism of fire. It was a happy event. "They were over here," we chattered amongst ourselves. "They were over there. They were every-fucking-where, man." And we grinned and we laughed, "Did you see the rockets? Did you see 'em fly? Did you hear the bullets smacking our sides? Did you feel the heat and the thunder? Did you smell the burn? Did you know? Did you know what the edge looked like before now? Did you ever know we'd be hanging over it so far?"

It was joy. I'll be damned if you could call it anything else. And I don't recall a moment from my first day in Iraq to the last, that I ever felt it so fully. Joy. Joy to have finally reached the battle after so many years of training, and talking, and praying. Joy to have finally answered the question of myself: Will I stand up and fight, or will I curl up and die? Joy to have found myself still standing when it was all over—still standing on my own two legs, still standing with my eyes, and my hands, and heart in place, still standing with my honor intact. That was the joy I felt on the afternoon of April 11, 2004.

I have often wondered if this joy we felt is an absolute of war, if it is felt by all combatants in all conflicts, or if it was conspicuous to us as an all-volunteer force. If we were, say, a force of conscripts, would we relish the battle so much? Perhaps not. And perhaps that is something to further consider amidst the constant insistence that we maintain such a robust standing military. I have often thought our country fortunate for having so many draftees in both WWII and Vietnam because it brought not only socioeconomic diversity but intellectual diversity as well. Such a wide range of perspectives among the soldiers is healthy, I think, if our nation must go to war, because they can provide the broadest interpretations of the events that ensued. In Iraq, there were only volunteers, only those soldiers who'd already accepted the notion of violent means before they ever engaged in it. I feel that may have narrowed the critique quite a bit in the aftermath. And I think it had a lot to do with all the joy we felt that day.

DISPARITY

I use that word *disparity* all the time when I talk about the war because it was everywhere. There was disparity between the policies and the operations. There was disparity between our objectives and our incentives. There was disparity between what was done and what was shown back home in the media. But the disparity that I am most concerned with now is the one that grew inside myself. It was a war all its own. The disparity I'm thinking about emerged in my consciousness from the moment I crossed the border into Iraq and it only widened with every passing operation. After that first firefight in Lutifiyah, I began to crave the elation of the kill. I think most of us did. And I don't believe it was entirely to do with genes or character. Embracing the violence was not a choice; it was a necessity. On the battlefield, a soldier must befriend the darker side of his nature to participate in the fight, to survive, to win, to pull that trigger—he must degrade his own humanity.

That is why I use the word disparity. Because we were there to demonstrate our humanity, not stuff it down inside. We were there for a liberation. We were there to do good deeds and to be a friend to the Iraqi people. That's what we said. But then we got there, and with every casualty we took our humanity was overwhelmed by a yearning to kill. It is surely difficult to help a people who you would prefer to shoot.

HERE AS A KILLER

There was still a fight to be had that April afternoon. It wasn't over yet. We heard firing to our north. A company was deployed to pursue the enemy while a handful of stragglers hung back and established a blocking position to make sure no enemy slipped away to the south. I was more or less a free agent at that point. I could latch on wherever I wanted, so I wandered to the top of the building where our blocking position had set up. The major whom I'd spoken to before was up there, too, checking things out.

A Marine stepped over to report his situation, and I quickly put up my hand and said cheerfully, "I don't want a report. I'm not here as a Captain. I'm here as a killer." It wasn't intended to be serious, but the sentiment was dead on. *I'm here as a killer.* Those words hung in my mouth for ten hours more until I wrote them down in my journal. "I'm here as a killer," I said sanguinely. "I'm here as a killer," I wrote sleepily that night. "I'm here as a killer," I heard myself say a thousand times over from that moment to this. Seldom have I spoken more truthful words than those. "I'm here as a killer."

Just moments after that, a handful of insurgents popped out, maybe two-hundred meters to our front, and we opened fire. Between the rifle platoon, and the major and me, they didn't have a chance. Years later, I discovered something else that I wrote down in my journal that night, something I find interesting now. I wrote, "I can't really take credit for these kills because there were so many rounds flying at that moment that it would be impossible to tell for sure whose took life and whose did not. And I think there may be some advantage to that—today and in the days to come. So I can claim their deaths as my own when I'm feeling like I'm feeling now, vicious and unforgiving. And I can deny them when guilt, someday, rears its ugly head."

It appears, even on that day of joyous killing, I knew that I would eventually be seeking an out.

UP ON THE ROOF

A few minutes later, another car pulled out and tried to turn up the street away from us. One Marine put his hand on the shoulder of another—a machine-gunner—and said, "Put fifty rounds into that car." I got the feeling he liked the way he sounded when he said that. But I found I didn't like it so much. Neither did the major. It wasn't sitting right with us. The gunner did as he was told, not reluctantly, and the car lurched to a halt and the driver fell out of sight, dead. The thrill was instantly gone. I wasn't happy anymore. I wasn't excited. Suddenly, everything seemed very quiet. A heaviness fell upon my stomach. I squinted at the riddled car in the distance and I said to myself, "Whoa…what was that? Should we have done that?"

I glanced over at the major and he looked disturbed—no, more than that—he looked angry. He was shaking his head and he muttered, "That was no good." He nodded toward the Marine and said to me, "You gotta cool him down." I was thinking the same thing. I got the Marine's attention and said something to that effect. "You gotta cool down," just like that, like he fouled in a game of basketball. The Marine was courteous and enthusiastic and he answered, "Yes sir" and went on his way.

The major left. Clearly, he was still disturbed. I was still disturbed. I thought to myself, "Was that a war-crime? Did we just witness a murder?" I passed by a Staff Sergeant who'd seen what happened, too, and he was shaking his head. "We checked out that vehicle," he said to me. "That guy didn't have any weapons. And he wasn't dressed in black, like the others. His clothes were yellow. Now they're just red."

Something wasn't right. We could feel it, all of us. But we really couldn't put a finger on what that was. "What's amiss?" we asked ourselves. "We were just in the middle of a firefight. We were in Lutifiyah. Everyone was hostile. What's amiss?" It's not that any one of us was afraid to call a Marine out if we had to. It was more that we couldn't convince ourselves thoroughly enough that he'd done anything absolutely wrong. We just didn't know.

How the hell could you not know? That's what I ask myself now. But then, in the thick of it...I didn't, not for sure. And when it came time to tell our story at the COC, to put it down on paper, my ambivalence would transmute instantly into cold hard certainty. My report said that that driver was an enemy combatant, even though he wasn't armed, because it was reasonable enough to say that he could have been.

Whether he actually was or he wasn't became irrelevant. He could have been shooting at us, we reasoned. He *could* have been shooting, and when he realized his time was running out, he could have thrown down his weapon and jumped into his car for a getaway. Maybe he had a rifle or an RPG in his lap and he was maneuvering to a better firing position. In the moment, we couldn't know. All we knew for sure was that he had just come from a place from which we'd been taking fire. Our justification to shoot lay in what we did not know.

The toughest thing about this fight was that we couldn't see our foes. Insurgents didn't wear uniforms. They didn't play by the rules...our rules, and they did some pretty underhanded shit in the course of a day—at least from our perspective. So who could tell one from another? We couldn't be sure who was hostile and who wasn't, particularly not in the middle of a firefight. But then again, it made it very easy for us to conclude, wherever there was reasonable doubt, that the people we did kill were hostile. So that's the conclusion we drew every time, and without hardly a word of discussion.

THE LUSTFUL

After the shooting ceased for good on that April afternoon in Lutifiyah, we waited for all units to report back in so we could gather the results. The result was that the insurgents were all gone. They'd dissolved into the city as quickly as they'd appeared. We had stormed through the neighborhood, searched houses and shot at cars that appeared to be fleeing. But no appreciable evidence materialized of the heavy ambush we'd just sustained. That was Lutifiyah, a city of specters that shot at us briefly, inflicted a few casualties, and slipped away out of sight while they waited for our heavy-handed response, the kind of response we claimed we'd never give, and the kind of response that swiftly undid whatever good we might have done. So the insurgency grew. That was the war in Iraq.

We'd barely been in country a month and SASO was already beginning to fade. I can say with confidence that no one gave a shit about SASO that day, and our operational focus from there forward reflected it. Under the circumstances, how hard could one really think about helping the people? It was tough to imagine ourselves driving down route Jackson with a water truck and calling out, "Hey you guys look really hot from digging in all those IEDs and shooting at us from windows and whatnot…why don't you come on over and have a cool drink of water?" From then on, the emphasis in northern Babil was on two things—raids and patrols—otherwise known as *combat operations.*

We called ourselves the Warlords, but we never got to taste the kind of succulent full-scale conflict we craved. We were doomed to this unrenowned province, this insidious suburb that jabbed at us with incessant IEDs, with minor indirect fire attacks, and these ancillary skirmishes, but never with decisive combat.

We craved battle. We lusted for it. But the Warlords were never given the opportunity to really fight, only to defend ourselves as best we could, to raid and patrol, and to contribute names to the death toll in the process. And every casualty made us still more thirsty for blood. Where there were ten "glorious" deaths in Fallujah for the television spectators back home to cheer or faddishly grieve, there were ten times that many inglorious deaths in other unknown provinces like ours, on unknown roads like route Jackson, where there was no fight, no media coverage, no victories, and no glory.

There was only death.

THREE

THE LAND OF OZ

When those four American contractors were killed in Fallujah back in March of '04, it was like the answer to our prayers. The Marine Corps laid siege to the city, and prepared for an all-out attack. That's when the Regimental Commander called our Colonel and said, "Grab your shit and get your people up here!" That was the best news we'd heard since we got in country. "What could be better?" we thought. Leave this shit-hole in Mahmudiyah, leave route Jackson far behind, and get into a historical battle in Fallujah? Fuckin-A! We were all in. I was picked to go on the advance party to Camp Fallujah to help iron out the details of our transition. That meant a few days away from the battalion, and as far as I was concerned, that was okay.

Everybody was still calling Camp Fallujah "MEK" back then, though we could never figure out what the hell it meant. We toyed with a few possibilities, tried to make various acronyms fit, but none seemed exactly right. People said it used to be an old terrorist training camp. They said there was proof, documentation, photographs…. They said a lot. At that point, I was prepared to doubt anything. But then I came home and discovered they were right and that "MEK" stood for Mujahideen-e Khalq—an Iranian dissident group harbored by the Iraqis and listed by the U.S. State Department as terrorists, and then subsequently invited into a dubious allegiance with our military for their ill-will toward Iran. Interesting, I thought, that we should adopt their name for our new camp. But we did, and it stuck. The new geographical designation—Camp Fallujah—didn't take immediately. Marines, as a rule, are resistant to arbitrary name-changing.

Whatever the name, it was our biggest camp in the country. It was no Green Zone, in terms of luxury, but it had nearly all the amenities. There was a general store (a PX), a Subway, a Burger King, a gym, and a recreation facility with a pool, and there were volleyball courts scattered all over the place with guys (and even girls) in shorts and bare feet playing and barbecuing, and drinking non-alcoholic beer.

Everybody seemed chilled out. Nobody looked worried about the war or about in-coming. Nobody wore their gear. I gaped wondrously at two Marines jogging down the street in their little silky shorts, and I said, "Man, we ain't in Kansas anymore." Running around bundled up in helmets and flak jackets, dodging mortars, rockets, and IEDs was our norm. That was our Kansas. This place was like the land of Oz.

The Regimental Command Post was a miniature palace with its marble floors, its eight-foot windows and its twelve-foot doors. The whole building was pretty magnificent. I walked into the foyer, which was probably bigger than the house I live in today, and found it lined with rows of ominous looking wooden crosses, about the size of a grave marker. On every cross hung a flak jacket and a helmet. It looked like a memorial site to me, but in fact it was more like a coat closet. Then I wandered on into the COC and found the place cool and quiet. There were comfortable chairs and great big flat-panel computer monitors hanging on the walls.

"I didn't even know they made 'em that big," I remarked, astonished, to a clerk as I passed by. He smiled at me dully and went back to work. The place was high-tech. It was laid back too. Nobody was screaming into phones or radios. Nobody was sweating their asses off, or sweating the war, or trying to pick up a detail or two from their units in contact. There were no units in contact. Nobody was calling in medevacs, or scrambling for the social security numbers of wounded Marines to type into casualty reports.

The people I met were dull and affable, and mellow to the point of lethargy. "Am I in the wrong place?" I asked myself. "Have I got the wrong war here?" We waited in the conference room to be briefed on the latest in Fallujah. The table was long and shiny. The television screen was so big I thought maybe they'd stolen it from a drive-in theater. We watched the news—Fox News. Finally, the Operations Officer came in and gave us the scoop.

"We're going in," he said optimistically. *Fuckin-A*, I nodded to myself. That was reason enough for optimism. He said, "This is going to be the biggest battle since Hue City." And you could see the glisten in his eyes. If I'd had a mirror, I would have seen the glisten in my own eyes too. Then he stepped over to a satellite image of Fallujah that covered an entire wall and gave us the plan.

He swept his arms very dramatically left, and then he swept them very dramatically right, and he showed us how the units would move through the assault, and then he smiled. "That's how we're going to do it." It was that easy. *Wow*, I thought. We used to sit around in planning meetings for hours, and that was just to raid one little house. He just laid out a plan to wipe out an entire city in about two minutes. This was indeed a different war. This was better.

As we walked out toward the front door, someone checked his watch and said it was chow time. It always seemed to be chow time on Camp Fallujah. A number of Marines started throwing on their gear. "What's up with that?" I asked one of them. "I thought you guys didn't wear gear around here."

He said nonchalantly, "Mortar hours. Gotta have your gear on during mortar hours or they won't let you in the chow hall."

I looked at him kind of funny and said, "What the hell is a mortar hour?"

He shrugged, "You know how it is. Some guy puts a pie chart together and tells the General, *this is when we're getting hit the most*, so the General says we gotta wear our gear during these times. Hence…mortar hours." Then he laughed, "Nobody was listening at first, until he told the chow hall not to let us in without our shit on. Now everybody wears their shit."

I shook my head. "Jesus, you had to be coerced with food to get you to wear your gear? That must be some pretty damned tasty chow."

He stopped and looked up at me surprised. "You've never been to the chow hall here?" He shook his head with a smile. "You have no idea, my friend."

The man did not lie. I really did have no idea this kind of sumptuous fare was available within the boundaries of war. It was a royal banquet every day. There were king crab legs, Cornish hens, and steaks to boot. There was a potato bar, taco bar, ice cream bar, pasta bar, salad bar with soups and breads and spices, fruit displays, and dessert trays, and they were all manned by Iraqi men stuffed into white shirts and black bow ties. I was pretty sure the Iraqi people outside the gates weren't eating so well. Hell, I knew a lot of Americans back home who weren't eating so well, either. "Jesus," I gasped, as I gazed across the splendor. "Who the hell is paying for all this?" No one answered. No one needed to. We knew who was paying, and we knew who was getting paid.

SOLDIERS OF FORTUNE

Now and then I think about those contractors who got shot, stabbed, burned, and hung upside down from that bridge in Fallujah. I bring them up again because their deaths precipitated the siege of Fallujah, and I never stopped to wonder about that. I never asked myself, "What the hell do we care about these guys for anyway?" Sure, they were Americans, but they weren't exactly representing the United States of America. They weren't one of us, one of the troops. They were mercenaries—soldiers of fortune. They were doing it for the dough. Kind of hard to shed a tear when they're killed. I guess we needed an excuse to attack, and that was as good an excuse as any other.

Aside from all that, their existence was always kind of curious to me. I never worked with any of them. I never even saw one up close, but I heard there were thousands and thousands of private soldiers running around the country. I knew a number of Marines who talked about getting out and joining Black-water, and Triple Canopy, and a few of the other security firms. They all had pretty much the same thing to say. "Better money, tax-free, and you ain't gotta wear all that heavy-ass gear."

Those were the perqs. It was unsettling to hear a man talk about money as he packed off to war. It kind of took the nobility out of it. That's how I figured it. But then it was hard to stand in judgment of them when I knew only too well how I'd profited myself from this war. And so I waved, smiling, and bid them farewell.

The military is a non-profit organization. In other words, we didn't spend all our time thinking about the dollar, about the bottom line. And that made us quite smug at times. But somehow we did spend a good deal of time thinking about that bottom line. I made a pretty penny as a Captain, especially with the combat pay, and just like the mercenaries, I made it all tax-free in Iraq.

I thought about getting out often enough over the years, but the same questions kept popping up. "What are you going to do for a paycheck? Who's going to bring home the bacon?" They say, once you've passed the ten-year mark in the Corps, you really ought to stick around for twenty. It doesn't make sense not to, being so close to retirement and that pension for life. And then there were the incentives and the bonuses and the special pays. The money was lavish for those of us who had no real prospects for work on the outside. It was a comfort.

The golden handcuffs existed in the military just the way they did back home. We all had mouths to feed and rent to pay. And the military was good about taking care of our every need. They gave us food, shelter, clothing, and medical. It was all socialized. It was all free—basically. We were never going be homeless as long as we were in. And the longer a Marine stayed in, the scarier the outside world became.

That's a strange notion, with all our contempt for civilians, to be scared of their world. Out there, people have to fight for their scraps. Americans live in a system of fierce competition, but I never had to deal with it personally. I was always in the Corps. Even in Iraq, when I was feeling low, low enough to hang up my cleats and get the hell out, I couldn't do it. I had that carrot sitting up there in front of me—command. And I had that big stick behind me—life on the outside, on my own. I didn't know what else to do but to stay. So that's what I did. Folks can say what they like about us in the military, about all our dedication and our commitment, but I say it's as much about the bottom-line as any other profession.

SHOOTING FOR THE STARS

For infantry officers there were no bonuses. There was command. That was the carrot, always. It was all the glory a man could ever dream of. It was all the power, all the salutes, all the men popping to attention and bursting into action at his say so. It was all the glamour an ego could ever handle. It was indisputably the most sought after job in the military, regardless of the level, and most officers would do just about anything to get it.

To get command—the really big commands—to reach the stars in a profession of arms, to develop his credibility and his mystique, an officer needs, above all, corporate knowledge. He's got to have combat experience. That's the goose that lays the golden eggs. And with respect to combat, I think it's fair to say that there is an unspoken hierarchy of experiences. The bloodiest battle is up at the top of the pyramid and it just goes downhill from there. So being *in* a fight is always better than being *near* one, and being near a fight is most certainly preferable to handing out soccer balls and attending town-council meetings.

We craved to lead men in battle. I never met an infantry officer who didn't. That was the kind of combat experience we were after. We wanted to be in the fight—bringing firepower to bear on an enemy and achieving crushing victories. That may have been partly the product of our natural inclination to fight. But I think for the officers, there was something more. We knew that our chances for promotion could only be improved by getting in the shit. When I was in the Marine Corps, there were only handful of commanders who had participated in those types of full-intensity operations in Iraq (the rest were bogged down in SASO), and when they returned home and went strolling through the officers clubs, they would invariably be watched with furtive envy.

It would have been unfashionable for us to openly concede a preference for combat, even while calling ourselves "Warlords," but it was no secret that the preference existed, and it seeped into our movements and our language all the time. For instance, I've always found it curious how adamantly we referred to our foot and vehicular movements in Iraq as "presence patrols" (a benign description for that activity), because it seems to me that whenever any Marine or Soldier, officer or enlisted, gives his resume of the war after coming home, he always emphasizes the number of "combat patrols" he did.

Before Iraq, the old careerists used to tell us that combat experience didn't matter. They said, "Just do your job, every job, well." *Sustained superior performance*—that was their mantra. There was almost a whimper in their voices when they chanted it. That's how they apologized for not having had their own wars. But in the new age of global war, young officers' eyes shifted skeptically left and right, because it was clear that times had changed. If a promotion board was faced with two Marines, both superior performers, one with a war under his belt, and the other without, we knew who'd be selected every time.

I spent my entire career as an officer thinking, planning, and dreaming, of the day I'd take command of a company. I don't know any of my peers who didn't. When I finally got there it was indeed exciting to be at the center of so much attention. I will say this for myself, and for a great deal of officers that I knew—the attention lavished upon us only made us strive harder to serve our Marines well. Our sense of obligation sprung directly, I think, from their loyalty and their faith in us as commanders. But when I decided to give up my command, I noticed nobody was trying to get me to stay. Nobody was twisting my arm, or even sad to see me go. There were fifty other officers waiting in the wings for me to move on so they could jump into my chair. I remember attending the retirement ceremony of an old colonel when I was a second lieutenant. He said to us, "If you ever want to know how important you are to the Corps, just jump out of the tub and look down to see how fast the water fills in the hole you left behind."

BENEFIT TAGS

I've talked a lot about money. But as I look over the whole situation, I know it's not all about the cash. There's something else that drives men to war. Life in the military, in many ways, can be an austere existence. So why do men fight? There are all kinds of theories. Why do they actually pull the trigger? Why do they kill in the thick of combat? I always heard it was camaraderie. I guess that's probably true. It does seem unlikely that a man faces the rage of enemy fire for the image of the flag that waves in his head. So maybe camaraderie is why they act under fire, in battle, but what brings them to the battle in the first place?

People join the military for all kinds of reasons. I saw enough of them in my time. Me, I was easy on the recruiters. I went in and I knew what I wanted. I wanted the worst they had to give. Gimme the hardest job, I said. Gimme the toughest boot camp. Gimme the hottest months. Gimme the meanest Drill Instructors. Gimme your worst. That's what I wanted. I wanted to be punished. They snapped on a video of Marine Drill Instructor shouting, "If you want to feel the pride of being a Marine, you'll have to earn it!" I smiled and I said, "Bring it on." And they did—hard. And there were a lot of guys out there who went in to get just what I got. So for us, the recruiters didn't have to bargain, or make it all sound like a good deal. Because we didn't want any good deals. Some people do. Some people want the sweet deals.

I was a recruiter's assistant as a Lance Corporal. So I got just a little taste of the world that recruiters moved in everyday. It was indeed sink or swim—a tough existence. Every month the pressure started anew. The recruiters had to make their quotas. They had to make it or they didn't get their time off. They had to make that quota or the boss was going to be breathing down their asses. They had to make that quota or get fired trying. I got to know a lot of recruiters over my years as an officer, and their stories were always the same. They had to make that quota, they all said. Like the rifleman on the front lines who kills to stay alive, the recruiter's survival as a Marine depends on it.

I wasn't a recruiter, but I ran close enough to their circles to understand the way the institution bears down on a man. Just like in combat, there was no "better luck next time" for the recruiter. There was only that adverse fitness report, waiting for him, hanging over his head every single month, month in and month out, and if he got just one it'd follow him to the end of his career.

Every promotion board he ever went up for, as long as he was a Marine, would know about the month that he failed to get his quota.

When I was a young recruiter's assistant, I listened to the pitches. I heard them say all the same things they'd once said to me. "Hey man," they'd rap with a smile, "it's just a nine-to-five job, except you're wearing cammies." (This was long before the war.) "You want the college money? You want the steady pay? You want the career opportunities? You want to dive out of planes? You want the girls crawling all over you in your dress blues? You want to feel the pride? Well dig in man. Join the gun club."

When I was in the Marine Corps, particularly when I was enlisted, a million guys complained that their recruiters lied to them. And I laughed every time at their whining. I laughed because I got the same sales pitches they did when I was joining up and I never felt lied to. But I did my homework, so to speak. I ate up all the war stories, and the sea stories, and the boot camp stories from every Marine I could find. I expected the horrors. I knew about the yelling and the beatings and the discipline. I knew it and I looked forward to it. Whatever the recruiters failed to tell me, I forgave them or didn't notice because I counted on the worst. I figured any guy who enlisted in the Marine Corps thinking he was going to fly a plane or be spoken to softly was just dumb anyway and probably got what he deserved. I figured they should have taken more time to know. I also understood that being a Marine was a tough business and that would mean dealing with a lot of tough characters. That's exactly what I wanted. I'd have been disappointed with anything less. So whenever I heard a man say he was lied to, I always answered back, "No. You just weren't paying attention."

By the time I became an officer, the Corps got wise and figured out that not everybody joins the gun club for the same reasons, so it wasn't necessary to pitch the whole ball of wax to every single kid who walked in the door. That's when they came up with the "Benefit Tags." They didn't have Benefit Tags when I joined. All they had were the brochures with a lot of cool photos of bad-ass Marines. I loved flipping through those thick, glossy picture books and imagining myself a bad-ass, too. But the Benefit Tags were a new approach. It was a key ring with about a dozen tags dangling in different colors. Each tag named a benefit. The recruiter would fan them out and tell a kid, "Pick one you like. Pick three."

Depending on the tags that kid picked, the recruiter moved into a pitch, tailor-made for those benefits. The tags were grouped into two categories. There were the "Tangibles"—that was the cash, and the skills, and the stability, and the medical, and the retirement—and then there were the "Intangibles." The Intangibles were all those things that drew me to the Corps. It was the loyalty, the pride, the *esprit de corps*, the camaraderie—all of it. The stuff you couldn't put your fingers on, but you could see it in those brochures, in the pictures, in that look in their eyes, in that straight in their back, in that sharp crease in their jaws. You knew it. I did. I knew from the moment I laid eyes on them, I wanted to be one of them. That's what the intangibles were all about.

So further on up the road, when I was training recruits, we used the Benefit Tags, too. Sometimes when we were having difficulty with a recruit who wanted to quit, we'd take him aside and have a little chat. We'd pull out our Benefit Tags and remind him of all the reasons he'd joined up in the first place. The Benefit Tags were mainly used by the recruiters to get the kids to sign up, but on the drill field we could use the same pitches to get them to stay.

What I noticed over those years of training recruits, was that there seemed to be one benefit tag missing. There was no "War" tag. There was no canned speech for that. No big discourse on the merits of killing in battle and possibly dying. Of all the benefits one might reap by joining the military, war—the very purpose of a military—was not one of them. Did that mean that war was a liability of service? Maybe to some, but that wasn't the rule, not by a long shot, not among the Marines I knew. The Marine Corps wouldn't call war a bad thing necessarily (it was their reason for being, after all), but then it couldn't really go around calling it a good thing either. They'd be more likely to express war as a tragic necessity. But privately war was seen as a good thing, a benefit.

The glimmer of exuberance one catches at the edge of so many war stories does not exude a heart-felt sense of tragedy. Nor do the popular t-shirts and the tattoos bearing the Grim Reaper and the caption: *Minister of Death, Praying for War.* The notion of battle is no doubt intoxicating to many Marines. It surely was to me. Great warriors are immortalized in movies, in books, and in television. They've been the subjects of rich portrayal since the birth of war itself. For a common man with no other aspirations to greatness, combat is an enticing proposition.

The officers, on the other hand, came from a different stock. They were college men. Generally, they came from a little money, at least middle class. They were a sporty crowd. They were athletes, most of them, cool and sleek—preppie even. I'd say I was one of the exceptions here. I broke down tires as a kid. I never played sports in school. And then I was an enlisted man. So it was tough trying to capture that persona. But for the rest of them, being in the infantry actually added to that sporty image. War is the ultimate sport.

We did a lot of tough physical training, training that carried the nobility of being deadly if we ever had to do it for real. That's the kind of sport you can brag about—and we did. But the snag is that war can't be sporty while simultaneously being tragic. You can't say in a deep voice, "This is our solemn duty" and then add, "but it's a blast all the same." It doesn't make sense, but you hear it all the same. Some can live with the contradiction. For others, like me, it pulls them apart.

A BIT OF COLORED RIBBON

Napoleon said famously, "A soldier will fight long and hard for a bit of colored ribbon," and that statement, callous as it sounds, is as accurate now as it ever was then. Glory in the wake of victory holds the ineffable allure that is still today marked by the campaign ribbons and decorations that stack up high on the chests of the soldiers who fight for them. So what kind of action is rewarded with medals? Would Marines, for instance, be awarded the nation's highest military decoration, the Medal of Honor, for kicking ass in stability operations? Would they ever earn the Navy Cross for doing a bang up job winning hearts and minds? No. That's the answer, pure and simple. The biggest medals, the most prestigious, would always be set aside for heroic action—in other words, combat action.

The incongruity in their message was like an invisible slap in the face. You couldn't see it in front of you. You couldn't put your hands on it. But you could surely feel it. You knew—I knew—that something was out of synch. One minute they were telling us, Hey Marines, be kind, be gentle, be humane. Give a shit about their culture. Show the Iraqis you care. But the body language was different. It was saying to us in no uncertain terms: You want to get promoted? You want command? You want your medals and your glory? You want your job? You want the cash? Then get your ass out there and get in a fight.

FOUR

STORY OF THE FELLED BRIDGE

The most common question that people have asked me since coming home is, *What was it like? What were you guys actually doing, day-to-day?* It's a simple question, and a very good one I think. But the answer is not so simple at all. What we were doing day-to-day was in fact quite revealing. So I often tell them the story of the felled bridge. It doesn't encapsulate the entire war, but it was a crucial development in the operations of my unit, and I think the problems that we subsequently encountered represented many similar problems in a lot of other units. So this is how the story goes:

When we first got in country, our only mission was to get along with the Iraqis. It was that simple. All we had to do was walk the streets, shake a few hands, build a couple of schools, and we were done. Easy day. Sure, we knew we were going to get in a couple of scrapes here and there. That wasn't going to take away from the main program though. But then one day an insurgent—who knows, maybe two—took a satchel of explosives and dropped a bridge on our main supply route. Boom—just like that—it was down.

Well that surely caused a ruckus upstairs. The brass was hot. They got us on the phone and they said to us: *Get your asses out on that highway and fix that fucking bridge. And when you're done doing that, stay out there, and make damn sure it doesn't fall again. And oh by the way, go ahead and guard those nineteen or twenty other bridges in your zone too.*

It took a reinforced rifle company to guard them all. An entire company taken out of action, in one day, by a couple of guys with a satchel charge. That's a lot of guys off the job. And the siphon of combat operations was always sucking away more. That's when we broke out our calculators and started doing the math. How many bridges were there out there? How many miles of oil pipeline and railroad might we have to guard? How many municipal buildings? Just how many weaknesses could be exploited? We'd never have enough troops to guard them all. We went from stability operations to defensive operations in the blink of an eye. The nature of the fight was altered—by the enemy—and nobody got that back home. They all thought we were still busy liberating Iraqis.

There was a whole section of our AO, suddenly unmanned because of that one bridge—a whole town full of Iraqis that had no one left to relate to. No Marines were out there glad-handing anymore, and passing out soccer balls, and cash, and medical supplies. No one was doing SASO. They were all out there on the highway, standing for days on end at the bridges, making sure they didn't get blown up, because that was our lifeline. If we lost our supply route, we lost the war.

On the other hand, if our Marines were too busy guarding supply routes to do those things that might actually *win* us the war, if they were too busy to win the people's hearts and minds, then we would quickly transform ourselves into what we loved to refer to as the "self-licking ice cream cone." And that's just what we became. The war was changed from how it had begun. We were merely defending our ability to remain. We weren't even trying to accomplish the mission anymore. We were just trying to stay alive.

That's the story of the felled bridge.

THE TROOP TO TASK RATIO

After a while, we started looking at the hours in. We were short-handed, and that was our bottom line. We lined up the all the jobs we had to do, against all the Marines we had available to get them done, and it didn't match up—not even close. That's what we called the troop-to-task ratio.

We went in to Iraq to do stability operations. That was our bid for victory. That was the main effort. Without stability operations, there would never—could never—be peace. We said that, the U.S. military. We wrote it in our doctrine. But we paid it little heed. Instead, we defended ourselves. We defended our roads. We defended our bases. We guarded EOD, VIPs, and detainees. We guarded landing zones, gates, Iraqi infrastructure, logistics convoys, bridges, checkpoints, Pathfinder crews, engineer teams…. The list was infinite. What few guys we had left at the end of the day were doing raids and patrols.

And then we started taking casualties. The troops became fewer, the tasks became greater. The ratio was stretching, so we stretched with it. We stretched those hours just a little bit longer. We pushed those eighteen-year old "kids" just a little bit further. When a battalion operation came around, we took one guard from each post on the base and half their reaction force to get our numbers up. We sacrificed our own security to accomplish the mission. We had to, just to get enough bodies.

We struggled to develop a relationship with the locals while at the same time struggling to stay alive, and of course, we gave a lot more attention to the latter. Stability operations were the first to go in a pinch. After a while, they all but faded away. There just wasn't enough time or people to do whatever good deeds that needed getting done, and without the good deeds, it proved difficult to win any hearts and minds. I think that played a big role in why the hostility we felt in ourselves and in the Iraqis around us began to really swell. It made one suddenly wonder what the mission had become or what it always had been.

FIVE

HATE

One day in Iraq at a commander's meeting, word got up to the Colonel that an Iraqi detainee "fell" off the back of a seven ton truck, with a hood over his head, and his hands flex-cuffed behind his back. That's one hell of a fall. Everybody in the room laughed—and these were officers. I laughed. The Colonel laughed, too. But he straightened himself up a bit and he said with half a smile, "Let's not have that happen again." We all laughed again. "No, seriously," he said in not such a serious voice.

This was treacherous territory for him because he surely knew that detainees "falling" off trucks wasn't a good thing, but then losing the esteem of his officers for being too soft-hearted wouldn't be a good thing either, nor would losing his own killer instinct, and both might just have come in jeopardy if he sympathized with the enemy too much. A detainee getting shoved off the back of a truck was just the beginning. The deployment was still young. The hatred had only begun to germinate.

There's always a lot of talk about developing hatred when it comes to war. You've got to hate them before you can kill them…that sort of thing. So whenever a war comes along, little anecdotes crop up about how we hated. We called them "Krauts" or "Japs" or "Slopes" or "Dinks" or "Gooks" or "Camel Jockeys" or "Hajjis". We called them "them." We broke "them" from humanity, and then we broke ourselves from humanity too, and we met them out there in no-man's land and we killed them. That's how we hated.

But there was a catch this time—a flaw in the program. This wasn't supposed to be a real war. This was supposed to be a liberation. And we weren't supposed to hate the Iraqis. We were supposed to respect them, to befriend them, and to make them want to befriend us. The officers in particular were cautioned never to fall into the habit of using racial epithets. "Stay mindful of your professionalism," they said.

Not every officer followed this advice, but most did. I tried, though I wasn't always successful. I did my fair share of hating, too. But I tried to remember the mission—the mission they claimed we'd gone to do. "Win their hearts and minds," they told us. "Win the support of the people and the insurgency will fail. The Iraqi people are a friend to the American people." That was the pitch, and I bought it.

The concept of winning hearts and minds seems ludicrous to me now. I don't know how I missed it. What would we do without hate? How would we fight? How would we kill? Hatred for Muslims in America didn't start on 9/11, but it sure got a whole lot more fashionable that day. For the attack against the United States—no—for the insult, for the audacity, I wanted blood. I just didn't know whose yet, but I was pretty sure they were going to turn out to be Muslim.

So I understand the anger. I understand the life-clenching rage at the people who attacked us on 9/11. I get it. I felt it. A lot of people did, and that rage was the fuel that sent us headlong into Iraq. I knew, of course, that 9/11 was never cited specifically as a rationale for war, but then I guess it really didn't have to be. The images were all there in the background of our collective consciousness. The crumbling towers, the great balls of fire, the people leaping hand in hand from flaming windows to their deaths; it was all so terrible and close to home, and the only appropriate emotion that I could imagine was hatred.

Suddenly, there was fear of a new kind of warfare, asymmetrical warfare, *Jihadism*, the kind of warfare where a single desperate man can haul a nuclear warhead in his knapsack into downtown Boston and light it off like a roman candle, or slip a jar under the seat in a subway of some pestilent virus that will spread geometrically across the city before even the first victim is found foaming at the mouth in the ER, his flesh necrotizing from the inside out. That's what they called WMD, Weapons of Mass Destruction.

Soon every Muslim became a suspect. Every family with an Arab-sounding name became a terrorist sleeper cell, just waiting for their orders to attack the infidels, waiting for their opportunity to martyr themselves for Allah. I've met a whole lot of people who never felt a bit of what I'm talking about, but then again I've met a whole lot of people who did. Our hatred was palpable. By the time we got to war, it was ingrained.

The trouble with preemptive hate on the battlefield is that it tends to hinder a soldier's ability to make clear-headed analyses of his circumstances and react prudently. Decisions are always impassioned, rash ... hateful. The hate blinds him. But conversely, for a soldier to enter the battlefield without that preemptive hate would be to hamper his ability to kill quickly and therefore survive, and so the hate stands.

When we got to Iraq, we weren't just calling the "bad" Iraqis *Hajjis*—that is, the Iraqis who were shooting at us—we were calling all of them *Hajjis*. Because insurgents live within the populace, and the bad guys could have been anybody, we had to be prepared to kill everybody. And that meant we had to hate everybody. It's tough to win the hearts and minds of people you hate.

In *Homage to Catalonia*, George Orwell gives an interesting account of a street-fight in Barcelona that broke out between the Communists and the Trotskyists (other Communists). Up until that moment, they'd been on the same team, fighting on the same side of the Spanish Civil War. Suddenly every block became a battlefield, every building a barricade. But the soldiers, whether on one side of the street or the other, were not inherently hostile toward each other. They were all workers. They were countrymen. They were neighbors. They passed food and water across the lines to each other. They joked from the building tops. They didn't shoot at each other. It was the basis for peace, if ever there could have been. But then orders arrived from on high. Orders to hate. Orders to open fire. Orders to kill. And that's just what they did.

The experience must have made an impression on Orwell. In *1984*, he imagines a people of the future who gather daily for "The Two Minutes Hate," a mandatory rage aimed at whoever is deemed the current enemy in a war that seems never to end. Throughout the story, the enemy alternates inexplicably. And whoever is not the enemy is praised as the ally. No one seems to notice the capriciousness of it all. They are all too busy hating. This caricature of reality is not so drastic, I think. We are, after all, in an endless war ourselves—the War on Terror—and the enemy is always changing.

In my time in Iraq, the Sunnis were the enemy. We hated them. We hated them for their connection with Saddam Hussein. We hated them because we were told to hate them. And we loved the Shia. Years later, I discovered things had changed. Suddenly I was reading articles about our efforts to work with the Sunni—the good Sunni—and to rid their towns of the evil Shia militias. I picked up a magazine which contained a story titled, "An Unlikely Ally," about the Sunni. The Shia became the current enemy, and the designated recipients of our hate. Orwell's notion of Two Minutes Hate was not so far-fetched after all.

AN AMERICAN DREAM

One cannot move deep into a discussion of the nature of our fight in Iraq without coming upon the "invisibility" of the enemy. They inflicted casualties from the shadows, through IEDs, through mortars and rockets, through short-lived ambushes in the night, but seldom did they engage us face to face. They wore no uniforms, held no ground, and bore no flag. There was many a night in Iraq when I stood with clenched fists and jaw, chagrined by our inability to see the enemy. We frequently described them as "cowardly," though I suspect now that that was more an expression of frustration than a clear-headed analysis.

The enemy's invisibility kept him vague in our minds. There was no image to apply to our hatred, no countenance. They lived in our consciousness more as specters than human beings. That was a reasonable enough attitude in training, where all enemies are imaginary, but on the battlefield we needed something more tangible. We needed a real human being in our sights. The ubiquitous danger in Iraq combined with the interchangeability of civilians and insurgents effectively transformed all Iraqis into the enemy. It wasn't entirely short-sightedness or racism; survival demanded we think this way. So with few exceptions, the Iraqi people—contractors, interpreters, police and soldiers, passersby on the street—were all looked upon with equal suspicion or contempt. They had to be, for the damage they might do. Therefore every unfamiliar face effectively became an insurgent incognito. And in this way, we gave flesh to the enemy.

But with the embodiment of the enemy, we simultaneously rendered the rest of the Iraqi people incorporeal. These were the very people we were dispatched to save. They slipped their skins and disappeared into an illusory ideal, an impossible standard. It seems to me that in our quixotic vision, the perfect "Iraqi People" would have had to love all that we loved and reject all that we loathed including themselves. And we would not have permitted them to feel consternation about our presence or regret for their complicity. They could not have felt any resentment when we killed their loved ones, whether the loved ones were dangerous insurgents or unwitting bystanders. They could not have vacillated, equivocated, or felt torn in any way. And they would have had to cheerfully accept whatever fate we put upon them without asking questions or taking umbrage. In a war for hearts and minds, "umbrage" would have made them, by definition, our enemies. That is all it would have taken.

It is true that individual Iraqis were, at times, well regarded, even trusted and great relationships were often kindled, but out on the street beyond the wire, and in the vacuum of combat where everybody and anybody was a potential insurgent, our Iraqi friends who accompanied us on patrol were compelled to look upon their own countrymen as we did, as a threat. And so the "Iraqi People" disappeared from the world. They were subsumed by our notion of "the enemy" and lost to us forever. That is how we turned them from tissue to myth and how the struggle to win their hearts and minds became an American dream.

MANUFACTURING KILLERS

I think it's fair to say that the taking of human life is something we, as a species, are inherently reluctant to do. I've read that in books, but I've felt in my gut too. But the soldier kills for a living—it is his reason for being. Killing is not a by-product or some shitty collateral duty like peeling potatoes or scrubbing the latrine. It is the institutional point. It's not a trade secret. It just is. So how does the soldier bridge that gap between his nature and his job? It is a process known as *desensitization*. Every soldier is desensitized. I was too. War is the graduation exercise.

As a training company officer at the Recruit Depot I participated in the transformation of high school boys into desensitized killers. As an infantry officer, I trained them to work together as a unit, to kill as a team. Back at boot camp, they had me spouting off the mission of the Marine Corps rifle squad: "To locate, close with, and destroy the enemy by fire and maneuver, and to repel the enemy's assault by fire and close combat." They taught us martial arts—the axe kick—a swift driving heel into the enemy's face as he lay immobilized on the ground. They promised if we did it right, we'd leave his skull a broken mess.

They taught us how to sneak up behind the enemy and dig a combat knife up under his rib cage, how to gouge out his eyeballs, how to cut off the supply of blood to his head, or air to his lungs, and how to rip out his testicles. We learned how to butt-stoke him in the face, thrust our bayonets into his flesh, and we practiced on hanging dummies. These weren't the inanimate tires stacks of the old days. These dummies were dressed in uniforms, and they were heavy and dense like a man, and we screamed "kill" as our blades punctured their skins.

Most of all, we learned to look upon the act of killing with nonchalance. It was all just a game—a sport. It was fun, and we went home and bragged to our friends about all the new ways we'd learned to take another man's life. Our friends were impressed, and they said shit like, "That's bad ass, man."

I watched the documentary *Sir, No Sir!* by David Zeiger about the veteran's antiwar movement during Vietnam. There was a former Marine talking about a survival class on the killing and disemboweling of rabbits. He described how they led the rabbit out on a leash, and slapped it in the head until it was dead. Then they gutted it out, pointed at the crowd and said: "Some day, you might have to do this, too, to stay alive. He felt the lesson was more about desensitization than survival—getting them used to killing.

His testimony made an impression on me because thirty years later I got that same class. They were still teaching the same lessons. They taught us to suck the eyeballs out of the rabbit's skull for water. Then the instructor put the rabbit skin on his hand like a puppet, pressing his fingers up into its brain and gave his own little puppet show. We got a good laugh. We took pictures. I still have mine. It was indeed a class about survival—survival of both body and mind.

THE KILLING CULTURE

Killing is the culture the soldier has entered. But when folks back home want to glorify what he does for a living, that fact is often forgotten. He defends, they say. He sacrifices. He supports. He secures. But he never kills, not in the posters, not in the speeches, not in the news, nowhere. Nowhere back home does the soldier kill. But within the gates of any base or any fort, the notion of killing is mentioned so frequently, and with such nonchalance or even zeal, that it becomes a completely acceptable element of every soldier's consciousness.

When I went back to boot camp as an officer eleven years after I was a recruit, they were still teaching young men how to use their bare hands, feet, and various sharp objects to efficiently steal away human life. When the recruits were given commands by their Drill Instructors, they were taught to respond, "Kill!" The motto emblazoned on our rifle range was "One shot, one kill." When Marines pass each other around base we often use the affectionate greeting "Oohrah!" which is the Marine Corps' modified version of the Turkish word for "Kill".

Everything in recruit training is related to combat and killing. We show them no mercy, and they soak up our mercilessness and store it in their minds, and their arms, and legs, and trigger fingers for the moment when they someday meet the enemy. Then they dispatch all that mercilessness onto him.

One muggy morning after a heavy rain, I watched my recruits crawl through the infiltration course, through the barbed wire, the tunnels, and the mud. The last recruit to go through was a pasty-skinned kid with thick glasses. He was weak and I wanted to see him toughened up. Before he reached the end of the course his entire body was soaked and muddy. His face was lost beneath a coat of mud that almost entirely obscured the outline of his glasses. He looked like a big brown blob. His mouth hung open limply as he gasped and wriggled helplessly toward the last obstacle.

The rest of the recruits were done and gone. The course was empty except for this one recruit. A flurry of Drill Instructors (known among insiders as "Hats") descended upon him with a vengeance. We called it a swarm. They stuck their fingers and the brims of their campaign hats in the recruit's mud-ensconced face and they screamed all together to replicate the best they could the stress of war. I looked on approvingly.

The recruit kept trying to get over that wall, but he just couldn't do it. All the mud his uniform had sucked up probably added another fifty pounds to his load. Between each attempt, he stood there panting with shoulders slumped forward, legs wobbling and dripping mud, and a half dozen Drill Instructors circled around him, screaming. But I could see in his face, even through the mud mask, that his mental toughness was building. His pain threshold was growing. His tolerance for aggression was increasing.

Finally he made it, and he staggered forward to execute the culminating movement of the course—the shooting, or stabbing, or bludgeoning of the enemy—the killing. All the hiking, and the running, and crawling, and climbing, and the jumping, and the swimming, are for naught if you can't kill once you get to where you're going. That's the lesson we were teaching.

WAR GAMES

The one difficulty we had in training when I was an enlisted Marine was our inability to actually engage our "enemies." We used blanks most of the time, which gave us the sound and the smell of firing our weapons, but not the satisfaction of hitting our targets. By the time I became a Rifle Company Commander, technology had come a long way.

Sometimes we used computer games to save money, but also to give Marines a chance to identify an enemy on screen and to kill him. The weapons in the game were all realistic. The graphics were realistic. The view of the screen could be made to look like the sights of a rifle or a machine gun and the Marine "player" could focus on an enemy combatant running or firing at him and he could shoot him down. The man on the screen would fall and bleed on the ground. It looked and sounded real—for a computer game. The Marines had a lot of fun playing it, and this was one of the ways we prepared for combat in Iraq.

Paint balls were the talk of the town when I got to be a Captain. They made a special projectile designed to be fired through our personal weapons. What made paint balls so valuable was that they stung like hell. No one wanted to get hit, so we'd duck, and that gave our training a degree of realism we'd never before experienced. It also gave us a sense that we had real weapons in our hands, and that shooting really inflicted pain. That went a long way to transforming the act of killing into a casual, if not entertaining, activity. Paint balls were as useful to us, as leaders—the trainers of killers—as they were fun for the young Marines, the killers themselves.

When we trained with live ammo, we didn't shoot at colored circles. We shot at black silhouettes of men, or plastic dummies dressed like enemy soldiers that popped up and fell down when they were hit. The Marines fired from fighting holes, and they wore battle gear—flak jackets and helmets—to give them the feel of war. We made shooting a target so much like shooting a man that it wasn't hard to make the transition.

And when a Marine shoots better than his peers, he's admired and he's handed medals and badges and promotions—all to encourage him to pull the trigger with another man in his sights and kill him. Like it or not, that's desensitization. But desensitization doesn't eliminate morality from the consciousness. It merely postpones cogitation. Sooner or later, when a man's had a chance to think things over, he will find himself standing in judgment before his own conscience.

"IT'S FUN TO SHOOT PEOPLE"

General Mattis, who'd been my Division Commander in Iraq, was once quoted: "It's fun to shoot some people...it's a hoot." The media went crazy. They splashed the quote all over the place. People were appalled. The papers described him as a monster.

That was an odd reaction, I thought. Nobody in the Marine Corps was ruffled, not even the Commandant. And that's because in the Corps everyone gets it. Marines know that you say what you've got to say to make men kill, and to make yourself kill. Everybody does it from Private to General—all the time. Mattis' only mistake, I suppose, was sharing it with the public.

He pulled the officers aside one night in Iraq, and gave us a memorable speech. Enemy activity was on the rise and he wanted us to get tough, he said, to get downright mean. He told us he wanted to see insurgents' bodies lying bloody in the street. It was an ugly image, but he was no fool. I think he knew exactly what he was saying, and why. So did we. For an infantryman, the thought of fighting and killing is all around him. It travels as an undercurrent to everything he does. It is how he wins in a fight, how he gets decorated for valor, and how he gets promoted. For the infantryman, killing is how he survives both on the battlefield and in his career.

THE BEASTS OF WAR

I've heard many veterans give testimony about the desensitization that they underwent in the military. As a man who has trained many men over the years and who was trained myself, I know there is truth there. But that's only part of the equation, only part of the truth. Having been to war myself, it is my feeling that the training, this *desensitization*, only carries a soldier so far.

The training only delivers him to the threshold of war, through that first shot down range, through that first kill. From that point forward, he finds himself moving into uncharted territory. It is up to him as an individual to negotiate all those moral obstacles on his own. The training means nothing anymore. War offers its own training.

In Iraq, feral dogs were like feral winds—ubiquitous, and sometimes troublesome. FOB Saint Mike used to be an old chicken factory. That was our home, where the chickens were once slaughtered. It was the home to many feral dogs as well. We knew instantly that we could not share our home with them. So we dispatched a posse of Marines to dispatch the dogs on sight…and their fuzzy litters. I could never do that. Some guys could. Some guys could pump a puppy full of shot, then hit the rack and get a good night's sleep. I wasn't one of them.

In the night, within the sandbagged bunkers, there were rats. They were everywhere. They would crawl over our bodies, under our cots, and inside our packs. We could hear the constant rustling in the darkness as they devoured all those nice snacks that the folks back home had sent to us. So we declared war. On the rats.

I fortified my cot behind ramparts of sticky pads and sometimes I'd catch one. I'd wake up to a squealing beside me, snap on my flashlight, and there it would be—a rat, stuck to a pad, wriggling in terror for its life with pellets of shit streaming out of its ass. I'd grab for my Kabar—a big knife—and I'd plunge the blade into its back.

That was tough to do the first time. I actually lost sleep over that little varmint. I felt guilty. Me, the big tough Marine, the desensitized killer, tore up over the death of a rat. I was stunned by my own consternation. But I grabbed myself by the lapels and said, *You better toughen up buddy. You're in a war here. If you can't slay some filthy rodent in cold blood, then how will you ever kill another man?*

So I went right on killing rats with my knife. My fingers would whiten around the handle. I'd lunge. The rat would squeak as I twisted the blade inside its body. It felt like a small furry pouch of Jello. But sometimes the damned things just wouldn't die. I could see their tiny organs dodging left and right as though trying to avoid being impaled. I'd stab and stab like a psycho-killer until tiny droplets of blood finally trickled from the thing's mouth and the squealing faded out. Then I'd lie back and stare at the bloody tuft of fur on the tip of my knife. After a time, killing rats didn't bother me anymore.

Soldiers desensitize themselves in war, all in their own ways, but they all do it because they know that they must in order to survive, to push through the killing and to accomplish the mission, whatever the mission may be. They push the humanity out of the enemy and out of themselves and soon become mere bodies of instinct and survival. What is often discovered only later, sometimes too late, is that one's humanity can be quite difficult to recover once it's been evicted.

SIX

WAR CRIMES

April of 2004 was a big month. The first siege on Fallujah began. Unfortunately, by the time my battalion pulled into town and was ready to fight, the brass had already agreed to hold off the attack for further negotiations. This disappointed us. We didn't want to talk. We wanted to brawl. Instead they sent us to a small town called Kharma midway between Fallujah and Baghdad. We called it "Bad Kharma" because it sounded ominous, I suppose, and because it was said to be the spot where Fallujan insurgents were getting resupplied. The bosses brought us in and they told us, "The last company to go in there met with some pretty heavy resistance. We want you guys to go in there and clear them out."

We saluted and said, "No problem. The heavier the better." But when we arrived into Kharma, everybody was already gone. The place was a ghost town. We still managed to find a few Iraqis lurking in the shadows to detain and throw behind bars. We always managed to do that. And we found a few stashes of weapons and ammunition. But other than that, the days in Kharma were dull.

That was the same month that the Abu Ghraib scandal broke. Abu Ghraib was a tough-looking spot, and drab. We used to drive past it all the time, and when we did, I could almost feel the evil heaving from the pores of its stony walls. Well, that's the way it seemed to me at the time. The first I'd heard about Abu Ghraib was back home on TV before I went to war. It was a documentary about *Saddam's Torture Central.* This was the place where he sent political dissidents. They had some grim stories to tell about the kind of business that went on there—some pretty horrifying stories. And all those stories would swirl around the walls and blow in our faces as we passed by. It had one hell of an aura. They said thousands upon thousands of Iraqis were executed there and thrown into mass graves. That's a lot of dissidents. But all that was under Saddam Hussein, the Butcher of Baghdad, and he was long gone—out of action. By the time we got into town it was already a U.S. facility. It was still a creepy place to look at, but one felt inclined to believe the worst was in its past. And I suppose it was, relatively, but then we got a look at those pictures for the first time, and we heard all the new stories of torture.

So it turned out Abu Ghraib was still a house of horrors. But these weren't Iraqis doing the torturing. These were *Americans.* That made a difference, and it made for a lot of hard reflection. I knew more than a few guys whose whole attitude toward the war changed the moment they saw those photographs. Of course, not everybody was appalled. I'd say the most prevalent take in the officer circles was that it was unprofessional—a bunch of dumb ass kids who got hold of a little authority for the first time in their lives. And I'd say that's just about where I stood on it, too. We were disgraced by a military unit run amok.

In all my years of service, I never heard torture described in any manual or by any commander as anything but absolutely intolerable. I can say with a high degree of confidence that, among military professionals, torture was universally viewed as unproductive and unethical. And that's a fact I'm proud of. Abu Ghraib marked the beginning of our descent into some perilous territory, and the American use of torture (or methods strikingly similar to torture) suggested to me that a sharp fissure had begun to form between the military establishment and its civilian leaders.

Elaine Scarry wrote in her book *The Body in Pain*, "Whatever pain achieves, it achieves in part through its unsharability, and it ensures this unsharability through its resistance to language." In 2007, U.S. Code was still defining torture as methods that cause "severe physical or mental pain or suffering" and defined severe pain as involving "damage that rises to the level of death, organ failure, or the permanent impairment of a significant body function." I don't know how a prisoner could ever express that kind of pain with such precision. I don't suspect anyone really could, and so the torturer is left conveniently with no ability to know when to stop. That may be precisely the point. It seems that pain's *unsharability*, therefore, provides the critical loophole the torturer needs to keep right on torturing.

In 1978, during the "Dirty War," an Argentinean journalist named Jacobo Timerman was arrested by his own government and sent to prison to be brutally tortured. He had spoken ill of their regime. They figured he must have been a terrorist. In his book *Prisoner Without a Name, Cell Without a Number*, Timerman described their horrifying methods and their excuses for using them, which sounded curiously like our own excuses. He wrote, "The members of the Argentine military claim impunity in the unleashing of brutality, insisting that the war against terrorism was imposed upon them, in which case methods matter less than destiny."

And when the world cast a disapproving eye toward Argentina and these methods employed by its government, they responded with indignation. Timerman wrote, "They hold this anti-Argentine campaign responsible for focusing world attention on the tortured, the prisoners, the disappeared, rather than on the fact that Argentina is the ground where terrorism for the first time is being mercilessly defeated." He could have just as easily been talking about America. I've heard those very same words uttered here, by members of our very own government.

THE JURF AS SAKHR BRIDGE

At Saint Michael, we had a torture incident of our own—a minor one. There was a temporary detention facility on the camp. It was small—nothing but a canvas tent girded by coils of concertina and razor wire stacked several feet high, and guarded by a half-dozen Marines. There was really no cause for my presence and so I generally avoided it. But the arrival of two particular detainees made me curious enough to check it out. They'd been detained at the Jurf As Sakhr Bridge.

The bridge was roughly twenty miles west of Saint Michael and crossed the Euphrates river from Yousifiyah of the Northern Babil province into the open desert of central Iraq. The bridge was named after the nearby town. It was the only crossing for twenty-five miles in either direction and was thought at one time to be the choke-point of an insurgent supply line. A platoon was deployed there to keep watch for suspicious-looking vehicles.

One night, a shiny new sport utility vehicle (grounds enough for suspicion in Iraq) was stopped at the bridge by our Marines. Inside they found two Iraqi men, a couple of exotic-looking machine pistols, and a briefcase containing half a million dollars, cash. The men were detained—hooded, cuffed, and brought back to base. That night, I fiddled with the machine pistols. I held the shrink-wrapped stacks of bills briefly before they were whisked away for *evidence*. I looked out the window through the darkness at the detention facility and thought about those two men. The scenario was so mysterious that I couldn't help but wonder about them. So the next morning, I went down to look at them.

I stepped into the tent for the first time and stared down a row of twenty cages that lined its insides. They were cages, not cells. Each cage held a man. Each cage was small. There was barely room to lie down or stand up. The place was more like a kennel than a jail. The stagnant heat, combined with the stench of sweating bodies, was asphyxiating. I had to step back out of the tent to catch my breath. Then I went back in. This time I was ready.

I paced down the aisle slowly, examining each man carefully, and each man examined me carefully back with steady eyes. In the last cage sat one of the two men from the SUV. He was fat. That's how I knew it was him. The others all looked the same to me—wiry and sullen. He looked sad. He was wearing a thin white disdasha and held a Koran in his lap. I stopped to look him over. At first he stared back at me dully, without a word, as one would expect from a man inside a cage, but then his eyes brightened. He'd noticed my shiny rank insignia and figured I must have been someone important. He figured wrong.

He stood up and started speaking rapidly. I didn't understand him. I didn't speak his language. But he chattered on nevertheless. He reached his hands out to me. His tone began to sound desperate and more alarmed as I turned away. "Shut up!" warned one of the guards. But he didn't shut up. He didn't speak their language. I motioned toward the guard that it was okay. The guard withdrew.

I walked slowly back toward the entrance. Each man rose as I passed them and began yelling to me. It wasn't a riot. Their voices weren't angry, but it wasn't mere prattle either. I didn't understand the words, but I knew what they were saying. I knew what they wanted. They wanted help. The struggle within me reared its ugly little head yet again. I felt guilty for not stopping, for not helping, and at the same time I felt guilty for wanting to.

It was twenty cages. It was forty paces. It was five minutes. Why was I torn at all? I was a captain, a professional infantryman, trained in the business of combat for over ten years, and now in the midst of a war, bloody and mean, and these were insurgents, criminals. These were terrorists. They attacked us. That's what I wanted to believe, but I just couldn't make it stick.

We had a Corporal named Wassef Ali Hassoun. He was a linguist, part of the Human Exploitation Team (the people who interviewed detainees looking for useful information). Corporal Hassoun was originally from Lebanon, but he moved to the States and joined the Marine Corps. His name hit the news in June of '04 when he turned up missing from the battlefield. Then we found a snapshot of him posted on Al Jazeera's web page. He was down on his knees in his utilities in front of a masked man with a sword. Things looked pretty grim for Corporal Hassoun.

We all crowded around the computer to get a look. There was no doubt it was him, but the kidnapping story just didn't ring true. On the day he went missing, Corporal Hassoun had been seen carrying a heavy backpack on the R&R bus, and he'd borrowed a fair amount of money from a friend of his. We kind of figured he'd teamed up with some locals and headed home for Lebanon. Our suspicions were partially confirmed when he suddenly reappeared back in the United States.

Corporal Hassoun was charged with desertion by the government, and he was cast out by our Marines, who felt that he'd abandoned them and that he'd broken faith with the Corps. I didn't have much of an opinion either way on the matter, but Corporal Hassoun deserved credit, as far as I was concerned, for something else he'd done back at our detention facility before he left.

It turned out that four of our Marines on guard had been punishing a detainee by shocking him with a live power wire attached to a converter delivering 110 volts. *Well, no wonder they were asking for my help*, I thought. But it was Corporal Hassoun who helped them. He reported what was happening to the command. That took a lot of guts, I thought, because it's not always easy to do the right thing in war, especially when it means turning in your fellow Marines for crimes that carry serious penalties.

The guards were court martialed, the facility was shut down, and the prisoners were all transferred out, perhaps to Abu Ghraib. When I flipped through the photographs of those contorted naked bodies, I thought about every man I passed in a cage, reaching out to me, shouting for help, and how I just walked on by. Not only could I imagine their fate, I could *picture* it.

THE CASE OF ILARIO PANTANO

As Watch Officer in the COC, one of my duties was to deploy our Quick Reaction Force (QRF) out into the AO, where an immediate presence was required. In other words, when the shit hit the fan, I sent in back-up. The QRF rotated from one platoon to the next, and they'd be on call for a few days at a stretch.

One morning in early April, before Fallujah and Abu Ghraib, we were approached by an Iraqi man who said he had a couple of insurgents holed up in his house, where they'd been storing weapons and explosives, and running their insurgent operations. He couldn't get them to leave and he wanted us to go in there and run them off, or drag them away. So I called in the QRF.

That day the platoon commander was Second Lieutenant Ilario Pantano. I gave him the skinny and sent him on his way. Ilario took his platoon to investigate the house and, sure enough, the man's story proved true. Ilario found weapons, explosives, and the two insurgents inside. The men were detained, but in the process of searching their vehicle Ilario shot them both dead. Of the factors in this case, two in particular raised suspicion among authorities. First, he'd emptied two full magazines—around sixty rounds—into the bodies of the two detainees. And second, above the carnage, he left a note on their car that read, "No Better Friend, No Worse Enemy," the mantra of General Mattis, our Division Commander. In essence, the General had asked for bloody insurgents, and that's what he got. Though Ilario reported the shooting as self defense, he was charged with two counts of premeditated murder.

Charging a soldier who has killed allegedly in self-defense is a tricky business, whether legally appropriate or not. The consequences are grave, not only for the individual, but for the rest of the unit as well. A commander, any commander, in a situation like this, finds himself in muddy waters. Nothing is clear. He walks a fine line in these cases, particularly the ambiguous ones, because the troops will almost certainly start to worry that, when it's their turn to pull the trigger, they too may find themselves on the wrong end of a court martial. The commander knows this is a bad thing, because he needs his boys unhesitant and willing to kill. That's what all that desensitization was about back in training, and that is what is going to give him his fire-superiority and his victory in battle. On the other hand, when a commander connives at the small war crimes, bigger ones inevitably crop up.

But there is another fine line that became much more apparent to me in the wake of Ilario's case. It is the line between fantasy and reality. The military accommodates a certain degree of fantasy in the minds of its soldiers—a high degree I would say. It is the lore and myth of battle, a potent apparatus for overcoming the reluctance to kill, and creating justifications for having done so. I think this is well understood, at least unconsciously, throughout the military, and so little effort is ever made to recognize its flaws. The fantasy of war can take a man's head into combat and out again without a scratch. His body, however, may get snagged in the reality. He may get wounded or killed. Or he may get charged for murder. What is troubling to the individual soldier is that the line between the two is indiscernible; it is not defined; it is elusive and ever-shifting.

On one day, a soldier may be encouraged or congratulated for his killing, yet on the next he may be frowned upon. The fantasy is that the law provides sufficient parameters to tell the difference. The reality is that it does not. That may be convenient at times, when circumstances get cloudy and the justifications to fire grow tenuous, but it can be inconvenient too for those who find themselves charged with a crime. While the facts of any given case may seem clear in the cool setting of a courtroom, they become decidedly less clear in the context of the battlefield where the soldier is continually bombarded by the mixed-messages of his leaders and a merciless enemy trying to kill him. So do they want bloody insurgents lying in the streets, or don't they? It is not always easy to tell, and the allegations that crop up periodically strike soldiers, I think, as arbitrary or as nervous deference to public opinion.

After Ilario was relieved of his duties as a platoon commander, he was sent to work with me in the Operations section while the investigation ensued. That is where I got to know him, and how we became good friends. That was unusual for a Captain and a Second Lieutenant. But Ilario was older than the other lieutenants—he was my age—and he'd gone to Marine boot camp before he took a commission, just like me. We were on Parris Island the same summer of '89. We'd developed a bond. We spent many a long night on the roof of that CP, smoking and joking, talking shop, and watching enemy rockets fly overhead and tracer fire stream up into the darkness from afar. We shared a lot of personal shit. So I gave a lot of thought to his case.

Though the charges against him were ultimately dropped, the case of Ilario Pantano churned up a lot of conflict for me. Because I was his friend, I felt naturally unsympathetic to the men he'd killed and bitter toward the men he had served (and whom I'd served too), and then been charged by. It wasn't about evidence. It was about camaraderie, I suppose. It was about loyalty. To stand by him meant to stand away from a lot of other things. My feelings on this matter were neither consistent nor rational, and I think that made them typical of war. Wars are innately inconsistent and irrational. War crimes are merely one of the many manifestations of that truth.

THE HERESY OF WINTER SOLDIER

It seems to me every war generates a certain strain of veterans who want to come home and talk about the less attractive realities of war. On January 31, 1971, over one hundred such men gathered together in Detroit Michigan to give testimony of war-crimes that they'd either taken part in or witnessed in Vietnam. They called it the *Winter Soldier Investigation*, a name inspired by Thomas Paine, who wrote, "These are the times that try men's souls. The summer soldier and the sunshine patriot will, in this crisis, shrink from the service of his country; but he that stands it now, deserves the love and thanks of man and woman."

Shortly before the *Winter Soldier Investigation* took place, Lieutenant William Calley's trial began for his role in the notorious *My Lai massacre*. Shortly after, I was born. A young John Kerry, serving as spokesman for *Winter Soldier*, testified before a U.S. Senate subcommittee on Foreign Relations about all that had been said. Thirty-three years later, in 2004, I was in a war in Iraq, John Kerry was running for President back home, and his famous testimony about *Winter Soldier* had returned to haunt him and the nation once more.

The television played and re-played segments of that hearing. I watched it from the COC in Mahmudiyah. He recounted the chilling tales of mutilation and killing and was nearly always followed by the voices of Vietnam veterans who felt betrayed by him. *John Kerry lied*, they said. *He sold us out. I will never forgive him.* So many years had passed since their war, and yet their hatred for him still seemed so intense. I was not from that generation or from that war, so I found their rage difficult to comprehend. Even if one accepted the possibility that some degree of falsification or embellishment had taken place at *Winter Soldier*, which was the common charge, one could hardly deny that war crimes did in fact exist (especially in the recent light of My Lai).

When the mind is pressed into such violent places, nobility simply cannot coexist. The My Lais, and the Abu Ghraibs, and the Hadithas, are only the most prominent and extreme examples of daily excesses that occur in war. War, after all, is a human endeavor, and humans are psychologically complex beings. They cope with war in a myriad of ways. Some soldiers revel in the violence, some abhor it. Some get scared in war; some get angry, bitter, or even vengeful. The stress bears down on everyone. And some soldiers reach their breaking points in sustained combat and act outside the parameters, whatever they may be, of acceptable conduct. Regardless of the efforts any military might make to kill morally, no matter how civilized the forces fighting think they are, and no matter how just the cause may be, there will always be incidents of excessive violence or inhumane behavior somewhere, to some degree, by some collection of personalities, under some set of ambiguous circumstances.

Atrocities will be committed, not by happenstance, but by definition. They are a natural feature of the battlefield. And the longer the war, the more break-outs will emerge. That's the way wars go. So to me, these veterans' objections to *Winter Soldier* seemed strange. It was as though they were objecting to the *exposure* of war's realities, rather than the realities themselves, as though public knowledge that war-crimes had occurred was more hateful than the fact that they'd occurred at all, as though this information was the esoteric language of some exclusive club, as though the American people should not be part of the conversation.

What appeared to evoke the most ire of all, among these veterans, were the allegations that, in Vietnam, the war crimes had elevated from merely a collection of isolated incidents to a systemic disease in the military. Or worse, that the military was knowingly employing these methods to accomplish its mission. The *Winter Soldiers* were accusing the whole of the armed forces from the bottom to the top of the chain of command. They were saying, *Everyone knew what was going on. Everyone knew—and they approved.* That was the heresy of the *Winter Soldier*; that was the betrayal. But it seems to me that what was being said at the *Winter Soldier Investigation* of 1971 was more important than just an indictment of the Army. It was an indictment of war itself as a place, a concept, an institution and an enterprise that, by its very nature, would inevitably yield exactly this sort of inhumane behavior. And *that*, I think, was the crucial message being sent.

In March of 2008, thirty-seven years after the original *Winter Soldier Investigation*, and five years into the Iraq War, a group of America's newest generation of veterans gathered outside of Washington D.C. to have their own *Winter Soldier*. The event was organized by the *Iraq Veterans Against the War* (IVAW). As a veteran myself, I was keenly interested to hear the voices of other veterans who, like me, had come to feel certain misgivings about the war in which they had participated, and so I attended as an outside observer.

Over the course of several days, there was much testimony that I found deeply stirring and resonant. Story after story was relayed by veterans, who had killed under dubious interpretations of the Rules of Engagement, who had behaved abusively toward Iraqi detainees and civilians alike, who had destroyed Iraqi homes and property, and who had felt a deep and irrational hatred for the

Iraqi people overwhelm their humanity and drive them to think and to act in ways that were in keeping neither with America's effort to win Iraqi hearts and minds nor with their own morality.

These veterans came from a wide range of areas of operations (AOs) and a wide range of military units. It was made clear that the problems they described, like in Vietnam, were systemic. And it was valuable, I think, that they reminded their audience that these actions and attitudes did not occur just in isolated spaces and times but frequently with the tacit approval of their chains of command, or under explicit orders. I could hardly deny that claim. I gave many similar orders in Iraq myself. I contributed to the violent climate.

There were, however, elements of the new *Winter Soldier* that struck me as discordant. From the moment I arrived, I sensed a conspicuous pressure, among those involved, to measure up to the *Winter Soldier* of '71. That would have been hard to do, I think, because while the two conflicts do share some attributes, in many ways they are distinct. Though Vietnam was often characterized, like Iraq, as a counterinsurgency situation, which presented many similar challenges, unlike Iraq the fighting remained, to a large extent, conventional and often against a conventional, uniformed foe. Vietnam was simply a bloodier war for the Americans. The casualties were much higher. The violence was felt much more broadly, sunk much more deeply into the soul, and so, I believe, yielded many more atrocities.

For those who served in Iraq, the experience was almost benign by comparison. Undeniably, there were extremely violent moments, which should not be overlooked; however, I never got the sense that the inhuman acts that began to pervade Vietnam ever took significant hold in Iraq. There were no large scale massacres, no "ears for beers," no detainees getting shoved from flying helicopters, no heads or genitals being cut off, no collections of fingers. Whatever mutilation may have occurred in Iraq was certainly not to epidemic proportions. Beyond those who served during the initial invasion and in the assault on Fallujah, most veterans did not see an overwhelming degree of carnage. Frankly, I didn't see much carnage myself. And yet the carnage was there.

By 2006, the World Health Organization estimated the Iraqi death toll was over one hundred and fifty thousand. That was at the low end of the estimates. Other organizations placed that number much higher. Compared to our own killed, the ratio was stark, and may have even exceeded the proportions in Vietnam. But most of our soldiers saw or took part in very little of it, probably because so many of the deaths in Iraq were caused by bombs and indirect fire attacks, beyond our field of view. I think this left many veterans, who were rightly concerned about our conduct in the war, struggling to justify their intense emotions with very few violent stories of their own to support them.

Measuring the Iraq War up to Vietnam in terms of atrocities and gore would be, I think, impossible. It is precisely how these wars are different that is most important to recognize, not how they are they same. In Vietnam, it was specifically the illegal activity that was the problem. In Iraq, it was just the opposite. Nearly all the killing and ill-treatment of the Iraqi people fell within the bounds of the law, or at least within one interpretation of the law. In the 1971 *Winter Soldier Investigation*, there was no question that the actions being described were wrong. (The question seemed more whether or not they had actually occurred.) In the 2008 *Winter Soldier*, it was the other way around. There was little question whether the actions described had actually occurred. The question became: Were they wrong?

SEVEN

FALLUJAH I

It was April 2004. Despite all our incessant patrolling and raiding, the Fallujah resistance was well out of hand. We watched the hearts and minds of the Iraqi people slip out of our grasp and into the clutches of the insurgents. They rebuffed our solemn attempts to talk and find peace. They answered our earnest promises of prosperity only with violence, attacks, IEDs, and rockets and mortars. The principles of SASO had failed. Diplomacy was dead. What were we to do? We did what was natural for us to do. We attacked.

Late in the month, we were given our orders and sent into position. Mouths were watering and broad with grins. The chance to inflict some real violence was upon us. "We gave 'em their shot at peace," we said to each other. "They had their chance to back down and they blew it. They wanted a fight. Now they got one."

It's the kind of thing you say to yourself when you want to hide away that lust for battle. No matter how you slice it, frame it, rationalize it, or reason with it, there's really no getting around what was obvious on the ground—we wanted to fight. We wanted it so bad, it ached. When we said, "This is going to be the biggest battle since Hue City," we weren't unhappy about that. We were bragging. We were looking forward to it.

I would be glad to blame it all on the officers, because they get most of the glory and the medals, while the enlisted men do most of the dying. I'd tell you they were cavalier because it wasn't their asses busting down doors and facing machine-gun nests at point blank range in alleyways. I'd say it was just the officers who were looking forward to the battle, but it wouldn't be the whole story. Because nearly every Marine I saw was smacking his lips for the taste of blood.

WAR-TORN

Here's a one-line war story: On the eve of battle we were confronted by a handful of Fallujan insurgents on the southern bounds of the city. I walked out onto the balcony of the house we'd commandeered to watch the fighting. A lieutenant came up to me and said with a smile, "You should've seen it. We gave 'em the old *shake 'n' bake*." (That was a mix of high explosive and white phosphorus mortar rounds.) He laughed, "You should have seen 'em burn!"

When I think about that story, I try to remember all the elements involved. Because it's more than just a simple war story. The very words "shake 'n' bake" are part of the story, and so is the grotesque reality behind them. The lieutenant's smile, his enthusiastic tone of voice and his eagerness to tell it to me, are part of the story, too.

His assumption that I wanted to hear the story is part of it, and so is my reluctance to say, "That was a terrible fucking story, lieutenant." Him telling that story back home to certain people is part of it, as is me telling that same story in my own way to other people. That story and how it exists in the collective consciousness is all part of that simple one-line story. "You should have seen 'em burn."

Another crowd of insurgents began firing at us from a distant building, so we dropped a bomb on them. The building turned to rubble; the shooting stopped. That was the unwritten, but much appreciated, SOP. We operated under the theory, Why bleed when you can call for air? There was no telling who else died in that building, and we weren't about to go check. I doubt anyone, including me, gave it a second thought. If we did, I doubt we'd have cared. To each other we would just shrug and say casually, Shit happens! To the people back home we would solemnly utter the phrase "Collateral Damage."

Up on the third floor of our Command Post the snipers set up shop with a couple of mattresses laid out by the window. They stretched out, peered through their scopes, and searched for targets of opportunity. An Iraqi man and woman emerged from a building in the distance waving a large white sheet. Out on the balcony a Master Sergeant paced nervously behind his Marines. "I've gotta watch these guys," he said to me. "One of 'em will wind up taking a shot." I was glad somebody was watching us. I might have found an excuse to take a shot, too.

Sounds like I can't make up my mind, doesn't it? Sounds like I don't know what I wanted, or who I was, or whether I cherished the killer in me or despised him. And that is exactly right. My moods swung across the war with the passing shifts, and moons, and meals. For example, there was a morning I woke up on the stone floor of a room filled with sun, and stinking piss bottles, and broken glass crunching beneath my back, and a phalanx of flies swarming in my face, and I was inexplicably happy and ready for whatever war had to offer. And on another morning, before dawn, I poured myself a cup full of vodka. It was meant to be a celebratory drink for some achievement or feat that I can no longer remember. I took no more than a sip before I collapsed on my cot into a desperate, lonely sleep.

There were moments when I looked into the eyes of the Iraqi people that I saw in the street, and I could not bring to mind anything more decent or beautiful. Other times, those same eyes brought a bile-like hatred up from my gut and it burned in my mouth, as acid burns. It burned away my humanity and cleared the way for that craving to kill, that taste for blood that I'd been harboring for so long. I was torn by the war. There really was no telling how

I'd feel from one moment to the next. There was no fixed point from which to navigate. No anchorage.

I was searching for something I couldn't touch or describe, but I could see it in the mirror. The horizon lay across my own eyes. The points I sought shifted and shrank with my pupils. The hunt was for the man deep inside me that I never knew. The hunt itself was the only consistent thing on the battlefield that I could attach myself to. War is a strange place to go "finding yourself," I'll admit, but for a soldier, where else is there? Where else can a soldier find out how he truly feels about killing? So at times, I can honestly say, I wanted to kill...I did. Even with my own ambivalence growing slowly inside, there was still that lust for battle.

NO FEAR

What I couldn't find anywhere was our embarrassment, or concealed cowardice, or humiliation. Where was the fear on the eve of battle? I couldn't find a trace of it. I saw a little fear on route Jackson. At its worst, that road was certainly dangerous, and a Marine might find fear slipping through his cracks once in a while. But then again, it wasn't that bad. He could push it away. The fear was there, I suppose, hiding, but it might have been closer to denial. Route Jackson was a crap shoot, and you told yourself, "I can't lose." The fact is, odds were with you. You probably wouldn't. It wasn't like WWI where you'd go up to the trenches and come back three days later with half your company dead.

In Iraq, you might do a year and lose fifteen or twenty guys out of your entire battalion. Sometimes it was less, sometimes more, but not by much. When I first got to Iraq in 2004, the death toll was sitting at almost eight-hundred. There were more murders in the state of New York that year. By the time I left, the death toll had reached nearly 1500—since the war had begun a year and a half earlier. The U.S. lost over 1500 men in WWII on D-Day alone. One day, 1500 dead.

Statistics like these live a tiresome existence in the aftermath. Back at home, nobody gives a rat's ass about them, but when those statistics are in the making, in life, they have real bearing. If you look around long enough and you think the numbers look good, well, you start to believe in immortality. So we were angry, and ready to kill, but I don't think anyone was all that scared.

BAD PRESS

As the battle drew closer, we searched beyond the mission statements and the speeches for our own rationale to attack. Most of us reasoned that the United States had attacked Afghanistan for harboring terrorists, and so in Fallujah, we would do the same thing. Actually, we employed a variation of that attitude all over the country. The way we figured it was that turning a blind eye to insurgent activity, or minding one's own business, was tantamount to connivance, which equaled complicity. That made anyone who did it the enemy.

In Iraq, a man's brain was pummeled by three things: the sounds of exploding ordnance, the screams of pain, and the voices of self-righteousness. No wonder we were ready to fight. Fallujah was often said to be a battle between Good and Evil. I think we were all quite willing to imagine it in such apocalyptic terms. Suddenly the place was crawling with embedded reporters from top magazines. Suddenly we were interesting.

They looked kind of funny wandering around the battlefield in their civilian clothes and their long hair. Generally speaking, Marines have a real disdain for civilians, particularly bleeding-heart reporters. But these guys were different. They were on our side. Hell, they were practically groupies. They wouldn't have gotten past the door if they weren't. So we were like rock stars for the first time in our lives, with flash bulbs popping in our faces. Who could argue with that? They were going to make us immortal.

But still, I scratched my head. Why all the interest now? We'd been fighting for months. Where were all the reporters back in Mahmudiyah? Where were they on route Jackson? Nowhere to be found. Because this was a whole new ball game—a conventional fight—it was what Marines do best. We knew very well that we would win in Fallujah, and that's exactly what the American public, and therefore the media, wanted to see—a win.

In response to Americans' appetite for decisive victory, the military adopted what became known as "The Powell Doctrine"—overwhelming force applied over a limited space of time. The problem in Iraq was that we weren't able to overwhelm the insurgency. But we could surely overwhelm a city in a conventional fight. We could surely do that. In Fallujah, we could hand a victory to the American people on a silver platter.

The war in Iraq was not like WWII, where we moved our armies across the map and Americans could see it; they could visualize victory. Victory was tangible, as would be defeat. Victory in Iraq would be subjective, a point of view, or an interpretation of events that would be invariably skewed by personal agendas. Even when I was still in Iraq I would hear the word *winning* and I would cringe because it had no real substance. It had no particular definition. What would victory look like? Where were the criteria?

There were a hundred and fifty thousand troops all scrambling around Iraq, striving to win, but nobody really knew what that meant, so we attacked Fallujah where victory would be concrete, where at the end of the day it would be perfectly obvious that we held the ground, that the enemy did not, and that we'd won.

INSTITUTIONAL VIOLENCE

There is what I would describe as an institutional violence in the Marine Corps—the cultural institution that is. They've got all the laws and ordinances against various forms of assault, same as any civilian district, but in the Corps it's more window dressing than substance. A Marine should be careful not to depend too heavily on regulations to keep him out of a fight, or to expect justice in the aftermath of one. Because it's rarely going to happen.

When there is no one else to fight, Marines are notorious for fighting each other. It is, after all, a fighting man's organization. How heavily could we stifle the instinct in a man to settle his disputes through violence, when in fact that is exactly what he is paid to do? The institutional violence that I'm talking about flows subcutaneously through the bodies of all Marines. It is the underpinnings of their consciousness. It is the buttress of their existence.

So let me share a couple of stories from back in my enlisted days, to illustrate what I mean by "institutional violence." If there is one thing Marines are especially prone to fight about, it's fire watch. Fire watch is the guy on duty who stands around in the dark watching for a fire, or for anything else that appears out of the ordinary. When it's the middle of the day, in the middle of a work-week, no one minds fire watch too much. But when it's night time, when it's the weekend, or when it's outside in the freezing rain, then guys start to mind a little more. That's when the disputes come about. It would typically start with the Marine who'd had too much duty, and he'd be pissed at the next Marine who didn't get any, or the other Marine who was late because he overslept, or the one who missed his duty completely. There was always a beef sooner or later, and it was often resolved by fisticuffs.

Amidst a chilly rain storm in November, 1989, I lay shivering in a sopping sleeping bag, beneath an old dripping canvas tent, in the middle of a puddle six inches deep. It was the School of Infantry. It was two in the morning. I wasn't sleeping. I heard voices outside through the rain. They were angry. They grew angrier and louder. They were fighting about fire watch. I stared into a pure wet blackness, shivering, and listening. The fight escalated quickly. The voices swelled into shouting and threats, and then the shouting dissolved into grunting, and lashing, and rolling in the mud. Then I heard a final shrill scream and a low wailing of pain. It was over.

One man had bitten off a piece of the other man's ear—over fire watch. We were all punished. We spent the remainder of that stormy night doing calisthenics and digging big holes with small shovels under the fiery command of our instructor. He said he was going to teach us about camaraderie. "How will you fight the enemy," he roared, "if you are too busy fighting each other? If you can't speak to each other without fighting, then you won't speak at all!"

We dug in silence until daybreak. We didn't speak for three days. On the fourth day, our instructor allowed us to speak again. He said with a dark glare, "Remember this."

And I did remember. I remembered every time there was another altercation about something petty, and there were a lot of them. And their cumulative effect, over time, cut me to the bone. There were so many ways that the Marine Corps fit me like a glove, and yet this thing of settling minor disputes with our fists just did not make sense to me. I figured there was a time and a place for the violence—war. I understood the business we were in. But these recurring episodes of ancillary violence, I simply could not reconcile. Thinking back, that should have been a sign. I should have gotten away quickly, while I had the chance. But I didn't. I stayed on.

Now, I was no angel. I don't mean to imply that I was, because I played my role too. And I was not always so queasy. I wasn't one to fight over fire watch, but I engaged in the institutional violence all the same, sometimes as an observer or an enabler, and sometimes as a participant. The violence did not exist exclusively behind closed doors, but often with the tacit approval of the institution.

For instance, back in '92 there was a Marine in my platoon named Gerald, who was fat and annoying and never shut up. I was his fire-team leader. To make matters worse, he had a habit of antagonizing everyone he came in contact with. One night he antagonized the wrong Marine. We called him "Country" because he was from somewhere out there in the cornfields of America. And the only thing Country really loved to do was to fight. Country never played sports back home, or worked, or studied. He fought. He liked to drive around with his friends from town to town back in the heartland, looking for brawls. That was just his thing.

Now the honest but unspeakable truth is that the quaint little myth of America's finest—our heroes, our soldiers—does not always fit. They are not all the candy-bar-eating, wide-eyed, small town boys, or the idealistic suburban boys, or the street savvy city boys just trying to get a leg up in life. The cliché of the savage with the heart of gold is not always true, because some of them just ain't that nice. Some of them are cruel bastards. It's unpleasant to say or to hear, but it's a fact. There are times when the polite rhetoric must be set aside for a bit of reality. The world is teeming with iniquitous people; it would be unwise to assume, in an impassioned desire to support the troops, that the military is impervious to this element of humanity. It is also valuable, I think, to keep in mind that these sorts of brutal characters are scattered across the battlefield as well, contributing disproportionately to the violent atmosphere.

So Country was one of these remorseless kinds of folks. He didn't care about fair, or weak, or right. He cared about laying his hands on another man, and hurting him. He liked to hurt people. He liked to destroy things. That's how he found the Corps, I suppose. Maybe he figured it was a place he could do some real damage. Not every last Marine is the best and the brightest. I'd been out in town with Country on more than a couple of nights in Okinawa that deteriorated into bloody brawls. He truly savored the pain of others.

So when Gerald started in with him one night, everyone saw the outcome before it ever happened, and encouraged it. Just a few words were exchanged before Country shot his arms out like a praying mantis, snatched Gerald's head, and pulled it into his own, smashing them together. The head butt was among his fondest moves, and he used it often. Gerald may have been unconscious before he hit the ground. But as he fell, Country landed another heavy blow on the side of his head. Gerald's body fell into a still heap on the floor beneath Country, who could be described as nothing less than pleased with himself. Several of the Marines rushed Gerald to the hospital, and the doctors said it was a good thing that they did—a few minutes more and he might have been dead.

Beyond the grave realization of how serious things can get—and how quickly—nobody felt a whole lot of sympathy for Gerald. Neither did I. Because he was fat and lazy, and because he was a pest, it somehow occurred to us that he deserved what he got. When Gerald came back to the unit he had two long scars on both sides of his head where the hair would no longer grow. Country had cracked his skull open—literally.

So Country was called off to the First Sergeant's office to be "chewed out," but when we gathered around excitedly to ask him what had happened, Country just shrugged with a smile and said, "He closed the door, shook my hand, and said 'Good job.'" That's the institutional violence I'm talking about. That's the wink you don't see in the posters.

BLOOD STRIPES

When a Marine is promoted into the NCO ranks (Non-Commissioned Officer), he's handed a set of blood stripes, which are the red trouser stripes that go on his dress blues. He's expected to endure a little pain in exchange for the stripes. We called it "pinning the blood stripes." With our knees, we'd strike him in the legs. With our fists and elbows, we'd strike him in the shoulders for good measure. I had it done to me when I picked up Corporal, and that gave me the right to do it to the next guy, and every guy after. Those were the rules and we all followed them.

Years ago, a Marine's home video, made it into the pulic eye. I saw it on the news. The video captured a roomful of Marines "pinning" jump wings onto each other for having graduated from the Army's paratrooper school. The pinned Marines wailed out in pain, while everyone else in the room looked on with approving smiles. The public reaction was shock and horror. Our reaction was nonchalance. We could barely comprehend all the fuss. To us, these sorts of episodes were commonplace. We all thought it was perfectly appropriate that a Marine receiving some new uniform device should have it ground into his flesh until he screamed out in agony.

In my unit, there was a Marine named Irving who was promoted to Corporal, and I could tell he dreaded his own pinning. He tried, I'll give him that. I think he tried to face the gauntlet with dignity. But we were a vicious lot. And in the Marine Corps, there is a cultural necessity to always top the last man's viciousness. Everyone wanted to be regarded as the meanest, the craziest mother fucker, and our efforts to gain that title always translated into someone else's pain.

Irving was scared. I saw it in his eyes. But I didn't care. Nobody else did either. Truth be told, I didn't like Irving much. Two at a time we threw our knees into his thighs, and we threw our elbows into his arms for good measure. I drew a bead on his leg as I drew my knee back, and I drew a bead on his contorted face and the beads of sweat that covered it. I wanted to hurt him badly. He buckled immediately under the blows. But that was of no consequence to us. A Marine NCO walks from one end of the gauntlet to the other—no exceptions. So we helped him maintain his pride by pulling him to his feet and positioning him for the next set of blows. He cried out, "No please don't!" But we struck him again, and again, and again. He begged for mercy a while longer, and then I saw his eyeballs roll back into his head as he fainted from the pain.

But there is no such thing as leave from honor, not even when passed out. So one of our bigger Marines picked Irving up from under his arms and carried him the rest of the way through—unconscious—while the remainder of us laid blow after blow into his dangling legs. Then we laid him down on his bunk for the night to recover. I was no angel. And the pinning of the blood stripes went on and on in our unit under the inaction or tacit approval of our chain of command, until one Marine's legs were fractured. He was medically discharged six months later. Then they started to take notice.

PACKING VIOLENCE THROUGH THE AFTERMATH

Turns out, it's tough to lose the violence when you get back home from war. When you tap into that primitive part of yourself and you break that seal, it's damned hard to plug the hole back up again. When I was a company commander, after we returned from Iraq, a Marine came into my office, and I said to him, "How you doing?"

He shrugged and said, "I'm not doing too good. I'm dealing with a lot of tough issues. I've got a lot of anger going on. Every little thing seems to make me crazy—my wife, my kids, traffic… I drop a set of keys and I want to tear the house down, just for the aggravation of having to pick them back up again."

After he left, I scratched my head and thought to myself, "Huh. That's funny. I've got a little of that going on myself." Then another Marine came by, and I asked him how he was doing. He said the same thing.

He said, "I'm not doing too good. I'm dealing with a lot of tough issues." He wanted out of the Corps. He said he couldn't go back to Iraq, though he was due to. Then he said to me, "When we were in Iraq, we were in a firefight, and all of a sudden a little pickup truck came up behind us. So I swung my machine gun around and I opened fire. I figured it must have been some bad guys. I figured it must have been, because who but bad guys would drive up on us in the middle of a firefight? But when the smoke settled, I went to that truck and I found out it wasn't the bad guys. It was just a man and his little baby girl cut to pieces by my machinegun." He said, "I just can't get the image of that baby out of my head."

I leaned back in my commander's chair and watched the remorse eat him alive. I felt for the kid, I did. I said to him in my most reassuring way, "Marine, you had no way of knowing who was in that truck. If it had been the enemy and you hadn't fired, every Marine in your squad could have been killed. You did the right thing." And then I said, "Carry on." Carry on, as in try not to think about it anymore. Try not to think about that baby that you shot to pieces. Carry on, as in we have a mission to accomplish and we don't have time to slow down to think about dead babies. We'll call it Collateral Damage, and we'll all just carry on. And for that, I began to feel a bit of remorse myself.

Two weeks later, I saw that same Marine. His head was shaved to the skin. He wanted to try out for the sniper platoon. Suddenly he was "motivated" to go back to war. I couldn't believe it. I was enraged. I thought he was trying to make a fool of me. So I said to him, "What the hell are you doing? You can't kill with a machine-gun any more, but now all the sudden you can put a man's head in your crosshairs, pull the trigger, and watch his brains burst out the back of his skull? You can do that?" He never made it to the sniper platoon, of course. I made sure of that. Then his motivation fell off again and he started back into looking for a way out. Eventually, he found his way to a "psyche-eval" and got processed out of the Marine Corps for a "personality disorder."

When I look back on that Marine and others like him, I regret my attitude and the things I said to them. I spoke with my commanding officer's hat on. I spoke with an institutional myopia. I did that a lot. I was unable to recognize their humanity, or their points of view as men, and not troops, until I got out of the military myself and put on my own hat. Then I recognized their troubles as quite similar to my own. A man's relationship with violence goes from inexplicable lust to inextricable loathing and dependency. A soldier may find it a struggle to live with the things he's done, but then he may find another struggle living without them. Many a man has escaped his tumbled universe by returning to war—to war where violence and rage is right and normal.

On the day I came home from Iraq, my son John was sick. We called the doctor and the doctor said, "If he's not better in three days, bring him in." In three days, he wasn't better, so we brought him in. The doctor said he had the flu and told us, "If he's not better in three days, bring him back in." In another three days, he wasn't better. He was writhing in pain and crying all the time. He couldn't sleep or eat or get comfortable. It was excruciating to watch. So my wife brought him in. She saw a different doctor this time. He was irritable. He barely looked at John. He didn't do any tests. He just told my wife, "If he's not better in three days, bring him back in."

He made her feel bad about herself for worrying. He made her feel stupid, and guilty. Three days later, John wasn't better, so we brought him to the emergency room. He had an empyema (a formation of pus) growing inside his lung, which was filled with fluid. He was drowning. He could barely breathe. He was three years old. They had to rush him to another hospital two hours away for surgery—to cut the thing out. That was my homecoming and my introduction to post-war rage.

I would drive into work every morning. Sometimes it was one in the morning. Sometimes it was two. I wasn't really sleeping. I was angry. I was so angry about my son that I'd start beating the steering wheel and the roof of my truck while I was driving, until I became so hysterical that I'd have to pull over and climb out. I'd walk out into the woods and punch a tree, or kick it, or just scream. I had to do that just to keep from driving to the hospital and finding that doctor and killing him—literally murdering him.

For making my son endure that pain for so long, for making my wife feel guilty about caring and being concerned, I wanted to tear his heart out. I wanted to stab him a thousand times with my combat knife like a rat in the darkness. Then I'd calm down, get back in my truck, and head off to work. I'd tell people about how angry I was getting, and they would be so understanding. They would and say, "Man I'd want to kill that son-of-a-bitch, too." They figured it was normal. But after a while, I started to suspect that it wasn't.

FUCKING RAGE

Long after the parades and the parties and the welcome home ceremonies, when the honeymoon is over, the rage emerges. But it's not just rage. It's fucking rage. Rage has a reason behind it. Fucking rage has no reason at all. That's what I've got. Suddenly the proverbial spilled milk is worth crying over, worth fighting over, worth every tear. I hate a blowing car-horn for the tumult it stirs inside me.

It's not just the noise I'm talking about. I'm talking about the hostility that comes through that horn's wail. I'm talking about that fucking driver behind the horn, behind the glass, with his pissed off face, and his lips moving, and his teeth flashing. That's what I'm talking about. I can feel those silent obscenities hit me in the face. I can feel the aggression. And just that fast, my hackles are up, and I want to fight more than I want to breathe. That blasting horn is like a shot across my bow. It's prelude to war. It'll take me an hour just to come down from a fury like that. That's what the blowing horn does to me. It's not just the noise.

But that's not all. I'm enraged by a missed turn, a missed time, a missed opportunity, or a missing remote. Screaming children are worse than incoming, and I've got two of them of my own. Suddenly all noise, all pressure, all responsibility becomes too much to bear. I opened the fridge one night and a salad dressing bottle tumbled out onto the floor. My whole body tightened up. I felt the adrenaline surging into my muscles. My wife, who was in the room, dashed over to pick up the bottle.

She'd seen all this before, so she said to me in a reassuring voice, "It's okay. The bottle's not broken."

But it was too late. I was already gone. I glared at her and I said, "The bottle? You think I give a shit about the bottle?" I could feel my face quivering and my heart pounding. "I'm not worried about the God damned bottle. I'm worried about my heart," I shouted at her, "because it's fucking breaking!"

Society is a system of restraints. In war those restraints are to a great extent lifted away. In normal life, problems are usually little more than inconveniences here and there. But on the battlefield, problems mean lives are in danger, and a fight is imminent, and killing and dying are close at hand. In those times, rage is the appropriate emotion, and violent reactions are acceptable.

Combat breeds rage. Combatants espouse it, and will often embrace it like an old war buddy. But when they come home that rage becomes more like a parasite. It won't go away. It feeds on the emotional disarray of its host, sucking away its life until there's only energy left for itself. When the energy for rage is exhausted, despair often enters into the vacancy, pulling all thoughts down into a relentless feeling of isolation. A combat veteran will come home and be expected to assimilate back into society and to reconstitute himself with the self-restraint he was once allowed to unleash in combat. Where he could once answer rage with violence, he will be expected quite suddenly to answer it with poise.

Many combat veterans will be carriers of anger for the rest of their lives and are disposed to unexplainable episodes of rage and bouts of depression. These are the battle wounds most difficult for the families back home to comprehend. These are the wounds that lead to sudden outbursts of domestic violence, to abuse, to withdrawal, to broken families, to drunken driving and disorderly conduct, to jobless and homeless veterans, and to an entire generation of soldiers lost between the battlefield and society. These are the wounds most difficult to heal.

SANDSTORM

My rage about the war is a lot like the sandstorms in Iraq. All life is stifled under the sandstorm. There is no movement other than the wind itself and all that it takes into its jaws and blows out across the sky. The wind howls hard, scourging the land, as if to demonstrate its might to the haughty armies who thought *they* ruled the earth. It absorbs everything. All the sound and the light, as far as a human's senses can reach, blend into a dark deafening howl, a force that denies the existence of any other, consuming the will of all humanity, assimilating it, and contorting it into its own wrath. The wind never gets tired. It never stops until it wants to stop. And just what makes a sandstorm want to stop, I cannot say. So all we could do was wait.

Our night vision goggles didn't work in the storm, neither did the thermals, or the radios, or the GPS. We couldn't communicate. We couldn't move. Our vehicles couldn't be driven. Our weapons couldn't be fired. The entire coalition was immobilized. When the wind died down, a heavy dust hung in the atmosphere for hours. The air was stifling and hot. All day the sun baked its heat into the desert floor. Then the sandstorm lifted it up, and all that buried heat with it, and scattered it across the dark skies. Sometimes the heat didn't dissipate for hours into the night. That's what my rage is like.

HUMANITY OF THE LIVING AND THE DEAD

I dropped into a pub in Charleston, South Carolina, where I met an old-timer at the bar. He stopped to share a pint with me and talk about life. After a while, I told him I'd been a Marine in Iraq. He raised his glass and said to me, "Ah, I'm proud of you boys. You're doing a good job over there." Well, I know I could have just let it go at that. But then again, no, I couldn't just let it go at that.

I said to him nonchalantly, "Lotta innocent folks getting killed over there…. Lotta innocent folks." The man waved his hand like he was shooing away a fly. "Fuck 'em," he said. But I could tell by the tone in his voice, that he meant it to be an affectionate *fuck 'em*, a sympathetic *fuck 'em*. It was his brand of loyalty, his support for the troops. It was *fuck 'em* as in, *I understand. You did what you had to do.* It was that kind of fuck 'em. I knew exactly what he was saying because I used that same *fuck 'em* tone with my Marines when I told them they did what they had to do.

But what this old-timer and I both failed to see was that there are times when the things our soldiers see and do in war cause them deep pain. The suicide epidemic among veterans speaks loudly to that truth. And meanwhile, the rest of us are left with a rather strange dilemma. Either we allow ourselves to feel that veteran's pain, truly as our own, and share his consternation about war, or, in an effort to support the troops, we deny the significance of his tragedies and, by definition, we deny his pain as well. To regard his guilt as unconscionable or plain silly is to walk heedlessly on by those veterans and leave them festering in the memories, alone, with nobody to turn to and say, "I killed." When we say *fuck 'em*, we not only exclude the humanity of the dead; we exclude the humanity of the living as well.

EVE OF DESTRUCTION

When it came to Fallujah, the Marines were happy because the SASO playbook was finally being shit-canned. They could finally do what they'd been trained to do—fight in a full scale offensive operation. They hated all that "semi-permissive environment" business of patrolling streets, getting waved at by some people and shot at by others. They'd have preferred the greater risk of getting killed or wounded in a straight fight, and having the chance to fight back, to sitting by letting insurgents pick away at them one by one, with each man wondering when his time was going to come.

They hated all the restraints in the world of SASO. "Fuck SASO," they would grumble. "Don't gimme rules. Gimme a fight." They hated never knowing if it was okay to shoot or not to shoot. It was never clear. The Rules of Engagement (ROEs) were far too vague to be useful moment to moment on the ground. ROEs were ostensibly created to delineate the restrictions of firepower for individuals and commanders. Though I feel they served more often to allow the freedom they needed from those restrictions to fire-at-will through cleverly conceived loopholes.

The most junior troops probably felt the paradox in our message more palpably than anyone. "Don't break the rules," we would press them ardently and then with equal ardency say, "Be aggressive. Don't hesitate. Hostile action or hostile intent is all you need to fire." The word "hostile" was given a wide berth in Iraq. But it was all a lot of legal mumbo jumbo and beyond the concern of the Marine on patrol, the guy who actually faced the ambushes and the IEDs. He just wanted a straight up yes or no answer. Can we shoot, or can't we? Finally, after months of ambiguity, the answer was a resounding yes.

Fallujah was going to be a no-holds-barred kind of fight. Finally the Marines weren't going to have to worry about whether the people they saw in the streets were insurgents or unwitting civilians. It wouldn't matter in Fallujah. Everybody was the enemy. Finally a Marine could blaze away with his machine gun if he wanted to, and nobody was going to chew his ass. And if a woman or a child got caught in the crossfire, well...nobody was going to chew his ass for that either.

If a Marine needed to go into a house, he didn't have to stand there knocking on the front door like a fool, hoping like hell there wasn't a band of insurgents waiting inside to kill him. He could blow a hole in the wall with a rocket launcher or an Abrams Tank or a half pound of C-4, lob a grenade inside, and kill everyone before he ever set foot in the place. This was Fallujah. This was full-intensity conflict. This was war in its purest form.

There would, no doubt, be some non-hostiles killed in the fight. But collateral damage comes with every war. And one thing was for sure, no damn insurgent was going to get a free shot at any Marine this time around, not like when they were out there doing SASO. Finally they could do like the t-shirt said: *"Kill 'em all, and let Allah sort 'em out."* Finally.

PSYOPS

We established a Command Post (CP) in an empty three-story house at the southern edge of the city. The large windows were adorned by golden drapes. The floors were polished stone. The big wooden chairs with purple velvet cushions were gaudy but exuded a certain sense of luxury. That night, I nestled under the comforting roar of bomber jets passing incessantly above. I don't know much about planes, but I knew these were ours because insurgents don't have planes. The sky belonged to us. I strolled out to the patio to look up into the sweet blackness through which they streaked, and I realized suddenly that the roar was not the roar of planes at all and it was not coming from the sky.

It was an Army PsyOps team (Psychological Operations). They were a crew of hot-doggers who tore around the country in pimped-out humvees with stereos, massive speakers mounted on the roofs, and a peculiar collection of soundtracks. They were the battlefield DJs, turning up at all the hot spots of the war to spin their wax.

"How ya doing?" one of them flipped me a nod as he changed CDs. The roaring jets disappeared and were promptly replaced by the upbraiding voice of a man yelling in Arabic at concert-level volumes into the city.

"What's he saying?" I asked him.

"Beats the shit out of me," the Soldier said off-handedly. "Your mother eats swine...shit like that—to antagonize 'em."

Soldiers have been shouting obscenities across the lines at their enemies as far back as they've been going to war. Modern soldiers differ only in that they do it with Hi Fi. I gazed out at the blackened cityscape and wondered if they could hear the yelling, if they could make out the words. Do they think it's real? Is this going to make them fight? Well, I guess that's what we wanted. I doubt we'd have been telling them their mothers ate swine if we wanted to see them back at the negotiating table.

When the man finished his harangue, a crowd of wailing cats took the mike. They were annoying and unrealistically loud. The barking dogs track struck me as pointless. They seemed only to blend in with all the real dogs barking through every night and every street across the country—hardly an agitation. But then the DJs threw on the ringer—a screaming baby. After ten minutes, I was ready to fight. I was ready to go insane. The one good thing about being at war, the only good thing, was that I was not home listening to screaming babies, and now this!

The b-side of the PsyOps compilation CD, which they loaded up in the early morning hours, transitioned the mood from eerie to kick-ass with the greatest hits from everyone's favorite heavy metal bands from the seventies. They jump started the morning with Quiet Riot's "Cum on Feel the Noize," our less sophisticated version of "Flight of the Valkyries."

"So you think I got an evil mind," the song blared, *"I'll tell you honey, I don't know why...."* I hummed along and tapped my foot as we prepared for our attack. They rolled from Quiet Riot, to Alice Cooper, to Black Sabbath, and to AC-DC. We were rocking out when the DJ called up through the electric guitars, "Got anything you want to play?"

And we looked at him surprised and yelled, "Anything?" We figured there must have been some kind of scientific purpose for each song, carefully calculated in a laboratory somewhere, to have some particular psychological effect.

The DJ just shrugged and yelled, "Anything you want!"

There was no rhyme or reason to the selections. There was no method to the madness. We were just cranking tunes. I know a Vietnam vet who goes into classrooms and talks to the kids about war. He always asks them, "What's unrealistic about war movies?" The kids shrug in the dull way kids do and he says, "Music. They're always playing music in the movies. But in war...there's no soundtrack." And I always smile off in the corner and think to myself, "Ah, I beg to differ, my friend. We had a soundtrack in Fallujah."

THE END

Just before dawn, we sent a rifle company to mix it up with the Fallujans at the southern border of the city as a precursor to the main attack. They were the envy of the battalion. Anybody who got any trigger time was the envy. I'd like to say that emotion wore off after time, but I'm not sure it ever did—not fully. There weren't enough horrors to go around. And just when the rest of us were going to get our share of the action, the brass pulled us all back for more negotiations with the Fallujans, and that was the end of our great fight, the end of our historical battle, the end of our glory. Our opportunity for payback was yanked out from beneath us like a rug. We were crestfallen. (The well-known Fallujah assault, the one that actually came off, occurred later that year, about a month after my unit left Iraq. I don't think it would be an exaggeration to suggest that the units involved were truly the envy of the Corps.)

So with the Fallujah business behind us, the order was "Back to SASO." Back to the business of patrolling and raiding. Morale took a conspicuous dip across the board from that moment on. The good news was that we weren't going back to Mahmudiyah. Not yet, anyway. We had a new spot on the map. The place was called As Sadan, across the street from Abu Ghraib. It was scarcely a town, though, more like a rural suburb.

The theory was that it was infested with insurgents stopping through for a little R&R. All we had to do was knock on a few doors and figure out which houses they were staying in. To avoid the commute from Camp Fallujah, we set up shop in an abandoned construction yard in the middle of town and dubbed it *Camp Suicide*.

CAMP SUICIDE

There's a popular T-shirt that says, "When it absolutely, positively, has to be destroyed overnight … *The Marines*." You can find it sold on any base and worn by any number of Marines—and their fans. The words are meant to be jocular and light-hearted. They bring a particular sentiment to mind and a knowing smile. It's not like it's an official credo or something, not meant to be taken completely seriously, but then again, maybe it should be. Because that knowing smile is recognition of a certain truth. If Marines love the destruction of the world, whole or in part, then as residents of the world, the destruction of their own bodies and minds cannot be left out. I think they get that underneath all the bravado. I certainly had a sense of it. Being a warrior, after all, is a self-destructive profession.

I've got no proof, of course, but I think most Marines come to the table with a rather pallid regard for their own lives. The phrase "die for your country" is thrown around all too often for them not to. The trick is to find those guys who relish life just enough to fight for it, but not so much that they mind risking it. In their search for recruits, I suppose the Marine Corps gets it right most of the time, but every once in a while, they get it dead wrong. Sometimes they find a character who doesn't relish life at all.

Suicide was a part of our daily language on the Recruit Depot. There was always someone threatening it, or attempting it, or getting away with it. Maybe that's what boot camp is all about. Maybe it's a suicide acid test. Maybe they figure, *if these kids make it through all this bullshit without slitting their wrists, then they'll probably do okay in combat.*

I don't know how many nights I spent up talking with young men at their wits end, begging me for freedom. They held their own lives hostage, as if to impress me, and in return I made a practice of toying with their fragility. Mercy had no place on the Depot. It was all melodrama to me, and I wouldn't shed a tear of pity for any display until a man made good on his claim. Even then, the pity came hard.

On my first week as a Series Commander on the Depot I got a call from one of my Drill Instructors. He said, "You better get down here." I ran down to our barracks where I found a recruit sprawled out on the pavement bleeding. He'd jumped out a third-story window and had taken the second-story window out with him. He lay twisted in glass and window frames but was still alive. He cried over and over, "I'm sorry. I'm sorry." But we showed no sympathy. We just glared down on him and told him to shut his mouth until the medics arrived. We had no further use for him after that, and so no further compassion was afforded. That was the general attitude toward suicide.

"Camp Suicide" really wasn't a good name for a residence, but Marines do tend to take pride in the precariousness of their duty. The more dangerous the circumstance, the better. All the more prestige they receive for having survived, even if that prestige comes at the price of those who don't.

In Sadan the precariousness came mainly from above. Sadan may have been a sleepy cow-town at one time, but our arrival brought a swift rash of insurgent attacks that were delivered primarily in the form of mortars and rockets. It was the great volume of attacks and their unusual accuracy that made life there *suicidal*. All a man could really do was duck.

The most prominent feature of Camp Suicide (aside from the ever-alight barrel fire used for burning human excrement, ever-manned by the Private who seemed never to learn his lesson, and who had no more stripes to take) were the bare steel frames of the old buildings that stood once walled and roofed before the invasion, but that had been since stripped down by scavengers for the sheet metal, leaving the structures like fleshless skeletons ravaged by war.

This had two notable consequences. The first—and this one was fairly important—was that there was no cover or concealment of any kind, no place to hide from the incoming mortars and rockets. The second, and more curious, was that, with all the walls long since stripped, chopped, and hauled away, the asbestos insulation, once tucked away beneath them, was now blowing around the camp like tumbleweed. Big fluffy wads of asbestos lay strewn everywhere across the ground and heaped up in ditches and even, every once in a while, balled up as pillows under the heads of the less discerning Marines.

Life on Camp Suicide amounted mostly to a long series of pauses between indirect fire attacks. We found ourselves perpetually sitting around, waiting for the next round to hit. When the firing began, we'd scurry around like roaches under a light looking for someplace—anyplace—to hide. Then we'd urgently (and quite predictably) launch our reaction force in hot pursuit of the attackers, who would always quite predictably get away.

When it finally became clear that the firing had stopped and the enemy was long gone, we'd settle back into our chairs or our sleeping pads and we'd wait for the next volley. By this time, it was early summer and the heat had become truly brutal, reaching a hundred and thirty degrees or more almost daily. I discovered that all foul smells grow only fouler the hotter it becomes. Sweet smells just succumb to the onslaught.

And then there were all those damned flies. One might nearly go insane from the flies alone. I'm not sure what the biggest number is in the world—my kids say *gazillion*—so I'll use it now. That's about how many flies there were, a gazillion of them, and they have a determined proclivity for the orifices of human bodies. All moments of serenity were dashed away by their infernal explorations. If you were reading, they'd crawl in your eyes. If you were sleeping, they'd be up your nose, or in your mouth or ears. If you were shitting, they'd surely be trying to squeeze their way through your sphincter. That was the grind at Camp Suicide.

THE MISSING POP TART

So amidst this mixed life of boredom and panic, and shooing away flies, I became quite attached to a tasty treat called the toaster pastry, or better known back home as the "Pop Tart." There are about two dozen variations of the MRE (Meal-Ready-to-Eat). The Pop Tart comes in just one. For me, getting a Pop Tart was like hitting pay dirt. It really was a cheerful occasion. I would set it carefully aside in my cargo pocket and save it for the proverbial rainy day. Then I'd sneak away and unwrap my Pop Tart with care. I'd hold it up in front of me like the Eucharist and admire it for a moment; then I'd take my first bite… heaven.

One warm afternoon, just as I was easing back in my folding chair to enjoy my latest Pop Tart, the rain came again—a shower of rockets began to fall from the sky. The impacts shook the ground like thunder and everyone lurched for cover. I sprang from my chair (setting my Pop Tart down carefully beneath it for later) and looked for cover too.

The irony of all our frantic scurrying was that there was never any cover to find. Everyone was perfectly aware of this, but I guess we felt like dashing to and fro in a panic was the right thing to do under fire, so that's what we did. There'd be fifteen of us huddled behind a lone girder, or a wall with no roof. We must have looked a little foolish. I'm surprised no one took a picture. Actually, looking back on it, I should have stayed right there in my folding chair and enjoyed my Pop Tart. The risk would have been the same as it was behind that overcrowded girder, and at least I'd have been comfortable.

Waiting for the shelling to stop was nearly always done with a sort of pathological nonchalance. It wasn't all that scary—to most of us. You knew it was dangerous. It just didn't feel dangerous...unless you got hit. One time a 120mm mortar landed within just a few feet of the lot of us. Those 120s are big suckers. We should have all been dead. Instead, it malfunctioned and detonated beneath the surface. Afterward, we dug up the shell and found it still basically intact, but split open across the body from when it exploded. We laughed and marveled and passed it around. But we didn't tremble.

Close calls weren't that scary, either, until your close call was another man's demise. Then it got a little scary. Anyway, when the shelling did finally stop, it was like the hushed barroom scene in a Western where a gunfight has just taken place. Once the shooting is done, and the body is dragged offstage, the piano begins to play again, and all the on-lookers pull their chairs back in, like nothing ever happened, and get back to their game of poker. I'd say that's just about exactly how it was for us.

On this particular day, I was concentrating more on my Pop Tart than on staying alive. I could almost taste it... Finally there was a long silence; then a voice yelled out, "All clear!" The phrase "all clear" was the technical term for "They haven't shot at us in a while now, and we don't think they're going to do it again for a while longer, so go ahead and take off your gear, relax, and carry on with life as if all was normal."

That was *all clear*.

But I wasn't complaining. I was ready to get back to that Pop Tart of mine, waiting for me under my folding chair. I'm making a big deal about the Pop Tart because it was a big deal. That's hard to explain to people who have never been out of reach of a convenience store in their lives. At Camp Suicide, there weren't a whole lot of breaks for us, nor a lot of treats. The Pop Tart was mine. It was my refuge.

So when I got back to my folding chair and discovered it missing, I became almost instantly consumed with rage. I tried to hold it at bay with a few perfunctory explanations to myself like, "Maybe it got kicked." I paced back and forth, meticulously scanning the ground. "Maybe you stuck it back in your pocket." I clutched my cargo pockets—about fifty times each, as I continued to scan the ground. "Maybe it's still under your chair." I re-checked under the chair almost as many times as I re-checked my pockets. All the while, I knew the truth. I knew without a shadow of a doubt what had happened. Somebody had *stolen* my Pop Tart. What rankled me most I think, beside actually losing my Pop Tart, was knowing that the culprit, whoever he was, had maintained presence of mind enough to steal my Pop Tart under fire, while all I could think about was ducking for cover.

I searched the faces of the Marines around me for a guilty smile, or the tell-tale crumbs falling from someone's lips, or the bliss smeared across a face that only a Pop Tart could evoke—anything that might reveal the perpetrator—but to no avail. The crook had vanished with my prize. I stood brooding for several minutes until a major walked up to me and asked what was wrong. I could barely speak. I was incensed. I fumed bitterly, "Sir, some asshole stole my Pop Tart, and if I find out who it is I'm gonna kick his fucking ass!" I was so blindly infuriated, I hardly noticed my own pettiness.

He turned to me with a distinct look of humored surprise and replied with a chuckle, "Shit, was that yours?"

FIELD MEMORIAL

Why were we out there in that exposed place? Why would we ever stay in a place called *Camp Suicide*? Well, for one thing, the CO never liked that handle. He preferred the euphemistic "camp incoming" which spared its glorious image while simultaneously brushing its futility under the carpet. For another thing, as the CO liked to point out, our presence was drawing out the enemy, and therefore allowing us to engage him.

My trouble with Camp Suicide was that we were *not* engaging the enemy. They were certainly engaging us. But I don't recall ever engaging them back—not there. So as far as I could tell, we were in the middle of nowhere, on ground that had no significance, no tactical value, no appreciable population to stabilize, and no consequential supply routes to maintain. We were in the middle of the countryside drawing fire, drawing casualties, just to drum up a fight we weren't winning. I guess that's what bothered me about Camp Suicide.

At the very moment I'd lost my Pop Tart, about a hundred meters from me, there was a Marine standing in the turret of a humvee. He was hit in the chest by one of the incoming rockets. His body was blown to pieces and scattered far and wide across the yard. The inside of the humvee was coated with his charred blood. There was nothing left of him. Among the scanty remains, was found one of his metal dog tags shrunk down into a tiny miniature by the intense heat of the blast. It was strange to look at. It was an image one would be unlikely to imagine outside the context of war.

Really, it was just a matter of time before something like this happened. Shortly after that attack, the CO decided to move us back to Camp Fallujah. I think the cost of our presence began to weigh on him more heavily than the gains. But before we departed, we waited for a lull in the fight and then held an impromptu memorial for our fallen comrade. It was an eerie thing to pause in combat to recall the name of a Marine who had so recently been in our presence.

When I was a young enlisted man, I went to the funerals of Marines all the time. I was on the firing details for the twenty-one gun salutes. This was before the Iraq War or the Gulf War, so the Marines being buried hadn't died in combat. They hadn't been in uniform for decades. They'd lived full lives and their funerals were relatively happy occasions. Everyone was always happy to see us and the old retired Marines would come up to tell us how sharp we looked in our dress-blues and how well we'd performed our duties, and sometimes they'd even buy us lunch or a couple of beers. After the Gulf War, I marched in many more Memorial Day parades, and though the fallen we honored were much younger then, and their deaths more violent, there was still a certain distance between me and those we honored. I'd never seen their faces. I'd never heard their names. I hadn't been to war.

Memorial Day after Memorial Day, I was always out there marching in uniform, remembering the fallen, paying my respects, but always having that removed feeling from the dead. But in the midst of war, it was different. There were no flags. There were no parades, or music, not even a bugle—just the gritty wind blowing in our faces as we stood at attention and waited for the First Sergeant to march smartly to the front of the formation and call the role. He called off the names, and each man answered, "Here, sir!" The final name always belonged to the dead.

The First Sergeant called it out three times ceremoniously. He called it out once and waited for a reply, but there was no reply, no "Here, sir." This was our time to think about the Marine, our friend, who only the day before was with us, alive, and answering to his name. But on this day he was not; he was silent.

His name was called out again, louder this time, and it reverberated in the silence as we all stood there stiff and numb. He was a family man. That's what I thought. I did not know the man well. That is to say, we shared a meal from time to time and some light conversation. What I did know was that he had a wife and a couple of kids. He would never be going home to them. His wife would be getting the call soon. His kids might not understand. Maybe she wouldn't understand. War is a hard thing for anybody to understand.

But the worst of my thoughts, the one I tried so hard to hold at bay, was the nagging gratitude inside me that it was his family and not mine suffering the loss. I tried *not* to be glad that I'd still be going home to my family, but it would be pointless to say that I wasn't. I was glad. Of all the emotions I felt in war, that gladness may very well have been the most despicable to me. That gladness stirred in me a real resentment for the war.

After a long quiet pause, the First Sergeant called out one last time, even louder than before, as though our fallen comrade might actually hear his name if it were yelled loud enough, as though he might answer up, as though he might just come back. We waited for a long hushed moment. All I could hear was the wind blowing through the trees of the date grove and through the bare walls of the buildings in which we hid. Fluffy wads of asbestos tumbled by. Finally, when there was no answer, the First Sergeant faced right and marched away without a word, as smartly as he'd come.

The formation broke, the piano of war resumed, and we got back to our hand of poker.

THE FUEL OF WAR

Sometimes when I look back on all our field expedient memorials, I wonder why we always got so enraged when a man died. Why were we always so sad? We might have known the man personally, and maybe we were even good friends. But that didn't quite explain the ambiguity. I couldn't figure it out. As charged as we were for the fight, as anxious as we were to get to war, and as familiar as we all most certainly were with the horrors that went along with it, I couldn't figure out why we were so upset when the inevitable finally came around—when someone was killed.

The whole process struck me like that shrunken dog tag—a little strange. But there we were, raging—me too, God knows, me too—together, an inferno of fury and hatred. We were primed by 9/11 to hate, and we surely hated, but I think we needed the occasional casualties to keep the pump going. If no one ever got hurt, if the only people ever to die were the Iraqis…well, maybe the hatred would burn out after a while. Maybe we wouldn't have been so interested in fighting. So we needed to get hit now and again. We needed the death and the sad memorials to fuel our own violence.

EIGHT

MALEBOLGE

SEMPER SOLUS

In Iraq, I wasn't alone. I was surrounded by people—Marines—an entire battalion of them. Yet, I *was* alone. I had no crew to go through it all with, to laugh, and bicker, and lean on. I had no buddies to lose, or to die for. All I had were professional acquaintances. I had the people that I worked for, and the people that worked for me. As an officer, you spend your time and energy putting distance between yourself and the ones you lead—distance and more distance—to make it easier to give those tough orders…the ones that could end in death.

All that distance adds up after a while, and it leaves you far away and alone, because they don't put captains in fighting holes with other captains. They spread us around so we don't see much of each other. Our only real companions become the regulations, and the orders, and the institutions that dreamt them up.

Then, to compound all that solitude, my attitude was drifting off the reservation as well. I wasn't relating to the people around me. I was straying quietly away. I spent my time off-duty isolated in my own thoughts. I spent my time on-duty isolated in my own thoughts, too, catapulting from one decision to the next and then hibernating again within myself until they needed me for another decision. That was my experience in war. Alone was exactly how I felt, and all the Marines in the Corps wouldn't change that.

LABYRINTHS AND STEREOGRAMS

The issue, as it first occurred to me, was that we, the military, had tumbled into a virtual labyrinth of impossible missions, unachievable objectives, and unattainable goals. Tumbled, as in thrown headlong into an unworthy pursuit. But there was more to it than that. I finally had to succumb to that fact. There was also the hand that we played in it. The labyrinth walls were built in many cases out of our own deceit. We, in the military, were deceived, I really do think, and manipulated, being the idealistic, yet sometimes naïve crowd that we are, but we deceived too. We deceived ourselves—first inwardly so that we would never have to knowingly lie—then we deceived the troops, and provided deceitful reports to our leaders so that they could deceive the American people. Soon, everyone was deceived.

The journey through this labyrinth, as I've imagined it, was a mental one. In the end, I discovered that there was no passage out. There was no exit. There was no happy ending. The further one traveled along the corridors provided, the darker and more hellish the travel became. Escape meant determining my own path and scratching through those walls. Of course, the dust would always be there, settled in my pores, and bits of the wall would always remain beneath my fingernails, but at least I would finally know where I stood. At least there was that.

In the more concrete sense, my journey was an exploration of the realities that I witnessed in war. It was my own attempt to codify them, to give them meaning in a larger context than I'd been allowing myself, and to find some explanation for the disparity between what I'd believed and what I'd done, and between what I'd been telling myself and what my self was yelling back. But to get my hands around that disparity, I had to see it first.

The war in Iraq was like a stereogram, a sea of shapes and colors apparent to all, that you could stare into endlessly, but only if you looked at it in just the right way would you ever see the three-dimensional image hidden beneath the surface. That's what my search was all about, to find those hidden dimensions.

I have chosen stereograms and labyrinths as the metaphors to describe the war because it was indeed a puzzle to me. There may be no solution, but if there is I could never find it under the weight of my commission. Having shed that, I enjoy greater freedom of movement, and the luxury of insignificance. I wander through my stories with a displaced consciousness, and that is good, because now I can watch my own moves with objectivity and care.

MYSTERY OF THE ISF

The Iraqi Security Forces (ISF) and the American attempts to recruit, train, and work along side of them was a long-shot at best, and yet in 2004 a U.S. withdrawal seemed utterly hinged to it. What we immediately learned was that police are not revered in Iraq the way they are in America. They are not glamorous characters. There is no Starsky and Hutch in Iraq. They don't have Crocket and Tubbs, Sergeant Friday, or Lieutenant Colombo. Cops are more like errand-boys in Iraq. They have the Godfather. They call him a sheikh, and he runs his show the way the mafia does. Sure, we could have thrown in some municipal leadership and a few policemen to go with them, but the people would always defer to the sheikh. He was the man in charge.

In our battalion we had a Civil Affairs officer, a major. He was the one responsible for all those humanitarian-type efforts that we advertised so enthusiastically back home, and that included working with the local police. He was a good man. He was hard-working and committed. But the war wasn't committed to him. I mean that, even though stability and civil-military operations were supposed to be the emphasis in Iraq, combat always managed to edge them out, and him too.

The Civil Affairs team was always the last in line for gear and for security personnel. When the colonel had nightly meetings with his officers, the major was given a seat in the back row, not up front with the Rifle Company Commanders, even though he outranked them all and his role was ostensibly more vital. He was never one to fret petty things like that. It was just a seat. But I think it was a clue, however minute, about where our priorities lay. And if that wasn't convincing enough, then the palpable indifference that one felt when he got up to brief should have been. It was as though we were all just waiting for him to finish talking so we could get back to the business of fighting our war.

Nevertheless, he stayed committed. He was the guy getting water and power to the locals. He got them medical supplies, food, and money. He brought the kids soccer balls and Frisbees. He put in the long hours and the sweat. But he so often came back to the room discouraged and frustrated with our system—an unwieldy bureaucracy that seemed strangely unwilling to provide him the necessary resources and support to do his job. *Strangely* I say, because they kept telling us that this was supposed to be the main effort. Whatever progress or successes he did achieve, he did it mostly through his own ingenuity, and not as a result of any coherent plan conceived by the military structure itself. He busted his ass trying to develop communities, but the reality was that he and his team were clearly not the main effort at all. The main effort was busy patrolling, and raiding, and attacking.

After Fallujah, the American push was to reassemble the Iraqi Security Forces. That was the Iraqi Army, the National Guard, the police and the special-forces. The task of the Civil Affairs officer was to get out and find new recruits for the Iraqi Police. In Lutifiyah, that was a tough gig. He would come back night after night worn out and exasperated. "This is pointless," he'd say. "They're all insurgents. Every one of these recruits is an insurgent." Then sometimes he'd come back hopeful. "We got a handful of good guys. I think it's going to work this time." Then it wouldn't work. It wouldn't work because in the end, any man who wasn't an insurgent was scared of all those who were. "They won't commit," he'd say. The major was a reservist and in law enforcement himself as a civilian, so he took this business seriously. He just couldn't get the Iraqis to.

After a while, we took what we could get. We'd ship them up to an American camp, train them for a couple of weeks and put them out on the street for combat. It was indeed combat, because they weren't out there directing traffic or handing out speeding tickets. They were getting shot at—all the time—and not with snub-nosed .38s, but with rocket launchers and machine guns. After all, they were the enemy. They were with us, the Americans. Soon they'd be killed or just stop showing up. We'd check in to the stations, and look around and say to the one or two Iraqi policemen that remained, "Hey! You've got thirty guys on the roster, all getting paid, and none of them are here. Where the hell did everybody go?" They'd hem and they'd haw and give excuses for the others.

"He is very sick," they'd say, pointing at the roster. "He cannot come. And him? He is very, very sick. And this man? He is dead. He cannot come. And this man had to go south to visit his mother. She is very, very sick." And that's how it would go, time after time. So we'd fire them all, and then the major would have to get back out on the street and start the process all over again.

The mystery of the ISF was not why they weren't working—that was obvious. The mystery was why we kept expecting them to. We took one look at them, and we knew they couldn't do the job. How could they ever control that which we, with all our might, could not? We had a hundred and fifty thousand troops on the ground with a hell of a lot of training and cohesion. They had a fraction of that, with little competence or cohesiveness at all. We had bombers, and attack helicopters, and UAVs, and Main Battle Tanks, armored vehicles with chain guns, and up-armored humvees with fifty-caliber machine guns, and oodles of cash, and a major supply system, and still we couldn't suppress this insurgency. They had AK-47s. They piled into the backs of pick-up trucks for patrols, and they did it in little or no body armor. We lived behind twenty-foot walls laced with razor wire and machine guns. They lived in the same neighborhoods they were being told to clean up. So did their families.

So what were their chances of success? What were their chances of survival? When we were tired or wounded, we could hop a flight for the coast and head home. Most guys did seven months to a year in country. Sometimes they did more, or maybe they went back for another tour, or even two or three more tours. But it was always a few years max—worst case scenario. The Iraqi men who volunteered to be police or soldiers were there for life. There was no escape. Once they committed themselves against the insurgency, they were committed forever. That's a fact they understood only too well. But somehow it escaped us. Iraqi police got two weeks to learn what any American police officer would have six months to master. Our officers walk into established police forces and get support, and mentoring, and more training. Theirs got nothing. They were lucky if they could get a car and a little ammo.

Then we started employing Shia police to clean up Sunni neighborhoods, and seemed stunned when they turned up executed or missing. We were amazed. We were flummoxed when they failed, or when they failed to show up. But why? Why, if it was all so obvious, were we surprised at all? Why did we keep right on insisting that, of all things, the strength of the Iraqi Security Forces was the single-most important factor in determining our withdrawal? That was the mystery of the ISF.

US AND THEM

I ask myself a lot, "What do you stand for?" The issues are complex and it is not always easy to know. Many people don't. They drift through life barely aware of the government at all. Politics is an enigma to them. Wars are but clips in the news. Voting is a waste of time. Life just goes on, whoever sits in the White House, or up on the Hill. Actually, it's not such an uncommon position. Until the war, I wasn't much different. Then suddenly, I started paying attention.

I suppose that to some degree the apathetic are correct. The range of perspectives from left to right is as narrow as the parties are different. They are merely shades of the same color. One party was insisting that America stay in Iraq and fight, and the other was arguing, just as adamantly, that we should stay in Iraq and defend. The first claimed we should leave all the troops there. The next said, No, we should leave just some of them there. Shades of the same color. If those are the only choices on the table, why bother picking? Those are not choices at all.

Questions that once seemed very simple to me have become manifold and beyond the grasp of mere logic. I must, for instance, continually return to the problem of deserters and how I feel about them. I read their stories in the papers and, like a heartbeat, an undeniable contempt lurches involuntarily into my head. I understand, at least rationally, that these are people who have followed their conscience, and that is admirable in its own right, and yet I find myself strangely dismayed by what they've done. "Cowards," I hear myself grumble. It's the voice of the Marine inside me, which I still find hard to quell. It can be difficult to reconcile all that conditioning and martial ethos with the notion that we, as a nation, have done wrong. But as I so hastily castigate these deserters for not having gone to a war that I do not agree with, I can hardly escape the bitter reminder that I went right along.

Even now I frown helplessly on deserters and conscientious objectors, despite my own "conscientious" objections to the war. The emotions can be intransigent and debilitating at times. I've been crippled by indoctrination or a sort of cultural propaganda. In an effort to find some middle-ground between these conflicting sympathies, I've manufactured all sorts of attitudes and platforms that support both. "I want to stand by the military as an institution," I have said. "I want to stand by war as a policy, so I can prove that this particular war was ill-conceived." It was my own brand of propaganda, but I quickly found that nobody was buying it—not the doves, not the hawks… nobody. Most importantly, neither was I. The "middle-ground" can be treacherous territory indeed.

The story of *Us and Them* relates to the propaganda we used in Iraq. We called it *Information Operations* or "IO". That was our term for the message of good will that we were spreading through the Iraqi neighborhoods in the form of leaflets, posters, banners and billboards. We handed out untold numbers of Frisbees, soccer balls, food, and cash, benefactions that earned us a spectrum of reactions from jubilation to contempt. We spread the notion of freedom. But when a man was caught bellowing anti-coalition sentiments through a megaphone out in town, he was quickly deemed a threat, arrested, and thrown in jail, by us. More than liberty for the people of Iraq, I suspect we wanted obedience, a characteristic that appears never to have had a niche in the desert.

Unlike the FOB, which emanated an aura of superiority, Information Operations reeked of disingenuous solicitude. I looked at a stack of posters in Iraq one day, all written in Arabic, and I picked one up and said to the IO officer, "What do these mean?"

He said, "They don't mean shit … as it turns out." I didn't get it. He said, "Bad software." We discovered that the translation programs we were using were only able to effectively translate single words, or at best common phrases. But when given complex sentences or confusing American jargon, or worse, confusing American ideology, the computer would regurgitate a very authentic-looking scrawling that amounted to a sort of limerick that a Mad Libs book might yield.

The second problem with the posters was that many of the Iraqis living around them were illiterate. So our literature was essentially incomprehensible to both us and them based either on our ignorance or theirs, and useful to neither. The cleverest insurgents, to whom both of these problems were obvious, made use of our posters by "interpreting" them as American declarations of sovereignty. This did not improve relations between us and them. *Us and Them* was a reality that we could never budge.

Us and Them would never become *We*. *Us and Them* was a line in the sand that could never be brushed away no matter how many bundles of leaflets we chucked from our speeding humvees, no matter how many chintzy Frisbees we dumped off at their schools, no matter how many town council meetings we attended with grand promises of money that tended never to materialize. You just knew when you looked in their eyes—you just knew when you looked in your own eyes—*Us and Them* was never going to change.

There was a place in Mahmudiyah we called "The Ghetto." That was about as *Us and Them* as it got. The stench was pungent and overwhelmed our eyes and noses on contact. Refuse of all kinds, of every shape and age, was strewn across the streets, on the sidewalks, over banisters and fences, in windows, and over doors. It was everywhere. Even at night the filth was unavoidable, with long arms that seemed to reach out and strangle us as we stumbled into its embrace. It was a panorama of rancid meats and rotting vegetables, of pools of fetid water blended with the rotting blood draining from the guts of rotting carcasses. There was rotting life everywhere you turned. That was the ghetto.

By day it was busy with throngs of bustling, bartering, scrounging, sweating humanity that flooded the markets and moved in and among the destitution and the filth like vivified cadavers as if none of it were apparent to them at all. Every human being hung with a deportment so grim that the air was heavy, not only with its odor, but with its mood. Old men squatted in broken doorways chatting while others leaned from windows watching children streak up and down the sewage-ridden alleys.

Gaggles of women, condemned to a life robed in black, thumbed through racks of colored dresses that were grimy from hanging in a squalid breeze for too long. They seemed no more aware of the dust that covered the dresses they intended to buy than they were of the irony they engendered by buying them. Young men hovered around kiosks, chattering intensely with the peddlers of every kind of junk recoverable, while they smoked cigarettes and watched us, the Americans, with suspicious eyes as we sped through their overcrowded streets.

At night the streets of the Ghetto were generally desolate, except for the few huddled men in shadowed patios, leaning back in rusted lawn chairs, smoking cigarettes as trash swirled around their feet and then scurried off under a thick breeze. Shops were barricaded for the night behind roll-down metal doors. There was no night life in the Ghetto, no parties, no late night frolicking. There was no warm yellow glow coming from their windows. Everything was dark. The only light in the Ghetto was that which poured off blazing white from the long fluorescent bulbs that were oddly affixed all over the city.

While in America the cities radiate brilliant light from colorful neon signs, which reflect almost magically across all the shiny new cars parked along the avenue, in the Ghetto there was no color, and for that matter, there were no shiny new cars either. There was only the antiseptic light of the fluorescent tubes hung all over the place, in the carports, over shops, in doorways, dangling off of kiosks, and from terraces. Everywhere that repulsive light seemed to flood the streets, blanching the strange cityscape, turning everything cold to the eye, even in all that heat, and lifeless, even with all those people. It had a dreary futuristic quality to it, the remnants of modernity dashed across a backdrop of persisting antiquity.

The people of the Ghetto, it seemed, had been bred, generation after generation, to think of one thing alone: survival. All thoughts beyond that were a luxury, and that included politics. That was not their choice; it was their nature I think, bequeathed to them by a history of neglect and sunken to the bone, not to be extracted by a few pamphlets hurled from moving trucks or by a lot of smooth-talking Americans who promised great things but seldom produced, and who ate better in their "expeditionary" camps, in the middle of a foreign war, than the people of the Ghetto did in their own homes.

It was going to take a lot more than that. Frankly, it was going to take a lot more than we were willing to give. The funny thing is, everybody seemed to know it, and nobody cared. Not us, not them, nobody. There was nothing we could give them that they needed, and there was nothing we could take away that they didn't already live without. The Ghetto would survive long after our departure, long after the war, and they knew it. So did we. That was *Us and Them*.

DISCIPLINE

THE CHAMBER

It seems to me, there is a sort of love affair, or an American obsession with discipline. As a child, I trembled at the sight of my principal. "Don't step out of line," my teachers would warn me with narrowed eyes, "or you're going to meet him." I met him often enough, though never for a failed exam. And at home it was the same. Life was mainly about staying quiet, staying in line, out of sight, and out of mind. I always had difficulty with that. I'd lie in bed in the darkness listening to the muffled revelry from the nightclub beneath my apartment floor, nursing the welt on my head, or the sting to my pride, or the emptiness in my stomach. I'd wait for hours until the apartment was quiet, and then I'd slip out of my room and steal food from the fridge or change from the change jar. No matter how heavily discipline was laid upon me, and it was surely laid heavy at times, I only grew more and more resistant.

Then I joined the Marine Corps, the last bastion of discipline (or so I imagined). I signed my enlistment contract in 1988 when I was seventeen years old. I still had to wait until I graduated before I could ship out. In the meantime I gathered boot camp stories from all the old-timers who'd been there and done that back in their own day. There were plenty of stories, especially from a guy named Butch. Every time he'd see me, his face would light up, and he'd start right in with a tale or two about Parris Island and the horrible things that Drill Instructors did. There was always another nightmare to tell.

Butch was proud of his stories and when he told them I could tell he was hoping I'd be a little scared. But I wasn't. I think half his stories were bullshit. But it wasn't because his stories were bullshit that I wasn't scared. I wanted them to be true. The scarier his stories, the more I looked forward to joining. The horrors only inflamed my curiosity. I wanted to experience something awful in boot camp. I wanted it to be a true rite of passage, an ordeal that would overshadow anything I'd ever done or seen. I think we all did. We ached for the worst they had to offer. Our title, "Marines," depended on it.

When I finally got to boot camp, I was nervous, sometimes petrified, but in that rollercoaster kind of way. I loved every minute of it. That moment a Drill Instructor shouts, "Get off my bus!" will live in infamy in the minds of every single person who's ever experienced it, even among the most terrible memories of war. "Discipline!" they made us shout at the tops of our lungs. "D-I-S-C-I-P-L-I-N-E. Discipline is the instant willing obedience to orders, respect for authority, self-reliance, teamwork, SIR!" And I loved it. I loved the screaming Drill Instructors. I loved their raspy voices. I loved the pain they inflicted on us ... most of the time. But above all I loved looking back and knowing that I'd survived. That's where the pride comes from.

I was a little daft in those days, one of those characters who kept drifting off into his own little world. One afternoon, we, the recruits of platoon 3065, sat in bleachers with gas masks in our laps and learned the nuances of combat in a chemical environment. The topic was: "Selective Unmasking." In combat, when Marines are not sure if there is still gas in the area or not, and they have no test kits to figure it out scientifically, they select someone to be the guinea pig—that is, someone to take off his gas mask while everyone else watches to see if he'll die or not. That's selective unmasking.

A diagram in the manual depicts two Marines, armed and noticeably burly, sneaking up behind the "selected" Marine when he's sleeping. The manual then instructs the reader to swipe his sleeping comrade's weapon and then wake him up at gunpoint to let him know he's been *selected*. I must admit, I always found that picture rather droll because it seemed just too ridiculous to actually be real. We did a lot of ridiculous things over the years in the Marine Corps, but we always assumed, I suppose, that in war the ridiculousness would fade away and that we'd finally get serious. That was not necessarily the case.

As the class moved into the drier portions of chemical warfare (and it got quite dry), my mind began to slip away. It was August on Parris Island, South Carolina. It was hot as hell. I felt the instructors really had too much to say on the matter, so I let the humid air pull my eyelids half closed and I wandered off into my dream world. I watched the grass blow and the willow branches sway in the distance. Suddenly there was a lot of yelling, and all the recruits around me were jumping down off the bleachers and getting in line, as they always do. I jumped, too, as I always did. I learned quickly that boot camp and school were very much the same. The academic classes could be taken rather lightly, but getting in line, that remained crucial, the crux of it all. Discipline was always the goal.

We filed up along the side of a small concrete building and we took a knee. The Drill Instructor told us to don and clear. I looked around me to figure out what that meant. All the recruits started to put on their gas masks, so I did too. Our Drill Instructor roared, "Ready ... pray!" Then he burst into laughter and stalked away. We stared at him sadly, and I started to wonder what the big joke was.

"Get on your feet," someone shouted, and we all did. "Get inside ... Let's go, move!" We filed inside the windowless building. I peered over the shoulder of the man in front of me to see what was coming, all the while puzzling, "What the hell is the big joke?" The building was dark inside. The walls were bare cinder block. The floor was concrete. The only light came from a small flame flickering in the center of the room. Two ghastly figures stood by the fire watching us file in and take our places timidly with our backs pressed up against the walls. They wore gas masks, too, with hoods over their heads, and baggy over-garments, and rubber gloves. They looked upon us with the fondness of executioners. One of them tossed a few tablets into the fire and a thick smoke billowed up from the flame and began settling on our skin. It burned mercilessly. I glanced around. Everyone stood fidgeting helplessly ... waiting.

Finally a muffled voice shouted, "Unmask!" I sucked in a deep, deep breath and I peeled off my mask. The gas particles swarmed my face, sunk into my skin, and smoldered. The two figures shouted orders. "Push ups!" We did push-ups, holding our breath. "Side-Straddle-Hops!" We did jumping jacks, holding our breath. "Sing the Marine Corps Hymn!"

We sang together, pathetically out of tune, in low monotone voices, trying to maintain a steady exhale. *"From the Halls of Montezuma, to the Shores of Tripoli..."*

"Louder!" they roared.

Our voices rose up for a syllable or two then fell again. *"We fight our country's battles, in the air, on land, and sea..."*

I noticed a steady withering of discipline around me. Coughing. Doubling over. Gagging. Hacking—the hardcore, emphysema kind of hacking. Guys started collapsing around me and bawling. Then one recruit made a break for the door. I popped my eyes open long enough to see him streak past me screaming.

The two figures in over-garments tackled him to the ground. The pinned recruit wheezed and cried. Shut your suck!" they shouted back at him. (Little did I know, ten years later, I'd be on the other side of exactly this type of encounter.)

After a few seconds my eyes could no longer take the burn. I squeezed them tightly closed, but the burning continued beneath my eyelids. Then another recruit yelled out for his mother. That's when I really started to get nervous, because I knew I was only a few seconds away from the end of my own rope.

We sang on, *"First to fight for right and freedom, and to keep our honor clean..."* I couldn't hold my breath any longer. I plunged my nose and mouth into my shoulder and sucked in a breath through my shirt. Cotton, it turned out, was not an effective filter for CS gas. It rushed into my lungs, searing my insides, turning my stomach into mush. I felt myself convulsing. I could hear the last words of the hymn being groaned in my ears as I tried to hold back the vomit. I really did think I was going to die. *"We are proud to claim the title of United States Marine!"*

"Turn to the right!" a voice called out. "Put your hand on the shoulder of the man in front of you and file out!"

My eyes were closed so tightly my eyebrows might have been touching my lips. I groped for the man in front of me, found his shoulder, and let the force of the line pull me forward. Then the shoulder disappeared! The man in front of me collapsed. I could hear him wailing . I stumbled over his body and groped again for another shoulder, tugging the rest of the recruits along behind me. I settled myself into a comfortable rhythm of short choppy breaths until I got through the door. The fresh air hit my face like a bucket of acid. The gas clung to my pores, burning incessantly. Long streams of snot poured from my nose. My eyeballs swelled in pain. Tears ran down my face.

"Shake it off!" somebody barked.

When I opened my eyes I saw that everyone else was in the same condition as me and I saw the Drill Instructor smiling at us. I finally got his joke. I noticed the poor recruit who'd made a break for the door was now standing at the rear of the line of the next group filing into the chamber. He was going back in. I laughed to myself. The joke was funny now. I wanted to experience something awful and that is exactly what I got.

RECRUIT STANLEY

On Parris Island we didn't eat much, especially out in the field. They handed out MREs, but we were only allowed to eat the main course and the crackers. Everything else, including dessert, was to be turned in and thrown in the dumpster. Our Drill Instructor would sit down in front of us and say, "You got until I'm done eating to suck down that chow." Then he'd hold up a canteen cup of water with a smile and say, "And this is all I got." We hardly required encouragement to eat fast. I recall being perpetually famished in boot camp.

One night a recruit named Stanley, overcome with hunger, snuck off to the dumpster under the cover of darkness to take back what we'd been denied. He gathered armfuls of cookies and brownies and brought them back to his hooch. There he sat munching for the rest of the night. Stanley was like our own Private Pyle. Every platoon has at least one. And these sorts of stunts never go undetected. Stanley was caught.

The next day, true to recruit training lore, the rest of us were made to pay with sweat while Stanley stood blubbering in the middle watching. The more sweat we lost, the more hatred we gained, and we lost a lot of sweat that day. One night back at the squad bay, our Drill Instructor emerged from his duty hut before Taps, only moments before lights out. He pointed at recruit Stanley, and he said grimly, "Somebody better lock his ass on!"

The lights went out. The Drill Instructor disappeared. And every recruit in that squad bay dove from their racks and ran towards Stanley like a pack of wild animals. We swarmed around his rack within seconds, bearing our teeth, and waving our fists. They trained us for months to be hungry for blood and then they threw us Stanley like piece of fresh meat. Stanley slept on the top bunk. When he saw what was happening, he leapt to his feet and kind of half squatted on top of his mattress, like he was taking a dump, with his hands out, and his face contorted with fear. "Please!" he begged us. "Please!" But please wasn't going to be enough that night. Recruit Stanley was long past please. He needed discipline. And we gave it to him.

THE YELLING

When I was a Series Commander at the Marine Corps Recruit Depot, I had a young recruit named Renee in one of my platoons. He was a tough kid. He was practically a Marine from the day his feet landed on the yellow footprints. All he needed was the training. But he had the attitude—mostly. We thought a lot of Recruit Renee. Then suddenly after a few weeks in, he quit on us. He didn't want to train anymore and it wasn't because he was weak, or scared, or tired. It was because he was sick of taking the shit. He was sick of Drill Instructors in his face all the time, yelling at him and telling him what to do (we did get those types from time to time). So he sat on a bench outside our office for eight hours a day, because that's what we did to wear down recruits who wanted to quit. But Renee showed no signs of fatigue. He was supposed to be sitting with his back straight and his feet together in a disciplined fashion. But Renee wouldn't have it. He slouched way back with his butt on the edge of the bench, his hand on his crotch, and a scowl chiseled into his face.

At the end of the day, the Gunny and I stepped outside to talk to him. Renee looked over at us and snarled, "I ain't gonna be nobody's bitch!" Now the Gunny could have reacted in any number of violent ways, but he was a wise man. He knew that not all men are gotten through to in the same way. Some men need a loud in voice in their lives. They respond to orders that are fierce and firm. Then they'll salute, about face, and get the job done. But then there are those like recruit Renee. The yelling only shuts them down. They don't care about what they have to do until they understand why they have to do it. They can be a stubborn lot, and that's just the way it goes. So Gunny looked Renee over, and I guess he saw something in him he liked. He knew Renee had the mettle to be a Marine. He saw a fire in his gut and a fearlessness in his eye. God knows we didn't shake him. So Gunny sat down with Renee and he explained to him about the yelling.

He said to him, "Listen son, the yelling isn't personal. It's not about you. It's about war. It's about making you work and think under pressure, just like you're going to have to do someday in a firefight. The yelling is the stress you're going to feel. The yelling is the bullets flying by. The yelling is the bombs going off, and the bodies coming apart, and the blood spilling. The yelling is combat, and it's the only way we can find out if you're going to crack when the shit hits the fan." Gunny looked him straight in the eye and said, "Are you going to crack?" That was all Renee needed to hear. He went back to training that day. Good on the Gunny, I thought.

But something about that speech just doesn't ring true for me now, because I've been to boot camp and I've been to war, and they are not the same. They're not even close. You could say, if you wanted, that a man who couldn't hack boot camp would most likely fold in combat, but you couldn't reverse that hypothesis. You couldn't say that a man who *could* hack boot camp was a sure bet to hold his nerves in a firefight. Nobody would make that claim because you just can't tell. No one knows how a man will behave under fire until the fire arrives. Boot camp cannot fully prepare a man for the stress or predict his behavior in war. So there had to be more to it than that.

I guess there were a whole lot of intents behind the yelling beyond simulating combat. The yelling was about urgency and speed. We had to make them think fast and act fast to survive. It was about overcoming fear and replacing it with audacity. It was part of the common trial that recruits had to endure together, producing among them a sense of camaraderie. It was the inspiration or the shock that got inside the recruit's head and precipitated his transformation. And it was the father figure he never had. It was all these things, individually and combined, but there was something more as well, something perhaps not planned on but produced all the same.

What the yelling and the intimidation instilled above all was discipline and that ever-crucial instant willing obedience to orders. But the instant willing obedience was not exclusively to the good orders, or to the moral orders, or the legal orders, but all orders. When a man is trained so vigorously to act instantly without contemplation, he is, by definition, denied the opportunity to distinguish between the good orders and the bad. He follows all orders without question. That is what is expected from a soldier. But he is expected to use judgment as well, and to know right from wrong. And like it or not, the two do not always go hand in hand.

THE EARLE ACCOUNTS

Boot camp is thirteen weeks, and really it could be no longer, though many a crusty Marine would like it to be. But the fact is, the recruits grow strong in those thirteen weeks, mentally tough, which is what we want, but they grow willful, too. Our grip on them begins to slip as we near the end of the cycle, and we can see the animal that we've aroused inside them. We free them in the nick of time. But while the level of strict discipline is lower in the regular units of the Marine Corps than in boot camp, the method by which we deal with their infractions remains ever the same. Yelling. Brute force. Physical punishment. The expectation for instant willing obedience never goes away.

My first duty-station was a place called Naval Weapons Station Earle, where security was only the façade of our daily lives—the excuse—and discipline was at the core of everything we lived and spoke. Those were tough years for me, in a lot of ways, and formative, too. I was at Earle when the Gulf War broke out. It was in New Jersey, of all places, and it was a shameful existence for an infantry Marine, mostly because we were missing out on the war. Being stuck in New Jersey was just salt in the wound.

To ease my pain, I'd swing up to Boston on the weekends for a few beers with my friends, but then after a while, guys would look at me dubiously and say, "Hey, you're a Marine right? Don't you know there's a war on? What the hell are you doing around here?" I'd try to explain that I was a guard, guarding very important stuff. But I never got the feeling they were convinced. Maybe I wasn't convinced, either.

Earle was an ammunition depot with groups of magazines littered across miles of woodlands. Of these groups, there was one in particular—M group—tucked away in the woods in a parallelogram spot that was known as the Limited Area (LA). Most people didn't know it existed. At one time, M group was guarded vigilantly by Marines for its contents. Those contents have long since been hauled away, but the vestiges of the Limited Area still exist in that naked parallelogram that remains hidden in the trees.

One night, one of the older Marines—a guy named Frank Lovejoy—yelled to me, "Boudreau! Grab your shit. We're going to the LA." It was January 1990. I was new. Until that moment, the LA had been only a myth to me. It was the place where all the salty war dogs disappeared to for three and four days at a stretch, the secret place that you could not photograph, or even speak about, the place where terrible things happened to the undisciplined—things that would never be discussed outside its forbidding fence line.

I was nervous. I guess that was the idea. It was just Lovejoy and me in a government pick-up truck. Lovejoy was not a model Marine. He carried a sizeable spare tire that pressed against the midsection of his uniform. His sagging jowls and droopy eyes gave him the look of an old beagle. His hair was as thick as regulations would allow. His manner was just as relaxed. And he wore glasses with wide, purple-tinted lenses, and an absurdly flamboyant gold watch, even when he was suited up in his combat gear. But Lovejoy had been around a while; he'd seen a lot and he liked to tell stories about it. Among the privates, he had a sage-like quality about him. So of all those who could have driven me out to the LA for the first time, I was glad it was him.

There was no moon that night. The air was black and cold. As we crept down a lonely road that stretched into the dark woods, he told me the eerie story of two Marines who'd been patrolling that very road some years before.

"They decided to pull over and catch a few Z's," Lovejoy said kind of sorrowfully. "They closed their eyes ... and they never opened 'em again." I stared numbly out into the passing darkness as he went on to tell me about a prison break that had occurred that same night. "The guy was in for murder," he explained. I turned to look at him. The shadows had carved a certain gravity into his face. Lovejoy shook his head. "Cut both their throats from ear to ear." Then he sighed. "He was long gone before anyone knew they were dead." Lovejoy had this weird tone, irreverent or stoical or something, almost like he thought they deserved it. Then he looked at me for a long hard moment, and he warned, "You don't sleep on post."

That was the imperative lesson of the Limited Area. You don't sleep on post. Of course, Lovejoy's story was ludicrous. I suspected as much even then. But I was eighteen and a sucker for any chilling anecdote, so I spent the rest of that short drive imagining the two Marines slumped dead in their truck with slit throats. A number of unsettling accounts emerged from Earle over the years, some of which were actually true. This one, I suppose had just the effect on me it was intended to. I was good and spooked as we arrived at the LA's front gate for the first time. It was the most menacing place I'd ever seen.

"Haaaalt!" a voice called out into the night. "Turn off your lights, turn off your vehicle, and proceed out!" Lovejoy and I did as we were told, and waited in silence before the entrance to the Limited Area. It seemed to snarl and bare its teeth to us. To think of that first moment, when the LA appeared so horrifying, is almost laughable to me now. But at the time, horrifying is exactly how it struck me. It looked like a vast basin of blackness with flood lights balancing on its rim every twenty meters or so, blazing forbiddingly outward over two fence lines that ran side by side the length of the perimeter. The fences created a path that was known as the *rabbit run*. Each fence was topped by a surly combination of barbed and razor wire and had mounted on it a tube filled with ball-bearings that created a circuit. If the fence was rattled, shaken, or climbed, the ball-bearings would move apart; the circuit would be broken; and an alarm would sound. Then came the Marines.

Gazing through the glistening fence line into the darkness of the LA, I had the impression of utter vigilance. A frigid wind assailed me from behind, stabbing me in the back of the neck and cutting down under my collar. I shuddered.

Suddenly a deep voice boomed across the land like the Wizard of Oz, *"Warning! You are in a restricted area. It is unauthorized to be in this area without permission of the installation commander."* The words were spoken deliberately, mechanically almost. Then, with distinct finality, it warned, *"Use of DEADLY FORCE is AUTHORIZED! Authorized... Authorized."* The last word echoed several times into the night. It seemed to travel for miles.

In fact it did travel for miles. The audible warning, I later discovered, was a recording played on an eight-track tape, which one late evening we decided to replace with a tape of our own. We got a big kick out of ourselves as electric guitars screamed out across the Limited Area and well beyond. The installation commander himself called out from his house a few minutes later. He was not amused. Despite the rebuke, we couldn't help but be impressed. We all agreed: that was one bad ass sound system. But that was many months later. For the moment, Oz was still quite frightening to me.

Deadly force was authorized. I gave some thought to that audible warning, to his voice, and to his words. That was a tough concept to grasp, standing there beside the truck waiting to enter the Limited Area for the first time. Several minutes passed and we were still waiting for approval to enter. The cold was no longer looming; it was upon me, sinking, biting, slicing me to the bone. I grew impatient. In the interest of saving a little time, I reached for my pack in the truck.

"Haaaalt!" A voice hollered instantly. *"Cease all unnecessary movement!"* Through the lights I discerned a shadow, which appeared to be aiming a rifle at me. I froze.

"I wouldn't do that if I were you," Lovejoy winked at me with a smile. I

shuddered again. Oz's voice rung in my head. *Use of deadly force is authorized!*
Yes, but he didn't mean on me, did he?

I was used to the beatings by then, and I was used to the discipline. I'd gotten plenty of both. But I'd never before faced the prospect of getting shot, not
ever, especially not over something like prematurely picking up a backpack. (It
is highly unlikely that I would have actually been shot, but I knew nothing of
that probability at the time.) I dropped my pack and stood deathly still, waiting
for someone to tell me it was okay to move. And there it was again—*discipline*.
We were learning all the time to elicit the behavior we wanted, to command
obedience, through the use or the threat of force.

To think that only weeks later I would be that shadow. I would be that voice
screaming *halt*. I would be that Marine aiming my rifle at some other shivering, undisciplined body. In that first moment when each of us faced the LA, we
were redefined—changed utterly. I stood outside a place where deadly force was
authorized. In my life, I'd never before done that. I felt a chill of fear, but once
I entered the Limited Area, I'd never feel that fear again.

Once a Marine went through those gates, he would be forever on the inside
looking out. The fear would vanish. The curtain would be ripped away and Oz
would be revealed for what he actually was—an eight track tape that could be
replaced with rock and roll. The words *deadly force* would lose their meaning—
no, they would change meaning. That's what it was. We went from looking
down the muzzle of a rifle to looking down its sights. The view was very different. Our position changed in relation to the words. In the single act of walking
through those gates, we were transformed from the potential subject of deadly
force to the potential instrument of it.

We wouldn't feel the fear anymore, but we'd always remember it. That's
what gave us our sense of power, I think. But, of course, power is a hierarchical
thing. We no longer feared the fence line, so to keep us disciplined and obedi-
ent, we were compelled to fear our superiors. The privates, like me, feared the
corporals, the corporals feared the sergeants, and we all feared the Gunny. In
this case it was Gunny Raines.

At Earle, discipline was of the utmost importance. We were the "elite" and
expected to act as such. Anyway, that's what they told us. So Gunny Raines
punished us daily by running us from one end of the limited area to the other,
wearing all our combat gear and our gas masks. I didn't even know what we
were being punished for. I really didn't. Nobody bothered to tell us.

They just said, "Shut up, boot, and run!" That's what they called me and
everyone else who was new, *boot*. I didn't like that name much. I fought back.
So they called me "undisciplined" and stuck me in a guard tower and kept me
there. That was the lowest post a man could have, and it was miserable duty in

the winter because there was no heat up there. I won a few battles at Earle; I won my name back, but they won the war. They stopped calling me "boot," but they didn't let me down from that damned tower, not for a long time.

My first night up in a tower was memorable for how cold it got. The towers were sixty or seventy feet high, so the wind-chill factor was significant. A bitter January wind whipped and whistled past my ill-dressed body. "Don't let me catch your ass sleeping," Gunny Raines warned me. "You'll never stop paying." I have no idea how anyone could have ever fallen asleep in such temperatures. But apparently he felt it was a possibility. Three hours into a four-hour shift, I could hardly bear the silence anymore, or my incessant shivering. The night seemed to be alive with terrorists peering in at me from every pocket of darkness waiting for their opportunity to attack. I picked up the land line and called the north tower.

"Yeah?" I heard a sleepy voice come on.

"Hey man," I whispered, "what's going on?"

The voice on the other end snapped back, "what?" then hung up.

Then I called the east tower.

"Yeah?" a voice muttered. This one was sleepy, too.

I whispered again. "Hey man. What time you got?" I could hear his body shifting around.

"It's like … three."

"What time they coming to get us?" I asked.

"In like an hour," he muttered with irritation. Then he added, "Dude, what do you want?"

"I don't know," I shrugged. "What are you doing man?" I said.

"What the fuck do you think I'm doing? I'm sleeping."

I looked down on the ground and spotted the pick-up truck used by our driving reconnaissance. It was crouched beside a magazine with its lights off. It hadn't moved in an hour. I called into the Alarm Control Center to see what they had to say. They didn't have much to say at all. They were sleeping, too.

I looked around me into the bitter cold darkness and realized that I was the only man awake in the entire facility. Nobody was on guard but me. As far as I could tell, a band of terrorists could have driven a tractor-trailer through the front gate, blown the door off a magazine and made off with a cruise missile before anyone ever noticed. I was even more shocked to discover was that this was not, by any means, a one-time occurrence. This was the routine. For a crowd of such disciplined Marines, I thought that was a strange routine. But I feel now that it was a routine with an explanation behind it.

Hazing was a major instrument at Earle, and probably everywhere else in the Marine Corps. I think it tended to crop up more vigorously in those independent commands, far from the flag pole. Always with the push-ups, and the beatings, and of course Gunny Raines' famous gas-mask drills. The formal system of military justice simply wasn't trusted to do the job. Taking a stripe or giving a man a little KP could never do what a swift kick in the ass would. The use of violence to elicit obedience was trusted, though, trusted utterly. We grew up taking beatings, and when we became grown ups ourselves, we turned around and passed those beatings on to the next generation.

Times got pretty hard at Earle. Aside from the beatings and the physical training, there was our liberty—our time off—which they were free to snatch away at any time they liked. Week after week, our liberty was shaved down until there was practically none. We stripped and waxed the decks a million times, through the nights, trying to get it shiny enough to earn us a break.

"The key is in the stripping," someone sagely announced. "You gotta strip it good to shine it good." So we argued back and forth about the best ways to strip a deck. We tried everything. We used chemicals, soaps, Coca-Cola, razor blades, even fuel. We squatted for hours wearing our "field protective masks," pouring high-octane gasoline on the floor, scrubbing like mad, sweating like pigs, just for a little bit of time off.

As the weeks turned into months, the stress swelled. "Someday, y'all gonna learn," Gunny Raines shook his head smiling. But I noticed we never did learn. Our discipline steadily declined. There were more fights, more stealing, more sleeping on post, more of just about everything they didn't want. And so the beatings continued. And the stress mounted. And the discipline deteriorated some more while the insanity thrived.

The east tower stood on a hill with one side that went almost perpendicular at the peak. The challenge was to see who could leave tire tracks the furthest up without flipping over their truck. Somebody was bound to reach the limit. Somebody did. The truck toppled over and was totaled. Then guys started shooting deer over the fence line with smuggled ammo. Then an armored vehicle full of Marines went tearing around a corner too fast, flipped, and plunged into a wooded ravine below. Then another one plunged right through the fence line. Then a marine shot himself on post. His name was Jakovic. I'd been his squad leader. The case wound up in Newsweek as one of a series of botched Naval investigations. It turned out Jakovic's partner had switched pistols before the police arrived. The bullet that killed Jakovic didn't come from his own weapon. Beyond that, I can't say what happened. His partner was charged but never tried. He'd been on cocaine—that much they could prove—but they couldn't make the case for homicide.

One year, there was a young marine sent to Earle by mistake. Actually, the mistake occurred some months before he arrived. He was meant to work in

Virginia at the battalion headquarters as an ammo tech, but instead he was sent to the security force school down the road to learn how to be a guard. The rest of the class were all infantry guys—grunts. He was out of his element from the start. He was a quiet kid and never thought to question his peculiar orders.

So he went through the training and was shipped up to New Jersey, to us. A few months later, when he'd had all he could take of the stress, he slipped a trash bag over his head and went to sleep. He was found later that night, still alive, and was rushed to the hospital. There was no permanent damage done, except maybe to his pride. We laughed at him for not being able to hack the hard life at Earle, and when he came around we called him "Mr. Glad."

Then there was the kid named Lipscomb. He was in my squad, too. He had a small body, a baby-face, and a lisp, so he took a lot of shit, on top of the shit we all took. He never slept on post, though. But still, he took a lot of shit from the guys, until one night he went berserk with a broomstick and gave the guys a little shit back. He went into a relief room and started beating them in the head in their sleep. He was screaming with a blood-red face. It took five or six Marines—big Marines—to hold him down. They kept him pinned for twenty minutes while they waited for the medics to show up. His veins were like superhighways bursting from his skin. His eyeballs twitched. His muscles throbbed. When they went to inject him with valium, the blood shot from his arm like Old Faithful. They hauled him out of the Limited Area strapped to a gurney and he never came back.

The next time Lipscomb was seen, he was in a rubber room playing with toy trucks like a toddler. He looked at his fellow Marines with no sign of recognition. He didn't speak at all. A few days later, we inventoried his belongings and discovered a Ouija board, which the Company Gunnery Sergeant held up triumphantly, shouting, "Ah hah!" as though he'd solved the mystery. Then one day Lipscomb reappeared at the base. He was his old self again, except that he had absolutely no recollection of the events that I just described. He'd shut it all out. The stress, the beatings, the hazing, all of it. All he knew now was that he wanted out, to go home, and the Marine Corps was happy to oblige him.

The peculiar stories that emerged from Earle were really endless. It seemed as though something off-the-wall, or completely insane, happened everyday. But aside from all those stories, the lesson that endured with me the longest was this: At Earle, the officers and staff appeared to only understand one form of discipline—discipline instilled through force. Furthermore, they seemed unable to fathom that whatever little discipline we did have was a product of our own desire, not their force. And the more force they inflicted, the less desire we had, and hence, the less disciplined we became. That is what they appeared never to comprehend so long as I was there.

In combat, in the field, there is the same obsession, as well as an ostensible requirement for discipline. Although, as George Orwell interestingly pointed out in *Homage to Catalonia*, during the Spanish Civil War, the Socialist and Anarchist militia troops, who were almost famous for their complete lack of organizational discipline, held the entire defensive line for months against the fascists army with virtually no support, no food, no pay, no firewood, and barely enough ammunition to fight. They held the line because they wanted to. Their discipline, he observed, depended on their "political consciousness"—in other words, their desire. No one was forcing them to fight, or even to stay on the line, and as far as he could tell, no one ever left.

In Iraq, we wanted the people to abide us, and to obey our orders. Come here, don't go there, do this, say that. It was happening at all levels from pedestrian to president. All Iraqis were under American control. And the most common method we used to make sure they did just as we pleased was force. When a little force didn't do the trick, we used a lot of force, and to our surprise the people grew only more recalcitrant.

THE CARROT OR THE STICK

I always knew of that old idiom, "carrot or the stick," but I never heard it so damned much as in Iraq. That was our attitude toward the people when I was there. We said, "It's our way or the highway to hell." The carrot or the stick. It made sense to us. We thrived on that kind of talk in the military. It was black and white. It was cut and dried. It was what we knew. We'd been living under it and through it our whole lives. We liked it. We liked precision. We liked our shit organized and systematic. That's why we had a detailed procedure down to a gnat's ass for every little thing we did and a pile of tech manuals to go with it. It's why we measured everything from paces in troop formations to fractions of inches on uniforms.

We would say, "This is the commanding officer. He's in charge, and he has the last word, period." It was a product of necessity, because we couldn't afford ambiguity in the combat zone. It's why we had to have a crystal clear mission statement. Mission success or failure needed to be clearly defined so guys weren't getting killed for no reason. Everything was worked into a formula. We calculated man-hours and troop to task ratios. Battle damage assessments, and mission go/no-go criteria were all numerical values, percentages of the total force. These were bodies, human beings, killed at war, but we talked about them like they were nothing but digits or values in an equation. Every piece of gear was weighed, and that weight was known and memorized. Every weapon system has a maximum range, a maximum rate of fire, an effective casualty radius, a muzzle velocity, and every other detail you can imagine, which were all figures memorized by the infantryman.

We even had statistics for the life expectancy of a Marine in battle. How many seconds will a rifleman survive in a firefight? How many seconds for a machine gunner? A point-man, a platoon commander, or a radio operator? Lives became mere seconds of combat, numbers, passed down from generation to generation of warriors and committed to memory. As a young Marine, I knew the seconds I'd live. I knew every one. The kind of institution that says, "You will live for exactly seventeen seconds in a firefight," the kind of people who thrive on that kind of morbid detail, also appreciate absolute concepts like, *good and evil*, and *allies and enemies*, and *right and wrong*, and *carrot or the stick*.

I know very well that this is a broad generalization I'm making. But no more so than the recruiters make when they go looking for new recruits. They make broad generalizations, too, all the time, about who they can most likely get to sign their lives away. Those recruiters haven't got all day. They've got quotas to fill and deadlines to make, so they've got to use their time wisely. They've got to go after the kids who are Marines in their hearts already.

When I was a young enlisted Marine, I thought I was an American original. I figured they broke the mold when they put those dress blues on me. But when I went back to boot camp as an officer, and I interviewed all my recruits and asked them about their backgrounds, I was stunned to find out that I wasn't an American original at all. I was an American statistic. I was just like all of them. We shared a common heritage. We came from broken, unstable homes. We lived on the fringes. We didn't play sports. We didn't do so well in school. We didn't have many friends. We didn't put a lot of stock in social norms.

We'd developed a low opinion of humanity and of life, because the life we'd seen was ugly. The life we'd seen was poverty; it was beatings and abuse; it was abandonment; it was molestation; it was neglect; it was addiction; it was failure; it was filled with hopelessness. Not every single Marine saw the same ugliness, and of course some saw none at all. We all had different stories, but I interviewed a hell of a lot of recruits, and there was an irrefutable trend of desperation. Now that isn't a coincidence. That's profiling. And that is exactly what the Marine Corps does. So yes, I'm generalizing.

The problem with the "carrot or the stick" mentality is that it forced every Iraqi into one of two existences. We would say, "Either you work for us, or you must be an insurgent." And the insurgents did the same thing. They would say, "Either you help us or you must be collaborating with the infidels." Meanwhile the local Iraqi farmer, or the peddler, or the laborer, the simple man who was just trying to survive and feed his family, was caught in the middle. He was either an insurgent or a collaborator—an enemy of ours or an enemy of theirs. Either way, he was somebody's enemy and his life was threatened.

UNIFORM OF THE DAY

When my unit went over to Iraq, we had four pairs of utility uniforms, two green, and two desert. In the beginning we were only allowed to wear the greens, to set us apart from the Army. So once the fighting got started, we only had two sets of uniforms to do it in, which could be a nuisance because clothes get dirty, and every once in a while a man likes to throw on a fresh pair of pants. But after a while it wasn't necessary to set ourselves apart anymore. We weren't really doing anything different than the Army anyway. When somebody shot at us, we shot back. Sometimes we shot back when nobody shot at us. Maybe we didn't want to be distinguished from the Army anymore. I don't know. But the order came down: All Marines don their desert utilities. The green utilities were prohibited from that moment forward. But that didn't help the laundry situation because, once again, we were left with only two sets of uniforms to live in, to patrol in, to sweat in, and to bleed in.

I spent most of my time in the COC, where there tended to be less sweating and bleeding going on. So I didn't have a complaint coming. But then there were the rest of the Marines who were out patrolling everyday. They didn't have a complaint coming either. A Marine would drag into the base after a nine-hour foot patrol with a patch of dried blood on his torn trousers and someone would burst from the shadows, and shout at him from across the lot, "Hey Devil Dog! Square away those camees! I don't give a shit if you were shot. You got soap and water? You got a sewing kit? Use 'em! You're representing the Corps out there!" ... or words to that effect.

For a while, we did have a laundry service. There was an Iraqi man who commuted from somewhere on the other side of Fallujah. He came every other day to pick up our dirty laundry, haul it to wherever he'd come from, clean it, then haul it all back. He was Catholic, so I guess we figured we could trust him to come back with all our clothes. One day he did not come back. The penalty for conspiring with the infidels (or doing their laundry) is often severe. For this man, it was death.

He was ambushed in Fallujah, on a road he traveled several times a week. He was pulled from his truck, Reginald Denny style, and summarily executed. Maybe he was shot in the head. Maybe his head was cut off completely. It could have gone down any number of ways. I don't know. I wasn't there. But I do know he was dead and that our uniforms never came back. Then a few weeks later, the I.D. card of one of our Marines turned up in the pocket of a dead insurgent in Fallujah. The whole thing was eerie, and inconvenient because now a lot of us were down to only one set of utilities with no laundry man. It took quite a while for us to find someone else willing to risk his life to wash our skivvies.

IN SEARCH OF THE BAD GUYS

MOTHERFUCKER

"You've heard the cadences we sing, right?" I said to a friend of mine once. "You ever heard this one?" Then I shouted, because this was a shouting cadence, not a singing one, *"Your son is dead! Shot in the head! Right between the eyes, with a one-oh-five! You should have seen his face! All over the place! First one on the block, to come home in a box!* I used to love that little ditty," I told him. "And there's a whole lot more where that came from, but you've heard them all before haven't you?"

He nodded. "I've heard them."

"And that's what confounds me," I fulminated. "Why, if everyone's heard them all before, why were we asking a bunch of guys who sing about mowing down children in school yards with M-60s, or getting their heads blown apart by one-oh-five artillery rounds—like it's a good thing—why were we asking them to pack their guns to Iraq, be men of the people, and try slap together some kind of stability? Why were we doing that? That's what I want to know."

My heart pumps out a lot of rage since coming home from war, and I ride the rapid blood streams like a lone paddler, thrashing to stay afloat. Sometimes I spew a head full of turmoil at the passing scenery and whatever passing people are in it, and sometimes I manage a little stoicism, but I'm angry all the time, and what I've found most frustrating is that I don't know at whom exactly I should be angry. Who deserves all this loathing? Who are the bad guys?

I'm not even sure there are bad guys anymore. I believe in survival now. But that doesn't make the rage subside. I'm reading about the war, and I'm shaking the newspaper, and I'm shouting like a lunatic, "There are no good deeds in war mother fucker!" I don't even know who *motherfucker* is. I just say it like there's someone in the room listening. Some mother fucker. Motherfucker is a space inside me that I scream at when there's no one to scream at, and there's usually no one around to scream at, so mother fucker fills in a lot. "Don't you get it, motherfucker? You don't hand out a few pairs of shoes to the locals and then bomb a town and call it a good deed. You don't build a school and then kill a kid and expect his parents to call you benevolent!" I kick a wall. I slam my fist down on a desk. I slump down into my chair like a melted candle, burnt out. And then I catch my breath and I look around an empty room and still I don't know who the bad guys are.

"You know a lot of veterans go through this," people say to me, like this is all in my head. Do I leap to rage? Sure. Am I disproportionately preoccupied with the war? Absolutely. Am I prone to talk about it for hours into the night with a guest until he's drunk and half asleep on my couch waiting for me to shut the fuck up? Definitely. But there's a reason for the rage. It's not a disorder. I just want to know who the bad guys are. As a boy, it was always clear. We were always the good guys, and they were bad. We were the cops and the cowboys. We were the cavalry. We were the U.S. fucking Marines. We didn't always have a title, and we didn't always have a particular set of credentials, but of course, I know now, looking back, that we always had a particular look, and a particular sound, and a particular attitude towards those who didn't, and there were certain attributes—certain hues—common to *them* as well.

I get the principles of Self and Other now. I get it. But astonishingly, I still can't define it for my own sons. Their play is immersed in the theme of good guys and bad guys. And I play right along. I let them make their assumptions about good and evil. I help them make those assumptions. I place those assumptions in front of them on a silver fucking platter. The stereotyping has already begun and they're only in elementary school. They know their daddy was a Marine, and they believe I was a good guy... at least I hope they do. They know the colors of my uniform, of my flag, and of my skin. How do I extricate the truth from all that? I look at my dress blues and all those shiny medals, and I look at all my dusty maps hauled back from the combat zone, and I look over my old desert boots, worn and sandy still, and I hold my sword, gleaming silver, and still I can't put a steady finger on it.

I let my boys hold my swords once. I've got two of them, one NCO sword and one Officer sword. They loved it. They held them proudly like those swords were the embodiments of good itself. Their eyes were big and blue. Their smiles were priceless. It was a magical moment. Then I took the swords back to stow them away out of sight, but before I did I caught a glimpse of my own eyes in the blade. I said to myself, "Are you proud of this sword? Are you proud of yourself?" Sometimes it really is difficult to know. Those swords do carry a magic in them, and it's potent. Even today I'm not completely immune. But you can't have swords without bad guys. You can't have dress blues. You can't have valor. You can't have medals. You can't have sacrifice in battle. You can't have armies. You can't have patriotism. You can't have any of it without bad guys. We need bad guys. The preservation of an age-old, time-honored, sacred institution depends on it. This institution is war.

So who are the bad guys? We spent a good deal of time trying to work that out before we shipped over to Iraq. They were the *muj*—the Mujihideen—they were al Qaeda, the Islamic extremists, the Saddam loyalists, the foreign fighters, the criminals and the thugs ... whatever. I don't know why we tried so hard to come up with a name. We should have done like the troops and just called them all hajjis. That's the way we treated them—the same, like their motives were irrelevant. It's not like we ever stopped to ask. A guy with a gun was a guy with a gun, and that made him the enemy. A bad guy by any other name is still a target.

THE NAME GAME

This name situation was always a tricky business. The bad guys were initially called terrorists. Then they were insurgents. But they were also Anti-Coalition Forces (ACF), I suppose because we wanted to stress that our fight wasn't a unilateral program, that it was a *coalition*. But then somewhere along the line, someone decided it wasn't good enough to call us a coalition anymore. We had to be a multi-national force. I don't know, maybe they figured people didn't know what a coalition was. So we dropped the "coalition" and became Multi-National Forces, Iraq (MNF-I), which meant, of course, that the enemy could no longer be an anti-coalition force, since we weren't a coalition anymore. And I think *Anti-Multi-National Forces* was probably too big a mouthful for anyone to deal with, so the enemy became Anti-*Iraqi* Forces (AIF). That had a nice ring to it. It was like saying, "This war is really all Iraqis against Iraqis here. We're just stuck in the middle trying to help them work it out." I got the feeling after a while that it was not so much the world we were trying to fool with our clever name game, but ourselves.

I noticed in the time I was in Iraq and since coming home that, of all the various names we assigned to the bad guys, and of all the various motivations we suggested they had for fighting, and of all the various organizations we said they represented, never were ordinary Iraqi citizens mentioned in that list. Never did we acknowledge that our enemies might not be exclusively political or religious extremists outside the periphery of daily Iraqi life, or that they might not be exclusively criminals or thugs. Never did we allow that the citizenry of Iraq might just be tired of the American presence and all the violence that went with it. Never did we permit the possibility that the fight against us was not necessarily the manifestation of a villainous plot by hardened terrorists, but of a steady migration of fed-up people toward such violent individuals and agencies. Whatever extremism emerged in Iraq (a historically secular country), I think it was, to a great extent, induced by our occupation.

INTEL

"Intel," the shorthand for Intelligence, is everything we can find out about the bad guys. It's always about the bad guys. Always. That's a cultural norm in the military. But this was a whole new ball game. The war in Iraq was all about the population and winning their hearts and minds. They said, "The only way to win their hearts and minds is to learn their culture." So the intel bubbas— that's what we called them, bubbas—had a new job. It wasn't all about the bad guys anymore. It was about the civilians, the locals, the *good guys*. What do they do? How do they think? How do we get them on our team?

The Colonel said to his intel bubbas, "Break it down for me. I want to know everything." The list of information that they had to produce was formidable. It was the culture, and the politics, and the history, and the media, and the religion, and the terrain, and the economy, and the civil, and the moral, and the tribal issues, and it went on and on. It was an endless list of details and tidbits I wouldn't expect a full-time Iraq scholar to get his arms around in less than a decade of study. It seemed preposterous to me that a young captain, who knew very little about Iraq, and his three-man crew, who knew even less, could ever succeed in finding all that information in less than three months time.

But the boss was determined, as bosses tend to be, and he pounded his fist and said, "We've got to know every detail about the Iraqi people so we can relate to them." We didn't get the answers to half that list even after we finished our deployment in Iraq, much less before we arrived. And I don't remember spending a lot of long nights worrying about it, either. We were too busy thinking about the bad guys, because that's what we do in the military, think about bad guys.

Every week there was a meeting, and every meeting began with the intel brief. The intel bubbas never mentioned Iraqi culture, or the people, or their points of view. I think if they had they probably would have gotten a swift kick in the ass from somebody. As a combat unit, we were naturally less interested in who we might have to help than who we might have to fight. So the intel bubbas talked about the bad guys and all the bad things they were doing. They talked about secret bad guy networks, and bad guy hideouts, and bad guy leaders. It was all about the bad guys.

The culture issue would pop up once in a while, and we'd wave our hands like we were shooing away a bug and say, "Yeah, yeah, yeah, the cultural thing, and hearts and minds and all that. Right. Sure. But let's talk about bad guys and how we're going to fight them." We had a picture of how it would be in Iraq. I had it too. We imagined the struggle to win hearts and minds, and the fight against bad guys, as completely separate events. "Yeah, it's all going to happen on the same block," we said knowingly, "but the bad guys ain't gonna shit in their own backyards." That's what we thought. We figured they'd be outsiders, night prowlers and such—easy to spot. We figured we'd buy the locals lunch, shake a few hands, kiss a few babies, and they'd all point their fingers at the bad guys for us, and we'd kill them. Done. Easy day.

Nobody in that room was stupid. Nobody was malicious. Nobody ever said, "I don't give a rat's ass." But we were infantry officers. We were trained hard, trained to think about one thing: the fight. That's an infantryman's business. And I think that's an important feature to consider in the effort to understand what all happened in Iraq. So the possibility of the good guys and the bad guys getting a little mixed up did occur to us. And the opposing demands of ingratiating ourselves with the locals and fighting an insurgency in the same neighborhood occurred to us, too. We got the picture. But it is truly amazing how easily we flowed from this picture to the one painted with nothing but bad guys. Our interest and acumen in problem-solving the fight were endless, while our enthusiasm for winning hearts and minds was clearly exhaustible.

In the infantry we say that a commander's plan is driven by intelligence. So when the intel bubbas hand him a limited package or one that is disproportionately heavy with scoop on the enemy, then the obvious product is going to be a limited plan or one that focuses disproportionately on the enemy. And that's exactly what we got. We flipped open the book on counterinsurgencies, and it said, if you want to be successful, you've got to know and understand the indigenous people. You've got know them like the back of your hand. So when we deployed really not understanding them at all, it probably should not have been surprising when we weren't successful. But success, I soon learned, was in the eye of the beholder.

THE DEFINITION OF SUCCESS

NARRATIVE

They say war is hell, but I say it's the foyer to hell. I say that a lot. I say coming home is hell, and hell ain't got no coordinates. You can't find it on the charts, because there are no charts. Hell is no place at all, so when you're there, you're nowhere—you're lost. The narrative, that's your chart, your own story. There are guys who come home from war and live fifty years without a narrative, fifty years lost. They don't know their own story, never have, and never will. But they're moving amidst the text everyday and every long night without even realizing it. They're out there beyond the wire, trudging through the sentences, tangled in the verbs, suffocating on the adjectives, wrecked by the names.

They live inside the narrative like a cell, and their only escape is to understand its dimensions. Once you get it, maybe you can start tearing down the walls. Every soldier's mind is different. There is no single code to break. It's ever-changing. I don't have a recipe, but there's one thing I do know and that is the power of the narrative. Put the story together. Understand the story. Ask questions of the story; make it answer you. Make it. You don't take no for an answer. You find the answer. You keep building that narrative until the answer comes around. That's the low road out of hell.

THE LOW ROAD

When I first came home, I wrote a novel called *The Low Road*. It was a genuine beast, over seven hundred pages. I actually tried to market the beast and the beast got shot down like any big game does. They used big slugs. But it was a success in the end because it was my first attempt to understand my own experiences, really the first draft of my narrative. It was important, because I wasn't really trying to figure out the nature of war. I was trying to figure out the nature of me.

Everyone said, "Hey I like the story, but do you have to talk so much about the war? Why don't you drop all that, and stick to the plot. Who knows? You might have something."

I said, "Don't talk about the war? What, are you nuts? Don't you see? That's the only thing I really do want to talk about. I'd rather drop the damned plot." So that's what I did. I dropped the plot and wrote a book about the war.

It's funny what war does to the memory and what it corners you into thinking about all the time. Nobody is built the same, but so many soldiers have found the extremes of war emotionally overwhelming. Fear, and anger, and joy. Love and hate. Sorrow. Vigor and fatigue. None of them has ever been felt so poignantly as in war, and yet somehow this is backwards. There is something incongruous about it. Emotions aren't meant to be stretched to such limits over such a short duration. They are supposed to correspond with a whole lifetime of experiences. Emotions are the topography of our memories.

But the emotional spikes of war, powerful as they are, can overwhelm and diminish the emotions associated with every other experience of a soldier's life. The memories of his past, while accessible, can become antiseptic, unfeeling events. So when the mind wanders through its memories, it will naturally tend to the experiences that have had the sharpest impact on the psyche, i.e., the experiences attached to the strongest feelings. When was I most scared? When was I most angry? When was I most sad? When was I most tired? For veterans, the answer is almost always war.

After talking to a few old vets one soon finds their memories, no matter how dulled, are razor sharp where it comes to their experiences in battle. For me, it's not as though I can't remember anything else. It's just that I don't care to. I spend the majority of my time thinking about the war, thinking about where it's going, where it's been, and how I participated in it while I was there. I think about the tactics, and the doctrine, and the politics. I think about the reports I wrote. I listen to the music I listened to when I was there, and take stark pleasure in the melancholy it brings on. I think about every element of the war all the time.

I told the doctors, when I came home from Iraq, that I wasn't sleeping well—only a few hours a night. They said it was normal, but that it would pass eventually. Two years later, I told the doctors again, I still wasn't sleeping. I was thinking about the war instead. My manuscript was written almost entirely during those sleepless nights. It wasn't a memoir. I called it an "analysis." When I finished, I passed it around to a few friends to take a look.

And my friends said, "Yeah brother, I dig it, but listen … do you have to wear your heart on your sleeve like that? Do you have to do so much shouting? When I read this thing, I feel like you're chewing my ass." And then they started pointing out certain passages, saying, "Man, if you write this you're going to piss off the liberals, and if you write that you're going to piss off the conservatives. And if you write this other thing, you're going to piss off the Marines. You're going to piss everyone off before you even get out of the gates, and nobody is going to give a damn about what you have to say."

So I listened, and I slashed and I burned out every bit of heart I had in there. Pretty soon it was finished. It was fair. It was polite. It had the information. But when I handed it back out to my friends to take a look, I noticed they all had the same reaction. I saw a glaze come over their eyes as they read. I saw the inspiration run right out of their faces. Suddenly, they just didn't give a shit anymore. I actually made the war boring. And that's tough to do. I stripped out the heart. I stripped out the me. I left out everything to do with what I personally saw and how it made me feel. This isn't just the evolution of my writing. It's the evolution of my self. My manuscript was my narrative, and my narrative and I were one. When I stripped the heart from it, I stripped the heart from me as well.

BREAKTHROUGH

I stood among nine people one night, and we talked to an audience about war. We talked about what it all meant to us. Each of us had a chance to say a few bits, so when it was my turn I told a couple of my stories. When it was all over I got a lot of positive feedback from folks. They slapped me on the back. They bought me beer. Suddenly they gave a shit. "Hey man, that was heavy," they said. "That was fucking deep brother. That was the truth. That was some serious shit. You got me right here," they said, pounding their chests with fists. One woman hugged me and cried. And I listened to all this, and I was glad of course, but I was confused. "I don't get it," I said to myself. "I told all these same stories in my manuscript. How come everyone's touched now, but they weren't touched then?"

Then I figured it out. They were touched because I wasn't polite. I wasn't fair. I wasn't watching my mouth. I wasn't trying to please the audience. I wasn't trying to please any motherfucker. I was just talking my narrative, telling my truth, and how I saw it. Maybe I'm wrong, maybe I'm right, but this is my deal, and I don't give a shit what anybody thinks. That's why they were touched.

CUSSING

I was rapping my "truth" to a friend one day when he suddenly scratched his head and asked, "Why do you do all that cussing?"

I laughed because it's true. I don't do it all the time (at home I use words like drat and shucks!), but when I'm in my narrative, I'm always cussing. I said to him, "You show me a Marine Corps unit that isn't cussing and I'll guarantee you they ain't grunts."

He said, "Yeah, but how does that help your point?"

I told him, "It doesn't help my point. It's not meant to help my point. A war is a fucking war by definition. They're the same thing, but people on the outside looking in call it a war. The people on the inside looking out call it a fucking war." When I step into my narrative, it's like stepping into character. When I saw the sights, and smelled the smells, and felt the heat, I was a grunt. I was cussing. So if I want to live it again, if I want to think about it, if I want to get in that memory and find some meaning to it all, I'm bound to be cussing.

SUCCESS STORIES

On September 11, 2004, my Battalion Commander sat down in his office in Mahmudiyah to write the final letter of our deployment to the families of his Marines, which included my wife. It had an optimistic ring to it. It vaunted our great successes. Of course, I did appreciate that his aim was reassurance, not cold hard realism, but I couldn't help wondering if he really thought it was true. In other words, while the Colonel may not have considered it proper to write home to our families and censure a war we were risking our lives to fight, did he actually believe we'd been successful, or was he just saving criticism for another more appropriate forum?

One problem, I think, is that it's nearly impossible to find an appropriate forum in the military. It's never appropriate to be critical. It's not appropriate when one is talking to the fretting families of those deployed. It's not appropriate when one is talking to the mourning wives or parents of those killed. It won't be appropriate when one is talking to the Marines who have to go back and fight again, or when one is talking to Americans who need to believe and who have sent their sons and daughters in good faith to war. It's never appropriate to be critical, and so an appropriate forum is never established.

Maybe the Colonel and all the other senior officers were working out the problems behind closed doors, beyond earshot, but I don't think so. I don't think he was reserving judgment, or being polite, or dignified, or any of it. I don't think he had much critical to say at all, other than perhaps the usual complaints of mismanagement. I think he believed in his heart what he wrote in that letter of his. And he was no rogue among commanders. What he was saying, they were all saying. It's not about the individual who was my commander (he was a fine enough man); it's about the state of mind one must assume to be a commander at all. I was no different as a commander myself. Attitudes in the military are not that hard to predict because they exist within such a narrow framework of regulations and tradition. It's not just the uniforms that are uniform; the consciousness is uniform too.

Most commanders had versions of what Iraq would or should look like when we finally accomplished our mission. They had a million success stories that they told their troops and the families back home. They had their own utopia in mind. I'd say the Colonel's letter represented his utopian war. He talked about moving in and kicking ass. He said we were the new sheriffs in town and every insurgent knew it. In a way, he inadvertently illustrated the shift in attitude that we experienced over the course of our deployment. In the beginning it was all about hearts and minds; in the end it was all about killing. He said our operational focus shifted from "No Better Friend" to "No Worse Enemy." That's exactly what it did. But he wrote about it like it was a good thing. And then he wrote about all our successes, all our glorious, life-costing successes.

What you'd have to notice immediately about all his success stories was that every last one of them was described in terms of our actions, not in terms of insurgent actions, or in terms of Iraqi stability. He never mentioned a word of how our Area of Operations had changed from when we'd arrived. He talked about all the things we had to do to mitigate the threats to ourselves but never uttered a word about the security situation for the people of Iraq. Nor did he give examples of increased local support. He didn't give them because they didn't exist. He concluded his letter to the families by writing, "Freedom has taken hold in Iraq, and it will not let go because of what these brave men have done." And I think he believed it. I think he believed in our success.

A year after our deployment, my battalion was back out in the same province of Iraq—al Anbar. The Colonel and I were no longer in the unit; the battalion had a new CO. And while the fighting was every bit as intense as when we were there and the casualties every bit as frequent (I know because I'm the one who had to report them to the families back home), when it came time for the new commander to write his own letter, he had virtually the same message as his predecessor, with the same dubious language. "The Marines performed beautifully, and success continues in our Area of Operations..."

What was perpetually unclear to me was how these commanders were defining success. How were they measuring it? Where were the numbers? What were the criteria for mission accomplishment and a stabilized Iraq? My commander and I were sent to the same war, the same area of operations, over the exact same period of time, yet our interpretations of the deployment and our operations were completely different. The true difficulty lay neither with his interpretation nor mine, but in that space that lay between. The difficulty was with the gray area that had been allowed to exist because of the lack of any concrete measurement for success.

Without any tangible set of criteria for success, commanders gravitated to what they knew to determine their effectiveness: combat operations. *How did we fare in this battle, or that battle?* they might ask, *or in this firefight, or that one?* How many weapons caches did we unearth? How many detainees did we capture? What were their casualties? What were ours? Body counts. Ground taken. Ground secured. That's how commanders measure success. And lacking any definitive evidence to the contrary, that's how success would be demonstrated to the American people.

There is a brief chapter in the Counterinsurgencies Manual that deals with this very subject. It's about the Measure of Performance (MOP), which is how well we did our job, and the Measure of Effectiveness (MOE), which is how well it worked. We had the Measure of Performance down pat. We planned an operation, executed it according to that plan, and then congratulated ourselves on a job well done. That's the material that filled all those letters sent home. But the Measure of Effectiveness seemed to consistently elude us and so remained ever-unmentioned. The measure of effectiveness in Iraq was an enigma. It was nonexistent, to everyone. Instead we had goals that remained ever-unanswered.

We were up to our eyeballs in goals. Every commander had a set of *goals* or he established *priorities*. Ours was to "Reduce insurgent activity in our Area of Operations." But at the end of the deployment, there was no reconciliation. The CO wrote in his own letter that the situation got worse at the end. That didn't sound like mission accomplishment to me. It sounded like it got worse. It sounded to me like we just kept pressing on with the same operations, month after month, pounding and pounding that same square peg into that same round hole. So much for goals.

In Iraq, we had an interesting device called the "relief tube." Relief tubes were clusters of plastic six-inch pipes that stuck up from the ground like rows of short white stumps and served as outdoor urinals. The theory was that the urine would run down the tube, deep into the ground, thereby mitigating the smell that might otherwise develop if everyone were to just piss on the ground.

Unfortunately for the contrivers of this invention, the tubes ended up serving more as general guides than specific targets. Nobody really aimed for the tubes; the holes were just too small. Most people figured near the tube, or on the tube was close enough; in the tube was simply too much trouble. This unspoken policy of the masses effectively negated the very purpose of the tubes and the stench gathered despite them, but their presence made the sanitarians feel better, so they remained. That's what our goals were like—general guides that everybody felt comfortable missing, but their presence made people feel better, so they remained.

NATURE OF THE BEAST

In Iraq, we moved by instinct. We flowed according to the gravity of our situation, not according to abstractions. We naturally drifted from the high ground. We adapted according to the casualties that were inflicted upon us, not according to ideals or lofty speeches. We did what we had to do to stay alive, and we did it in accordance with our nature. As Marines, our nature, synthetic though it may have been, was violence.

That's what we knew; it's what we understood; it's how we'd been conditioned to deal with our problems and to resolve our conflicts. It is surely how we dealt with our problems in Iraq. "We're taking more casualties?" we'd say. "Then we've got to fight harder. We've got to hit back. Run more patrols. Be more severe." It always came down to combat. And nobody ever scratched his head and said, "Is all this violence actually producing stability? Is it reducing casualties? Is it working at all?"

Grunts hate counterinsurgencies. I didn't know that until I got to Iraq. Too many mixed messages. During the workups before we deployed, we pushed the Marines to be more gentle, more sensitive to Iraqi culture. We said to them, "Don't be so rough. We want to win their hearts and minds." After a while they were acting more like Avon ladies than Marines. We just couldn't stomach it anymore. It didn't sit right with our infantry sensibilities. So we said, "Hey Marines, get tough! Don't take shit off these people? Let 'em know who's in charge." They looked at us like we were plain dumb. "Which is it buddy?" That's what their faces were saying. But their mouths were saying "Yes sir," and they went about trying to find some happy medium between the extremes of violence and kindness. And that is where the psyche starts to split. Right there.

STAY IN YOUR LANE

Back in the Corps, they used to say to us, "Stay in your lane." That meant, if someone asked you a question about the war, you'd only tell them about your specific role in the war and not one iota more. If you were a machine-gunner,

then you'd tell them about machine-gunnery. If you were a platoon commander, then you'd tell them about platoon commanding. You didn't start answering
questions above your pay-grade. You didn't try to guess what it might be like to
be a General. "You don't speak for the Corps," they'd warn, "or for the United
States. So don't even try."

Then something unusual happened. On January 10, 2007, the President of
the United States got up on television and drove the conversation straight into
my lane. He stepped up to the mike, and in front of the nation, started talking
about small unit tactics. He was throwing doctrinal terms left and right like he
was Patton himself. He even ginned up a tactical analysis on why things had
fallen off-track in Iraq. Of course, as Commander-in-Chief, the whole damn
war was his lane, but until that moment, I'd never heard a president's war
policy resting so fully on the soundness of his infantry skills. He threw around
terms from the Counterinsurgency manual like "clear, hold, and build," probably because they sounded smart, and technical, and out of reach to the aver-
age American who wouldn't know the difference between a bulkhead and a
scuttlebutt if one hit him in the face. But the moment the president started
talking shop, he opened the door to a lot of military people who would know
the difference, who had read the manual, and who had been in Iraq to see how
it had played out on the ground.

As a Marine, I read the manual pretty carefully. In hindsight, I think there
was much that it neglected. For example, it did not seem to account for the inevitable feelings of imperiousness that we, the American soldiers, would begin
to feel in such an environment. It did not account for the rage that would ensue
in the wake of our casualties. It did not account for the natural degradation of
humane sensibilities that occurs in all wars. It did not account for the institutional aggressiveness pervasive throughout our military. It did not account for
a lot of things, nearly all of which were factors that ran counter to so many of
the ostensibly sensible principles found in the book.

The book said, "Some of the best weapons for counterinsurgents do not
shoot," and it said, "The decisive battle is for the people's minds," and it said,
"Often insurgents carry out a terrorist act with the primary purpose of enticing
counter-insurgents to overreact," and that "Sometimes doing nothing is the
best reaction." These were wise maxims, and yet we never behaved accordingly,
not when I was there. It was as though we'd never heard a word of it. The book
said that, in a counterinsurgency, "If a tactic works this week, it might not work
next week; if it works in this Province, it might not work in the next."

But the examples of isolated provinces were pounded and pounded into the
ears of America as evidence of our success. Meanwhile the violence persisted,
and the insurgency continued to grow, because an insurgency—any insurgen-

cy—is a dynamic entity. It moves through provinces as insurgents move, but also as an energy force, a general feeling that ebbs and flows through the people. An insurgency is amorphous, shifting size, shape, composition, attitude, and tactics all the time. It doesn't necessarily mean they're ghosts. It means that an insurgency exists more as an idea among the people than as a unit of aggressors from within them. Hence the slogan: winning hearts and minds.

But soon into my tour I began to regard this business of winning hearts and minds as mere lip-service because everybody else read the Counterinsurgency manual just like I did; everybody heard the slogans, and yet nothing changed. And my cynicism stuck because I kept hearing politicians telling me, and everyone else, that they had a handle on the war. They kept telling us that our battlefield commanders were making adjustments to the plan, adjustments to the enemy, adjustments to the tactics, techniques, and procedures, and yet I couldn't find a trace of change. I saw more troops deployed, but what were they doing differently than what I was doing when I was there? Where were all the adjustments? What changed?

Of course, I have no claim on the pulse of the Iraqi people, but I have come to believe that their will is fundamentally at odds with ours. I think so because I cannot imagine them feeling any other way while living under such a heavy hand as our own. I cannot imagine myself living here in the U.S. under a similar occupation, and under the fear of foreign soldiers all the time, and of what they might do to me and my family. It must be an oppressive feeling to them, and therefore, as an American who deeply appreciates his own freedom, I cannot imagine how they would not deeply yearn for theirs.

And that is why I look upon any stories of tactical success with skepticism. Because it seems to me that, no matter how many troops are deployed to Iraq, no matter how many rifles are squeezed into a given city block, and no matter how submissive the people are forced to be at gunpoint, their actual contentedness, and the overall stability of their country, can only be accurately measured in our absence. I think that reality, inconvenient though it may be, transcends any tactical successes we may or may not have had.

THE OLD WAY, IN SHEEP'S CLOTHING

When President Bush gave his "New Way Forward" speech back in January of 2007, I noticed a conspicuous shift in the rhetoric. Suddenly the Iraq War wasn't our problem anymore. You could see it in the murky language he used in his address. A certain ambiguity emerged about the responsibility for success in Iraq and the ownership of its military operations. He talked about us succeeding in the fight against terror. He talked about the need to change our strategy. He talked about the comprehensive review of the situation by *his* national security team, *his* military commanders, and *his* diplomats, and how America was changing *our* approach. He talked about "taking other steps to bolster the security of Iraq and protect *American* interests in the Middle East."

But then he went on to say, "*Only Iraqis* can end the sectarian violence and secure their people. And *their* government has put forward an aggressive plan to do it." He added that the Iraqi government would be appointing a military commander and two deputy commanders for *their* capitol, but for this plan to work, he stressed, "*Our* commanders say the Iraqis will need *our* help. So America will change *our* strategy to help the Iraqis carry out *their* campaign to put down sectarian violence and bring security to the people of Baghdad." Our strategy, their campaign. Our help and support, their commanders. Our approach, our policy, our interests, our views, their plan.

Whoever wrote that speech, clearly was not a military man. No Marine or Soldier I've ever met could listen to all that and avoid asking the obvious question: All right, so who the hell is in charge? The obvious answer was us. The United States would always be in charge. What President Bush was showing us was not a new way forward, but the old way in sheep's clothing.

FROM THE TRENCHES

Since coming home, I've thought a lot about the war, but not always about the same things. In the beginning it was all technical. It was doctrine. It was procedures, and policies, and speeches. It was all a formula, an algebraic equation, and I strove to demonstrate the imbalance of it all. I would curl up my mind into to a fist and pound out the variables. The Army/Marine Corps manual for Counterinsurgency Operations became my bible. I referred to it incessantly, citing passages like scripture and quoting generals like prophets. I was a desperate man.

If I could only prove scientifically that the war was astray, if I could demonstrate through inviolable texts and inviolable men that this equation just wasn't adding up; then perhaps a few more people might inherit my view of the war. It wasn't just about activism; it was about the displacement of my conscience. It was about finding a community for myself, or creating one. To feel bad about a war that everyone else seems to feel good about can be very estranging. To prove my point was to justify my agitation.

So I wanted to make my case with pristine objectivity so that folks—even the blue-collar folks I grew up with, the die-hard supporters of the military— would understand where I was coming from. I wanted to say to them, "I'm with you, man. I'm one of you. I was out there busting down truck tires as a kid. I was on the grinder at Parris Island earning my title 'Marine.' I was crawling through the mud with the grunts. I was chewing the dirt in Iraq, getting shot at and IEDd. I was burying my fellow Marines. I get the sacrifice. I understand the duty. I know what it means to serve. I came from the trenches. So when I see my fellow Marines getting blown away for nothing, for no good reason, and with no chance whatsoever of success, I get angry. Don't you get angry, too?"

I wanted to tell them about our slogan: "First: Do no harm." I heard the general say it a million times (he was the one who coined it), and then, like a dutiful officer, I repeated it myself a million times more to the Marines below me. "First: Do no harm. First: Do no harm!" I wanted to show people the counterinsurgency manual. I'd wave it around and say, "Look what it says. It says, 'An operation that kills five insurgents is counterproductive if collateral damage leads to the recruitment of fifty more insurgents.' You see. The general was saying it. The book was saying it. They were all saying: Don't do that! We knew what we were doing wrong, and yet we kept right on doing it.

"We were cutting down families at checkpoints, blowing down their cities with shock and awe, sniping midnight meanderers from afar, trashing out homes night after night, killing hundreds of thousands of people, and displacing hundreds of thousands more. We were generating new insurgents faster than we could ever capture, kill, or incarcerate the old ones. Every raid we conducted, however justified, every Iraqi we killed, every city we attacked, every patrol we ran, every detainee we took, every bomb we dropped, however justified, only contributed more strength to the insurgency." That's what I wanted to say.

The activists in my life used to tell me I was barking up the wrong tree with all this talk of tactics and doctrine. They'd say, "Man, it don't matter. The whole thing was a moral travesty from the start anyway. So who gives a damn if it was mismanaged?" Well, that may have been true, but what these activists didn't get about me was that the discussion was never strictly about what was rational or sensible. It was about the talking, and the ruminating, and the obsessive desire to examine through my mental microscope every inch of the war, every cell, every molecule. I wanted to press my face upon the glass and feel my eyeballs quiver in synch with the palpitations of battle. I wanted to know the war, feel the war, become one with the war. War is irrational; I guess to become one with it meant that I, too, would have to be a little irrational. I didn't necessarily want to make sense. I really don't think there is such a thing as perfect sense, particularly in war.

I weaved a lot of rhetorical questions in the early days of my return, and crafted a lot of Socratic arguments to hem in my opponents, but in the end they were not effective because they were not me—not purely. They left out the true agenda, and the true agenda was reconciliation with my conscience. The true agenda was finding, beneath all this expostulation, amidst the core of myself, what I believed about war and how I'd come to believe it. As time passed, I forgot about the manuals and the doctrine. I left them in the dust. I stopped obsessively jotting down the remarks of generals and politicians. I was once cautious, near-paranoid, about who I was seen in conversation with, or which organizations I spoke for, or how I might be viewed by the public. Strict neutrality was my method. Objectivity was my religion. I dropped all that too. I lowered the façade of resolute impartiality and finally spoke my own truth. It was roiled and ambiguous and emotionally charged, but it was me, and never had I felt such clarity until then.

FAILURE IS NOT AN OPTION

NO FAILURE V. NO ZERO DEFECTS

We used to say all the time, "Failure is not an option." Really, it was an absurd maxim, because of course failure is always an option. It's not that we opt for failure. It's that sometimes failure opts for us. But meanwhile, there we were, living it, thinking it, reciting it all the time. "Failure is not an option!" It made us sound determined I guess, and uncompromising, like the kind of great steely-eyed leaders you'd want to read about or see in the movies.

But then we also spent a lot of time talking about and trying to generate an environment with a "no zero-defects mentality." In this case, we said failure was an option. Because we didn't want guys afraid to risk their asses. We didn't want them afraid to make mistakes. "Go ahead and make your mistakes," we'd tell the Marines. "Just don't make 'em twice." We wanted them on a perpetual hard charge, full-speed ahead. We wanted them to take it all to the wall every last time. We wanted them to be bold. We wanted them to be fearless. The fear of failure is a fear of everything. And then failure has already occurred.

THE ART OF WAR

One difficulty with war, from a theoretical perspective, is that it's more art than science. It's based more on philosophy and gut instinct than data. It's a human endeavor. In other words, it's subjective. Coming up in the infantry, I always had a real respect for the aviation community. It wasn't the gold wings or the sporty fly-boy shades. It wasn't the glitz or the glamour of streaking through the azure that I admired. I enjoyed my place in the mud. What I liked about the aviators was the technical nature of their job. You can't bullshit when you're a pilot. You can't hide behind platitudes. You either know how to fly or you don't. The manual tells you exactly how far you can go on how many pounds of fuel, and how high and how fast you can fly, and how much weight you can haul, and how many hours you can stay in the air before you've got to come back down to the ground. It's all right there in black and white. If you don't know it, or choose to ignore it, you crash.

In the infantry, there's room for bullshit. And there's room for a lot of loose opinions. The fine line between what is actually achievable and what is not, and the difference between what is very difficult and what is impossible, is seldom black and white. It's almost always a matter of perspective. So objecting to a mission based on its achievability is a tenuous stance for the officer who wants to keep his job and maybe get promoted someday with the recommendation of the very boss he's telling, "I can't." Very tenuous indeed. To make matters worse, the boss's job depends on mission accomplishment every bit as much as his subordinates. So, no shit, failure is not an option!

That's the art of war.

BETWEEN THE ROCK AND A HARD PLACE

In the peace-time years, the Marine Corps sent its infantry battalions to Okinawa, Japan. We used to call it "the Rock" like it was tough duty. From Iraq, it looked like Club Med. Before any infantry battalion walked out the door on deployment, they did works up—that's training—and they were tested to make sure they knew what they were doing, to make sure the Marines could handle themselves in a fight, as individuals and as a unit, should a fight ever come to pass. The test was a big deal. It was called the Marine Corps Combat Readiness Evaluation (MCCRE). Failure would almost certainly mean termination of the battalion commander's job and the end of his career. And so they rarely, if ever, failed. The evaluators were the staff and officers of a sister battalion—a sympathetic audience to be sure. The lead evaluator would be a fellow battalion commander, a sympathetic man.

My unit was set to deploy to Okinawa in the spring of 1999. I was still a second lieutenant. We'd received the vast majority of our Marines only two months prior to going through the readiness evaluation. That wasn't an aberration or some kind of mistake. It was just the way the Marine Corps did business in war and in peace time. You could think of it as just-in-time manning. But two months wasn't enough time to train so many new Marines in so many skills, individual and unit, and expect any level of real mastery. Yet that is exactly what was expected, or more precisely, that is what the commanders were expected to report or risk losing their jobs.

When the test was complete, the evaluators prepared a brief for the Division Commanding General to facilitate a discussion on the strengths and weaknesses of the deploying battalion. The officers were all present to provide comments or ask questions. The evaluators stood up in front of the General and said, "These guys were great! They really know their stuff." They painted a glowing picture of us. The other lieutenants and I shot concerned looks at each other. We rolled our eyes. We knew the truth.

For example, my company assaulted its own machine gun position in a night attack—a pretty significant mistake—and yet it never came up, not a word of it. We spent eight hours on a night foot movement that should have taken no more than two because we couldn't keep ourselves organized in the woods. For an infantry outfit, that's not a good thing. The examples of our inexperience were boundless, and still they never came up. The evaluators just kept right on talking about how shit-hot we were.

Then the General, who'd been in a while, nodded and asked, "Where do you think you need improvement?"

And this collection of officers, ours and the other battalions', shrugged and shook their heads and said, "No, we're good sir." The young lieutenants in the room were bewildered or appalled, but most of all we were silent. We watched our own bosses say nothing and we followed suit. We said nothing, too. Nothing but, "No, we're good, sir."

But in looking over the General, I got the faint impression that he knew what was happening. I'd say he must have, because after all he was a General, and he'd probably been through this same drill himself a million times before. He seemed to be saying to us, "Okay, you pass the test, acknowledged. Now let's really talk tactics, because I enjoy this stuff." But nobody budged. We stuck to our story. "We're ready," we said.

When the brief was over I went to my Company Commander. I was alarmed, as if I'd witnessed a crime. I saw what we did and I felt it was dishonest. Shit, I thought it was downright dishonorable. I said, "What just happened here? Why did we lie?"

And he said with a straight face, "We didn't lie. But you don't air your dirty laundry with the boss." I was stunned, and I'm not one to keep stunned to myself.

"How the hell is the General supposed to employ his maneuver units if he doesn't know their capabilities?" Then I asked him, "Is this what you expect of me? To keep my problems to myself?" To my astonishment, he said, "Yes." And I was baffled and more ashamed of myself and my officer corps than I'd ever been.

This is a minor anecdote, to be sure, but it underscores an important symptom, I think, of our military's condition. It is the story of *failure is not an option*. This is how we did business. I never said, or even thought, that we should have detailed every last error for the General. I did, on the other hand, think we should have been honest. But we just couldn't do that. We couldn't say to him, "General, we've got some damned fine lads out there, and they're busting their asses trying to get it right, but they've only been with us for two months. So it's not so much that they're bad, but that they're only two months good." What the Majors and the Colonels knew that I didn't know was that honesty is not always the best policy. If everybody else was cheering, "We're ready!" and one man came around saying, "I'm not so sure that we are," then he'd surely find himself out of a job, and fast. That's what we called a zero defects mentality, and that mentality reared its head in Iraq from the moment the war was conceived.

From the first time a lieutenant sees what I saw, from the moment he witnesses this institutional dishonesty, he begins to learn what he must do to survive. And by survival, I don't mean that this mentality is driven by selfish ambition alone. Most officers accept a degree of bureaucratic compromise precisely so that they can get promoted into positions that will give them the opportunity to more positively affect the Marines they lead. "If only I could be the commander," they say. "Then I'd un-fuck this situation and do it right." That's the rationalization of the officer. Seldom are they facing black-and-white ethical dilemmas, where the decision is clear. The compromise is most frequently gray. The further the officer goes up the chain, the more he'll have to compromise, and compromise he will or he won't survive. But ultimately, a man cannot compromise his conscience to achieve some practical good on some later day. The dividends in his hands will never outweigh the loss in his soul.

I do think it would be imprudent to move past this discussion without acknowledging the presence of careerism in the military, because it is there. Undeniably, there are some officers who live their lives in hot pursuit of individual glory. Ambition can be a difficult impulse to manage. It gives us the drive to excel, but in our headlong pursuit for success, judgment can sometimes be clouded. I don't like to belabor this point, because it tends to reduce the problems we were having in Iraq to the quality of the officers in the military, and that's just not what was happening. In my experience, most officers wanted deeply to do the right thing. But careerism is a factor worth considering because it did play a role in the decisions many commanders made on the battlefield.

Unfortunately, as often as we chanted at each other, "Failure is not an option," failures did occur from time to time. In the real world, whether we'd like to admit it or not, failure is simply a matter of course, even in the military, because the military is made up of humans, and humans are not perfect. So what did we do when we failed in reality? What happened when we zigged when we should have zagged? What did we do when we failed in areas where failure was not an option? In Iraq, we created a version of the truth that avoided the failures, and that everyone was pleased to hear. We generated statistics from cleverly articulated reports. Then we provided those statistics to people who could use them to show the world how everything was right on track.

STEALING

CORPS VALUES

I've seen some stealing in my time. Some people claim it's all the same. The self-righteous ones say, "Stealing is stealing." But I always figured there was a range of stealing, and the range was wide. When I worked at the tire shop in Boston, I got to know a lot of folks down there who didn't have much. So I saw a lot of stealing. But even as a kid I didn't look at it all the same. For instance, there were the guys who'd pocket a sawbuck now and again because they were breaking their backs 'round the clock for five bucks an hour and they barely had enough to pay the rent. And then there were the characters like Gary Coolidge, who divided his life between prison and drugs.

He divided his time at the tire shop between snorting coke and sucking down oil cans of beer. I don't think I ever saw the man sober. When Gary ate fried eggs, and he ate fried eggs often, the yolks would ooze out all over his lips and drip down onto his chin. He'd tell stories with his mouth full, and bits of egg would fly out with the bullshit. Gary was always telling me how he'd given up a full-ride scholarship to college to join the Marine Corps. I looked him over, with his torn plastic sneakers, his dilated eyes and the yolk dribbling from his lips, and I judged him. I didn't like Gary much, so I didn't believe much of what he had to say. One day, Gary went out on a road job to fix a flat on a tractor-trailer. When he got to the job, instead of fixing the tire, he tried to sell his service truck to the customer for a little drug money. I always figured that was a different brand of stealing.

Then there was a Marine back at Earle by the name of Lance Corporal Toombs. Looking back on it, I think he must have been bipolar or something, because his personality was divided between just two forms of expression: long periods of stony silence and abrupt episodes of unexplainable jubilation, during which he would suddenly grin and burst out, "Who stole the soul?" Toombs was a kleptomaniac, if I ever saw one. He couldn't not steal.

One day I was standing in the hall of the barracks, with a guy named Hannah, when Toombs strode by wearing nothing but a kinky-looking pair of banana yellow bikini briefs. Hannah stopped mid-sentence to stare at him as he passed. I stared, too. Then Hannah looked at me with astonishment and said, "He's wearing my skivvies!"

My eyes shifted dubiously to Toombs and then back to Hannah, and I said, "He is?" I don't know if I was more stunned that Hannah owned a pair of yellow bikini briefs or that Toombs had ripped them off and was now sauntering up and down the hall with them on for everyone else in the barracks to see. That had to be a different kind of stealing.

Toombs stole a lot of stuff while he was there at Earle and I think the guys got used to it. He stole my dress blues once, right off the hanger. Actually he traded them for his own. I only noticed because when I went to put on my jacket one day, it was about four sizes too small. It was too small for Toombs, too, which is why he swapped it out with mine. I went to see Jackie down at supply and he told me there was only one guy in the platoon who was issued that size—Toombs. I checked in with Toombs that afternoon and he apologized right away and came up with a pretty elaborate explanation of how he'd switched them accidentally. He was good-natured enough, and I had my blues back, so I let it go.

One morning, up on the east tower out at the Limited Area, I found a crumpled piece of paper. I opened it up and found it covered in Toombs' handwriting. "Statistics" was the heading. It was kind of an odd compilation of facts and figures about himself. I scanned it over briefly, past his eye-color, his height, and his best time on the hundred, down to the line titled: "Bad habits." Next to that was the word "stealing." You had to feel sorry for the guy.

Of course, Toombs wasn't the only one stealing. In my time, I saw Marines steal everything from deuce gear to rifles to night vision goggles. ATM cards went missing. Cash vanished. Rubber checks were written. Taxis were ditched. Electronics, bikes, tools, jackets, shades—you name it—it was probably stolen at one time or another by some Marine somewhere. Even the "geedunk" machines weren't safe. I know I helped flip a few of them over in my time for their tasty proceeds. Once, after a field event, I even pocketed a smoke grenade. I figured no one had counted them. I figured wrong. The command launched an aggressive investigation to find it, so I had to give it back.

In the greater scheme of things, in the framework of international law and all that, I don't suppose petty theft is really of any major concern. But internally to the Marine Corps, it does carry weight with respect to a man's character. We'd recite incessantly and with vigor our *Corps Values*: "A Marine does not lie, cheat, or steal!" But I'd say that was more of a goal than a statement of fact. The Marine Corps, being chock-filled with guys like me bearing looser interpretations of stealing, was bound to run into a few cases of larceny.

To remind us all not to sully the good reputation of our Corps, the Commandant came up with an interesting invention called the *Corps Values* card. It was a small plastic card that a Marine could tuck into his wallet and pull out at a moment's notice when the urge to rip something off reared its ugly head. All new recruits and Marines alike were encouraged to carry their *Corps Values* card on their person at all times for just such moral dilemmas. There were, however, more practical uses for the card. In Okinawa, Japan, for instance, when I was the Regimental Officer of the Day for the 4th Marine Regiment, I locked the master key inside one of the offices. I was reluctant to confess my mistake to the Colonel, who called in the middle of the night asking me to unlock his door and retrieve something on his desk.

I said sheepishly, "Can I get back to you on that?"

He said, "You got ten minutes."

I was distressed and the clock was running, so I shared my predicament with the Staff Duty. He unhesitatingly whipped out his *Corps Values* card and said, "No problem." Within a few minutes the Colonel's door was open and I was saved. But the Staff Sergeant had had a little trouble at first. As he wriggled the card into the doorjamb, he grunted through gritted teeth, "Usually I can break in much faster than this!"

LAW OF WAR

You don't steal from the enemy. Marines are taught that from day one. Stealing from the enemy, or from the people of a foreign country, has always been one of the cardinal sins of the Corps, even more than stealing from your buddy. They told me that much when I was still a Private myself. "Not only do you tarnish our image as Americans," they warned us, "but you invigorate the enemy as well. It is always easier to fight an immoral enemy than a moral one."

But war alters the dimensions of morality within a man's consciousness, and what is clearly wrong on the home front becomes natural on the battlefield. Killing, for instance, is a sin, unless you're in war, unless your life is threatened. Shooting an unarmed man is generally considered wrong, even in war, unless you think he's maneuvering against you. Then it's okay. Firing on the wounded or surrendered is not allowed, unless you believe they're faking. Then, by all means, fire away. So there are exceptions to the rules. That's what you pick up in the combat zone, the exceptions. The lines of morality shift and fade away, and so the soldier often doesn't even realize it's happening.

In Iraq, we had a couple of Marines in the battalion who stole. Someone found them sitting on a pile of dinars and there really wasn't any question. They'd gone into an Iraqi house on a raid, *official business*, and they came out with a pocketful of cash. It was a bad thing they did. I don't think there's any talking around that. But I also don't think that what they did was terribly surprising. We spent a lot of time and mental energy dehumanizing the Iraqi people. They were called hajjis. Those under suspicion were manhandled like animals, and those whose houses we raided were, no doubt, under suspicion. They were detained with bags over their heads, stuffed in kennel-like cages and sometimes abused like dogs. Small wonder our Marines felt okay stealing from them. The very concept "stealing" is only applicable among humans.

What I learned in Iraq is that sometimes stealing goes far beyond the pinching of sawbucks, or bikini briefs, or a few dinars from the locals. Sometimes it is much more than a minor episode of skewed ethics. In Iraq, we stole their dignity. We came in like gangbusters, fired all the professionals and the soldiers, wreaked havoc wherever we roamed, and told the Iraqis they were going to start living our way—the American way. We called it a liberation—liberation from a tyrant—but I think we really meant liberation from themselves. We stole their dignity, and so I think it was natural that they would fight us to the death, because a people without dignity have but a vestige of life. They are dead already.

WHO STOLE THE SOUL?

That's what Toombs always said, and if I had only known then how prophetic those words would turn out to be, maybe I would have listened. Who stole the soul?

There was an Iraqi police station in Yousifiyah. They called us one afternoon in a panic to report that they were being attacked by "many men." Many men quickly turned into dozens of men. And soon dozens turned into hundreds. Hundreds of angry men with assault rifles and rocket launchers were attacking this little countryside police station of Yousifiyah. That's what they told us when they called us for help. But it was too late. The hundreds of angry men with their rifles and their rocket launchers had already overrun them, rifling through the barracks like pirates, stealing their weapons, and ammunition, and radios, and freeing all the prisoners. They'd been overrun and not a shot had been fired.

We went of course. We sent a platoon. By the time they got there, the streets were clear and quiet. There was no sign of a struggle, or a riot, or the slightest disturbance. People carried on with their lives as if nothing had passed. The police station was empty. There was no blood, or smoke, or any other evidence of a fight. The policeman or two that remained—unharmed—gave a gripping account of the takeover. We suspected right off that the whole story was a hoax or an embellishment of the truth. The Iraqi Police had proven themselves consistently melodramatic. Maybe some men had come and made demands, but clearly there was no attack initiated. The question was more this: Were these policemen cowardly or ill-disciplined for having not defended themselves? Or, were they complicit in the takeover? I was many miles away at the time. There was no way for me to know for sure.

But the theft of all these weapons, and equipment, and prisoners was probably inevitable, given the strength of the insurgency in the area and the impotence of the police. Being powerless to prevent it, the policemen had only one choice to make: live or die when it happened. The insurgents knew all this, and perhaps they pointed it out to the policemen. Or maybe, obvious as it was, the policemen knew it already. And maybe, if we'd thought about it long enough, we'd have known it, too.

So what is a man to do when the theft of his possessions is inevitable? Does he live with it? Or does he fight and die in the embrace of that which he has lost already? The moment I crossed the border into Iraq, I knew my faith would be stolen from me. I saw the tragedy in the distance like the rippling heat waves that wash the desert horizon. All I could do was to load up into my gun-truck and drive into them. They stole my faith. *They*, I say now, like the Iraqi policemen who spoke of great hordes of men streaming into their barracks. They, I say now, like I didn't have a hand in it. A voice whispered inside me before it all began, saying, "We will have your faith. We will have your soul. You may live or die. It matters nothing to us." I, like the policemen of Yousifiyah, nodded sadly and looked around at what I'd already forfeited. I opened the door, and I showed them the way to my faith. I was overrun and there wasn't a shot fired.

THE MIXING BOWL

MIKE AND TONY AND THEM

So then there was Mike and Tony and them, up at the bridge. We called it *the Mixing Bowl*. But what you've got to understand is that this bridge was all bridges, and all checkpoints, and any place at all where American soldiers had to stand guard on a road and say, "Stop!" They were all the same. The Mixing Bowl was everywhere. The Mixing Bowl was the war.

And Mike and Tony and them weren't just a few of guys in my unit; they were everyone. Mike and Tony and them were the guys we sent up to keep the bridges from being blown. They were the guys that kept our supply lines open. Without Mike and Tony and them, we didn't eat, and we didn't drink, and we didn't shoot. So Mike and Tony and them were pretty important to the big picture. But they didn't feel important when they were standing up there in the heat all day, just staring down a highway that disappeared to a point on the horizon.

We pulled Mike and Tony and them together and we said, "Whatever you do, don't let anyone pass this point." And we told them, "The only thing in the world that you have to worry about up here are the car-bombers. That's it. So if you see a car coming, and you signal it to stop, and it doesn't stop—you shoot it. Don't hesitate! Because that's the only way to tell the difference between the good guys and the bad guys. The good guys stop. The bad guys don't." That's what we told Mike and Tony and them.

In thinking about car-bombers, one should avoid the assumption that they attacked checkpoints with the exclusive intent to kill Americans, because that just doesn't get to the heart of it. There is no question, of course, that a man who has committed himself to a suicide attack against our troops would like to see a few of them killed in the process. But it's doubtful that that was ever the only objective, because that wasn't where he achieved his most significant victory. His victory was achieved from the grave, long after he was dead. Because he wasn't just trying to kill Americans. He was trying to scare Americans. And that is exactly what car-bombers did. They scared Americans. When Mike and Tony and them saw what a car-bomb could do, when they saw all that it could destroy, it scared the shit out them.

From that moment on, they didn't hesitate. They shot at any car that didn't stop because they remembered, all too well, what we told them. But Mike and Tony found out that sometimes the good guys don't stop either. Sometimes Mike and Tony and them would blaze away into a car, and then they'd come to find out that there were no bad guys inside, just dead, unarmed civilians. But the car didn't stop, and Mike and Tony and them couldn't, for the life of them, figure out why.

What the insurgents realized, and what amazingly escaped us on a daily basis, is that for every unarmed Iraqi we shot at our checkpoints, there was a family out there, mothers and fathers, brothers and sisters and cousins and uncles, there were friends, and lovers, and colleagues, and co-workers, and they'd all be mourning the deaths of their loved ones. And they'd all be enraged at us, the Americans. And then suddenly, they would be a whole lot more sympathetic towards the insurgency.

For every actual car-bomb attack in Iraq, there were dozens more innocent people shot at checkpoints like the Mixing Bowl. Because when Mike and Tony stared down that highway, week in, and week out, the only things on their minds were the car-bombers. And every time a car came ambling down the road towards them, they thought just one thing: "Is this one going to be a car-bomber? Does this one have my name on it?" Good guy or bad guy? If that car didn't stop, Mike and Tony and them were going to open fire. And that is how the car-bombers helped build an insurgency.

So that was life on the Mixing Bowl. Mike and Tony could tell you all about it. They could tell you about all the cars they shot up, and about all the people they killed and wounded, and about all the times they found those cars with no bombs, and those people with no weapons. The great unanswerable question was, *Why the fuck don't they stop?* Mike and Tony and them would get frustrated because they were decent guys. They didn't like to see innocent people killed. They'd shout out, "What's wrong with these people? They see us out here with our guns and our jersey barriers. We've got stop signs up, written in Arabic. We're waving our arms. We've got spike strips. We've got lights. We've got everything. So why the fuck don't they stop?"

The toughest part about that question was that we really didn't want the answer. When we said, "Why the fuck don't they stop?" we really weren't looking to understand what was going on in those drivers' minds. It was a rhetorical question, and we always had the pat answer. We said, "Because they're fucking stupid." We did—all the time. And it wasn't because we were ignorant or malicious, but because that's the only answer a man could really come up with after he found out he just shot up a family, or a child, or an old woman. That's the only answer he could live with when he knew that he'd probably have to do it again. "Because they're fucking stupid." So Mike and Tony and them carried on like this, week in and week out, shooting unarmed Iraqis until we had a long line of bloody cars sitting along the fence line of our camp.

After a while, the brass started to take notice. They looked at Mike and Tony, and then they looked over at that long line of riddled cars and all that blood dripping from the seats, and they said, "Hey! What the fuck is going on up there at the Mixing Bowl?" Because you see, the brass knew this was bad for business. They said, "We don't need all this bad press."

So they sent me in to "investigate," to gather the facts. I collected photos from every perspective. I took statements from every witness. I diagramed distances and angles. I studied the procedures. Then I put it all together into a statement of innocence. That's what it was. A statement of innocence. Because I wasn't trying to prove that Mike and Tony and them did anything wrong. I was trying to prove that they were exactly right. Right to shoot. Right to fear for their lives. Right to defend themselves. Right to kill. I didn't want those boys to be persecuted for doing what they had to do to stay alive.

In essence the brass was asking the same question we'd been asking ourselves: "If you guys are following all your procedures, then why the fuck don't these people stop?" And in essence my report was giving them the same answer we'd been giving ourselves: "We are following our procedures. We're doing everything we can possibly do to let them know we want them to stop, and these people are just not stopping, so they must be fucking stupid." That's about what I was saying. And so the brass looked over my report, nodded approvingly and said, "Roger that. Carry on."

To be clear, I never left out any incriminating evidence. If Mike and Tony and them were murdering folks, I would have said it. But Mike and Tony and them weren't murdering and they weren't lying. They were surviving in an impossible situation that we put them into. So I did what I had to do to protect them. And what I had to do was absolutely nothing. Nothing. As long as I didn't go trying to answer that question, "Why the fuck don't they stop?" then everything would be okay. All I had to do was stick to the party line—*these Marines are just out there defending themselves the best way they know how—* then everyone would stay happy. At least I thought they would stay happy. So I stuck to the party line, but everyone did not stay happy.

A funny thing happened. After a while, I found we stopped having to justify our shootings up the chain of command, and we started having to justify them down the chain of command. Mike and Tony and them started to take notice. They looked at themselves, and then they looked over at that long line of riddled cars, and all that blood dripping from the seats, and they said, "Hey! What the fuck is going on up here at the Mixing Bowl?" Because there's only so many innocent lives a man can take and only so many children he can see ripped to shreds by his machine guns, and by his hands, before he starts to question his own morality. Mike and Tony and them started asking themselves, "What the hell are we doing here?" And the brass damn sure knew that was bad for business.

So they sent me in to straighten things out. All the officers were on damage control. And we said, "Listen Marines, we've seen the facts of the case, and you're clear. You had no way of knowing if it was going to be a car-bomber or not. So you did what you had to do. You did the right thing." That was the speech. I don't know how many times I gave it. But I don't think Mike and Tony and them were buying my brand. I believe they were feeling a little hesitation, maybe a little remorse. I believe the images of all those dead innocent people were stuck in their brains.

But then one day a car turned up at the Mixing Bowl. It didn't stop. Mike and Tony and them opened fire with their machine guns the way they always do. The car lurched to a halt and then it blew sky high. It was a car-bomber. They said the engine block must have sailed two hundred feet in the air. When it landed, it left a crack in the asphalt from one side of the street to the other. Hearts were pounding in the COC. All murmuring stopped. We held our breaths while we waited by the radio to find out if Mike and Tony and them were okay. And after several long minutes, we all let out a long sigh of relief when we found out they were.

Then we rushed out to the Mixing Bowl to look over the wreckage. There was no body. It was vaporized. There's wasn't even any blood. Then we looked over at Mike and Tony and them. We got in real close, and we pointed our fingers at the mess, and we said, "You see that? *That* is why you don't hesitate."

That was the case clincher. Our argument was iron-clad. All we had to do was make sure that when the next car load of innocent people got shot to bits, nobody went looking for the answer to that fatal question, "Why the fuck don't they stop?"

HYPOTHETICAL

I'm going to describe a scenario, which is hypothetical to the extent that I don't know the people involved and I don't know their thoughts. But I can imagine it because it was typical in Iraq and ongoing. In this scenario, an Iraqi man is driving down the highway with his wife and his son. I'll call him Hamal. All of the sudden Hamal looks down the road and sees that he's coming up on an American checkpoint. Now maybe Hamal has never dealt with any Americans before. He's never spoken a word to them, and they've never had cause to speak to him. But they will now. And maybe that's not such a bad thing, but then again maybe it is.

Maybe all Hamal knows about the Americans is what he's learned from his neighbors, and they all say "Watch out Hamal. Watch out!" Now Hamal's a simple man. He doesn't want any trouble. He doesn't care about the Americans or the insurgents. He just wants to provide for his family. But his neighbors are warning him all the time, "Watch out Hamal! They're going to get you. You'll see. One day they're going to get you."

Then one night the Americans come and they get Hamal's neighbor. Hamal thinks to himself, "Hey, he wasn't such a bad guy. He was a hard worker, a good Muslim, an honorable father. He did what he had to do. So why did the Americans take him away?" Hamal will probably never know the answer to that question, but all the other neighbors are pointing at his empty apartment and they're saying, "You see that Hamal? You see? This is what they do."

So now Hamal is driving with his family and he's about to deal with the Americans for the first time. He's scared. He's seen the pictures of Abu Ghraib. His neighbors showed them to him. They pointed at the stacks of naked bodies and they said to him, "Just look at what the Americans do." And they said, "Hamal, these weren't terrorists. These were taxi-drivers and farmers." And there's a chance they're right because in Iraq every time an IED went off, we used to round up the closest five people we could grab and haul them away in hoods and cuffs. We didn't know if they were innocent or guilty. They were just onhand, so we took them away.

Well, Hamal isn't much into politics really, but whatever the Americans are up to, it seems pretty clear that it's dangerous to tangle with them. And now he's about to face them—the Americans. If he was alone, he wouldn't be scared. Well, maybe he would be scared, but not as scared as he is now with his wife and son sitting beside him. He doesn't want them to be taken away to Abu Ghraib. If he stops, they might be. Maybe he'll be taken away. He doesn't know. In the four or five seconds he's got to think about what he's going to do, he imagines all the awful things that might happen. And he's scared out of his mind.

The checkpoint is drawing closer. The Americans are now pointing their weapons. "So it's true," he thinks, "they do mean to harm us." They're waving at him to stop. There are signs. There are barriers. But Hamal thinks, "No way. You're not getting my family." And he mashes his foot on the gas pedal, he prays to Allah, he tells his wife that he loves her and their son very much, and he tries to break through.

Meanwhile, there's Mike and Tony and them. They've seen what a car-bomb can do. They've been out on the Mixing Bowl, out on that checkpoint, out in that fucking heat for weeks now. Maybe it's been months. Time all blends together when you're out there for so long. Fear and boredom can make for a deadly concoction. Suddenly Hamal's car appears. It's moving fast. It's not slowing down. Mike and Tony and them start to panic. They start to sweat, even more than they were sweating before. Their hearts are pumping fast. Their fingers are wrapped around their triggers. Their eyes are fixed on that car as it gets closer and closer. Mike and Tony and them wave their arms. But the car keeps coming closer. Then they raise their weapons because we told them it's a good way to let drivers know you want them to stop.

But Hamal's car doesn't stop. And Mike and Tony and them finally reach their limit. Fear, and panic, and rage, and training, and orders, and procedures all kick in at once. They pull their triggers back and the figures inside the car disappear behind the bursting windshield. Then the car finally stops. But it doesn't explode. Everything is quiet. The barrels of the machine guns are smoking hot. The passengers are all dead. Mike and Tony and them don't find any weapons or bombs, just the horrible bleeding bodies of Hamal and his family. They shake their heads in horror and confusion, and they ask themselves with wringing hands, "Why the fuck didn't they stop?"

So as a Marine, I am left in this hypothetical, while sadly plausible, and in fact real, situation with a predicament—a question. Who am I supposed to feel sorry for? Should I feel sorry for Hamal who didn't stop because he was scared? Or should I feel sorry for Mike and Tony and them who killed Hamal because they were scared, too? I think of Hamal and his family, and though I don't speak their language, or understand their ideas or their customs, I do recognize their humanity. They are people with dreams and passions and loves, like all people have. Their deaths are tragedies as all deaths in war are.

But then I think of Mike and Tony and them. I know these guys, and I love them. They're Marines. They're my brothers in arms. I've shared some long drinking nights with them and a few tough scrapes, too. And so I ask myself, who am I supposed to feel sorry for? And *that* moment right there, that moment of hesitation that I just expressed—who should I feel sorry for?—is exactly why we could never answer the question, "Why the fuck don't these people stop?" Because a Marine can't hesitate when he's trying to survive. He can't identify with the Iraqi people, not even the innocent Iraqi people. He can't win their hearts and minds when he's out there on the Mixing Bowl trying to live through all those car-bombers. And so Mike and Tony and them were left with an impossible dilemma. Either they did not fire and risked dying, or they did fire and risked further jeopardizing the mission. It was a lose-lose scenario and it would never change. The Mixing Bowl was a permanent fixture of the war.

OPERATION TRASH LUTIFIYAH

PAYBACK'S A MOTHERFUCKER

Lutifiyah was the small Sunni town to our south. We called it *little Fallujah*—that's how poorly we regarded it. We had a hell of time with those people, a hell of a time. They killed a few of our guys down there and wounded a lot more, and we were pissed about that. So before we left Northern Babil for al Anbar, we vowed to get some payback. Of course, nobody really wanted to go back there once we'd left, but when it turned out we had to, payback was exactly what we had in mind, and it was a mother fucker.

We called it "Operation Trash Lutifiyah." That wasn't some crass side joke from within the ranks. That was the official title of the battalion operation order, distributed by and to the officers and copied to higher headquarters. I know; I helped to draft and distribute it. Everybody knew about Operation Trash Lutifiyah. When I talk about this kind of thing, I've found there are people who have a tough time hearing it. I think it's because they want to believe in our military so badly that they can hardly fathom little anecdotes like this. They want to believe that we were really trying to win hearts and minds. But we weren't. Not with the kind of American drive that, for instance, put us on the moon. Once that first blood was drawn, hearts and minds were shifted to the back-burner. Combat came to the forefront.

In Iraq, we spent most of our days doing three things. We attacked. We patrolled. And we raided. We called that last one a "Cordon and Search," but it was still a raid. And sometimes we even called it a "Cordon and Knock" when we wanted to raid politely. And sometimes, when we didn't exactly know where the bad guys were, or when we figured everyone in the area was at least a little bad, we cordoned off the whole town and we raided them all. That was Operation Trash Lutifiyah.

But first, let me describe what I would call the best-case scenario when it came to raids. I went out on a cordon-and-search one night, and there was a little farmhouse on the periphery of our target, so we figured we'd better check it out. I watched the whole thing unfold. The Marines went in, knocked on the door, and a man came out. He had just sat down to dinner with his family. We politely explained the situation to him and asked if he wouldn't mind stepping outside with his family for just a few minutes while we looked the place over.

A few Marines went inside and gently looked about, while others kept the family company in the yard, chatting as best they could with them in Arabic and giving the children pieces of candy. There was a lot of smiling going on. After about a half an hour, the search was complete. The place was clear. We apologized to the man and his family for the inconvenience and thanked them for their patience. We shook his hand and then went on our way to search his neighbor's house. Now unless we were to give up raids altogether, that was about as good as it was ever going to get.

But the truth is, every time we went busting down (or knocking on) someone's door and searching the place, we made a dozen new enemies. Our own manuals said, "Don't do that!" Yet we kept right on doing it like we didn't know the difference. I'm not talking about humanity. I'm talking about effectiveness. It made no difference how polite we were, or how much candy we dished out to the kids, or how many "God be with yous" we threw at people. We went into their homes, uninvited, and started rifling through their personal shit. So of course they were going to get sick of it. Of course they were going to get angry. I think I'd get sick of it and angry, too. I think anybody would. Of course they were going to start hating us and start supporting people who were fighting us. I can't imagine any other outcome.

THE HITS JUST KEEP ON COMING

We were up to our eyebrows in IEDs and petty harassing attacks in Lutifiyah. We were up to our eyebrows in casualties. And we were fed up. "These people have no idea the kind of combat power we can bring to bear," I used to mutter. "They ain't seen nothin' yet." I'm pretty sure we were all thinking along those lines as we geared up to go. In reality, Operation Trash Lutifiyah turned out to be relatively uneventful—at least from our point of view. There wasn't a shot fired.

We cut off all means of escape, as planned, and we went through every last space in the town: every apartment, every shop, every house, every room, every closet, everywhere. It was systematic and yet it was chaos. We detained every military-aged male, that is, every man between eighteen and fifty-five. It was a full day's work. Then we pulled out and went home, leaving fresh wreckage in our wake and new reasons to hate us.

There were certain homes that we'd specifically identified as the residences of High Value Targets—insurgents. There were about a dozen of them scattered through town. Those were the places we trashed with particular vigor. We tore them apart and tossed their furniture, their clothes and their personal belongings out into the street. We called them hits. None of the men were home, so we dealt only with the wives. We were sending their husbands a message. As we smashed whatever was smashable, we were saying, "We know where you live, motherfucker."

I use the word "we" in this case, not because I was down there personally putting my hands on people's stuff—I wasn't, I was in the COC—but because it was my unit; I wore the uniform and I gladly participated in my own capacity. I coordinated activities on the radio, I gathered reports, and I smiled as it all went down. I approved. I was practically cheering. That's why I say *we*. And I know fully what we did because it was my job to know. It was my job to hear the stories, from peers, seniors and subordinates alike, and they were relayed with equal enthusiasm. We were all pleased to trash Lutifiyah.

Operation Trash Lutifiyah was technically a one-day gig, but for those dozen or so households we suspected in particular as being the homes of bad guys, we extended the nightmare a little longer. On the wall of the COC, we hung a satellite image of Lutifiyah and we drew circles around each of the homes. As every patrol went out for the night, I instructed them to pick two or three and go on down there and trash them out again. It didn't matter which ones they picked, and it didn't matter what time they showed up, or how long they stayed, or how bad they trashed the place. I didn't care.

The point was to keep sending our message: "We still know where you live, motherfucker. And we're not going away." We sent our message to these men by rousting their wives and children in the middle of the night and trashing out their homes. Every night for the next two weeks, I directed another few homes to be trashed, and every night, as Marines carried out those orders, the insurgency grew a little stronger. We called it Operation Trash Lutifiyah, but I think a more apt title would have been *Operation Trash all rapport with the Iraqi people.*

STRENGTH IN DECENCY

The manual says be careful how you apply force—it could come back to haunt you. We read it, we knew the deal, and we told the troops what they had to do. And yet there was a hollowness in our voices, a hollowness that was drowned out by the sounds of exploding IEDs, of mortars and rockets impacting in the FOBs, of bullets snapping overhead, and thumping RPG rounds impacting to the left and right, until our voices could no longer be heard at all.

The message wasn't heard by the Marines who saw their friends lying twisted, pulled apart, on the ground, burned, bleeding, and silent. It's hard to hear over that kind of silence. It's hard to use force carefully when casualties are being inflicted daily from the darkness and progress is clearly not being made. It's hard. Their minds were on the fight, on killing, on making it to the end of the patrol, to the end of the operation, to the end of the day, or the week, or the month, to the end of the deployment. Their minds were on survival.

The Generals understood the nature of the fight. They knew it wouldn't be a strictly kinetic battle—that is, one using firepower alone—but one that should be primarily non-kinetic. They understood. Hell, they wrote the book. But the message wasn't getting down to the lowest levels where the soldiers were out on the streets interfacing with the Iraqi people, and it wasn't because the soldiers couldn't read.

It was because from the moment they they joined their units, the talk was of the fight. They were desensitized to the brutality of war from boot camp. Their training was about battle, about shooting, and calling for fire, and reactions to enemy contact, and everything else to do with combat. Cultural training was an afterthought. We didn't know the language in Iraq, or their culture, or their history, and we didn't want to know it. Our operational focus was on fighting, because our intelligence was about bad guys, because our attitude was about warring, not about helping.

Our system of promotions and decorations were centered on combat; they were about valor in battle, about learning the war-fighting business, and about being recognized for accomplishments made under fire and being rewarded for those accomplishments with command. They were not about stability operations. We told ourselves failure is not an option. We said: First, do no harm. And then we told the Iraqis that we'd come as liberators not occupiers. We offered them the carrot or the stick, but there was conspicuously more stick than carrot, and then we wondered why we weren't winning their hearts and minds.

Counterinsurgencies are meant to be a blend of civil and military operations—says the book and the men who know—but then the infantry units were left to their own devices, their own ingenuity and their own knowledge of war to sort our their own areas of operation. They had to rummage up their own armor. They had to struggle with poorly functioning equipment and communications gear. They had to rebuild a country with hard-to-procure resources from obstinate bureaucracies. They had to drive countless miles on

IED-infested roads. There was no substantial effort to improve the lives of the Iraqi people, none that did not pale in comparison to our effort to fight. Our message of help was weak because we insisted on projecting strength through firepower, when we should have been projecting strength through decency.

REPORTING—THE REST OF THE STORY

WAR STORIES NEVER TOLD

Martin Luther King Jr. said ,"He who passively accepts evil is as much involved in it as he who helps to perpetrate it. He who accepts evil without protesting against it is really cooperating with it."

There were so many times in Iraq when I felt like that was me: *the passive acceptor and cooperator of evil*. As a watch officer in the COC, I didn't live the war stories for the most part, I collected them as they occurred, entered them into the computer, and pieced together the fragments. I was an observer of war, of the decision-making process within, of the battles that ensued, of the conclusions that were drawn, and of the subsequent actions that were taken. That was my job, to observe and to take all those war stories as they poured in from the battlefield and record them in our operations log, that is, to transform them into palatable, antiseptic language that incriminated neither the teller, nor the chain of command. As I did, I discovered another war story, the biggest story of them all, and day by day, I helped to bury it away so no one would ever hear it.

I never told a lie. I just left out a lot of important truths. Or maybe it would be more accurate to say that I left out the truthful conclusions. The conclusions we wanted to draw relied on certain possibilities being absent, so that's what I did. I made them disappear. I let all those episodes of gray lethality whither away into the silence. I shoved them into our memory hole. Except our memory hole wasn't a furnace. Our memory hole was an institutional blind eye. If we could fail to see it, we would not see it, and if we did not see it, it did not get recorded. And if it wasn't recorded, then it didn't happen.

One afternoon after we returned from Iraq, one of my lieutenants remarked off-handedly to me, "You have no idea all the shit we didn't report." It was an unsettling comment to be sure. The omissions were as much a part of our war as the killing. Everyone was involved in shaping the battlefield in terms that were convenient to us. As an officer who drafted many hundreds of operational reports in combat, I'd say that any report coming out of a war should be considered immediately suspect, based on politics, based on ambition, based on passion, or depravity, or unawareness, or fatigue. In fact, the only statistics I would credit as being absolutely accurate are the American casualty reports. It's hard to fudge the numbers on our own body bags.

I was talking to some people once and somebody asked me, "Does the President know what's happening in Iraq, or is the military distorting the truth so badly that he can't tell what the truth is anymore?" I thought that was pretty good question, and the obvious answer was that I didn't have the foggiest idea what the President did or did not know. On the other hand, it would be impossible for me to believe that he couldn't have known the truth if he wanted to. So I think that he probably wanted a particular version of the truth, and the military was inclined to give it to him. God knows I played a part in that process. From the beginning of the war, I'd only heard President Bush express optimism about our prospects of success, so I just came to assume that that's the kind of truth he wanted to hear. And therein lay the downside to the bright side.

In Iraq, the reporting facade was ubiquitous. There was always a positive spin within reach, and everything in the reports we produced was designed to create a perception of success. I drafted a Daily Operations Summary every single day of our deployment, and every single one of those reports started out with the phrase, "The battalion conducted *offensive* operations in zone." Beyond revealing our natural inclination to aggression, that phrase immediately implied something about our initiative on the battlefield. That word "offensive" created the illusion that we were in charge and in control, and that our operations were proactive.

But if you looked down over the rest of the report, you couldn't escape noticing a conspicuous trend toward *defensive* activities. It was all there in black and white. We were spending all our time defending roads, defending oil pipelines, defending bases, defending infrastructure, defending ourselves. And yet we called them *offensive* operations. Because "defensive operations" would have sounded entirely too reactive, like we'd lost all control of the war. But the truthful conclusion, the one we chose to let slip down into the memory hole, was that everything we did in Iraq was a reaction.

Attacks and raids are generally considered offensive operations, even if they're in response to enemy activities, but I never saw an attack or raid conducted in Iraq that we weren't baited into. We were not determining our own path. We were being pulled, pushed, and driven into exactly the types of reactions that the insurgents liked best: hostile reactions. Yet the reports I wrote always depicted the battlefield as well contained, and our commanders always raved about our successes. And if ever there was an incident that challenged that perception, well, I'd just find some other way to think about it, some different, yet plausible way to convey it. It's not like I had to work at it. It came naturally to me.

ONE DEATH TOO MANY

Outside of Lutifiyah, our snipers spotted an Iraqi man skulking around by the side of the road. It was the middle of the night, it was route Jackson, it was fucking Lutifiyah, and he had a shovel. They figured he must have been up to no good. They called me up and requested permission to engage him. "Engage him," they said, like they wanted to have a conversation with him. They said, "Can we engage him?" and I said "Sure. Sure, go ahead and *engage* him." The question of this man's life—whoever he was—was decided in the night with the question "Can we engage him?" And my answer, "Sure."

The language we use in war can be astonishing sometimes. When I asked my wife to marry me, I "engaged" her. In Iraq, we were using that same word, "engage," to kill a man. I've used it that way for years without thinking about it. I still often do. But now it makes me wonder about all the other words we were using. Like *liberation* for instance. What did that turn out to mean on the ground? It meant snipers calling me up and asking to engage strange men in the night, and me answering "sure" without a second thought about it. I'm not sure I gave the matter five minutes of my time. I'm not sure I gave it five seconds. He was carrying that fucking shovel after all. What was I supposed to think, that he was a farmer?

Actually, it turned out that the Iraqis did farm in the middle of the night. I'm always impressed when I find that people around here—civilians—know that, because in Iraq I'd never heard anything about it, not for several months into the deployment anyway. When I was finally told, I didn't even believe it at first. I thought it was ridiculous. I said: Wait a second, you're telling me that these people wake up in the dead of night, haul out of bed, pick up a shovel, and what? Go farm? But that is precisely what they were doing, and there were some decent reasons for it, too. For one thing, there were issues with the electricity and their irrigation equipment, which at times came on only at night. Furthermore, it was a hundred and forty degrees during the day, which made it pretty damned uncomfortable just to stand still, much less do a lot of digging. So they farmed at night.

But then again, there were still all those IEDs up and down Jackson. And every guy we stopped in the night with a shovel claimed to be a farmer. All of them. Every last Iraqi carrying a shovel at midnight was a fucking farmer. We thought to ourselves: Well someone's burying these god-damned IEDs. So some of these guys with shovels must be lying. I guess we got to where we figured they were all lying. We got to where we didn't even ask anymore. Snipers would just call in and request permission to engage a man with a shovel from two hundred meters away. And I'd say, "Sure."

Now and again, I think about death-row, and about the kinds of heinous crimes a person has to commit to get there, the incontrovertible evidence of guilt that the government has to produce, and the unanimous decision of twelve jurors that has to be reached to get a death-sentence. But in Iraq, a man with a shovel, on the side of the road, in the middle of the night, could be sentenced to death—by me—and there would be no judge, no jury, no appeal, and no stay of execution. The snipers would ask to engage him, and I'd just glance up from my magazine, take a sip of coffee, and I'd say, "Sure." I said "sure" a lot in Iraq.

So they shot him. He lay dead by the side of the road, and we'd never know if he was truly an insurgent or not. But he could have been. And so he was. And so that's what I wrote down. I wrote, "One insurgent engaged and killed." Of course, the possibility has occurred to me that this man actually was an insurgent. And I know he could have been. But what is significant is that we stopped caring to know for sure. It was too hard to tell, and it was too easy for the bad guys to get away, so we relied on straws of evidence and decisive action in the still of the night. We killed them all, or we tried to. But they couldn't have all been insurgents. Nobody guesses right one hundred percent of the time. So that means we engaged at least one farmer out there. It means that I gave permission to shoot at least one innocent man—at least—and that one death is one too many for me.

UNSPOKEN LIES

I've said I never lied. I've said it a lot. But all the while, I was lying in a way. I was lying to help accomplish an un-accomplishable mission. The lie was not what I said in my reports. The lie was what I did not say. It's what I packed into the blank spaces between the lines. So I wasn't lying when I said that the police station was blown up. I wasn't lying when I said the local medical clinic was serving as an aid-station to the insurgents. I wasn't lying when I said that the police we trained turned out to be insurgents themselves. I wasn't lying when I said corruption in the Iraqi Army was rampant. I wasn't lying when I said that the insurgents we faced were dangerous and determined. I wasn't lying about the casualties we took. I wasn't lying about the IEDs that went off, or the rockets that landed, or the bullets that flew by. I wasn't lying. There were problems. And we were trying to sort them out. That's not a lie, either. We were trying in the best way our infantry minds could figure. But we would always gravitate to violence, by our nature and by our desire to stay alive. And by political necessity we would always frame our reports to justify that violence. That was the lie.

I found that the conclusions of success in Iraq did not need to be based on any kind of factual analysis, because they never were from the start. We never really asked ourselves, "Is this working? Are we being effective here?" We just skipped right to the conclusion that we were. We never flipped to the page in the book that said, "Here's how you know." We just said, "We know."

Actually it's tough to know if you're being effective in a counterinsurgency situation, and even the experts will say there's no one way of telling for sure. But there is a list of indicators by which you can estimate, and those indicators are in our own manuals. But I don't think we looked at those, either, because right there at the top of the page, at the top of the list of ways you can tell if your counterinsurgency efforts are being effective or not is "Acts of Violence."

I thought it was interesting to read, two years after I came home, in the Baker-Hamilton, "Iraq Study Group" report, that they'd found "significant underreporting" in Iraq. And the example they chose to illustrate their point was "Acts of violence." They wrote, "On one day in July 2006 there were 93 attacks or significant acts of violence reported. Yet a careful review of the reports for that single day brought to light 1,100 acts of violence. Good policy is difficult to make when information is systematically collected in a way that minimizes its discrepancy with policy goals."

ROTTING TRUTHS

Back when I was growing up and working down at the tire shop, I used to steam clean the meat trucks after they dropped off their loads of quartered cattle. It was just one of the services we offered. We did it all. A couple of guys could work on your tires while a kid cleaned the guts from the back of your truck. That was me. The kid.

Inside the trailer was a frigid gory mess. A hundred blood-spattered meat hooks were scattered over the corrugated floor with large hunks of fat, and stray kidneys, and hearts, and other ruddy organs mixed among them. The smell was thick, even in the cold. It was foul. The sprayer I used got burning hot, which made the stench even more pungent, but still it struggled to get up all the blood. It was sticky. It just wouldn't go away. Neither would the stench. Everything was greasy from the fat. The steel hooks had to be stacked neatly in the back. It was like handling bloody icicles. All in all, though, it wasn't that gruesome a scene. I never saw any slain animals dangling from the hooks, just the blood they left behind. I never witnessed a slaughter, and I was never affected so badly that I wouldn't eat a steak. I kept right on eating. My job was simply to wash away the remnants of this ugly business. That's what writing reports in war was like. It was every bit as grisly, for the blood I washed away.

One summer at the tire shop, we found out that all the blood, organs and fat that I'd sprayed off into the drains was accumulating in the pipes beneath the yard. When there wasn't room for one more drop of blood or one more chunk of flesh, we had to climb down into the sewer and clean it all out with our hands and shovels. The rotting flesh had been piling up for years. I've never experienced a more horrendous smell than that—even in war. We took turns shoveling it out, and the smell clung to our bodies and lived in our pores for weeks. Someday, all the truths of this war that we've shoved down into the sewers of our reports may clog, too. And when the time comes that we have to shovel them all back out again … they're going to stink like hell.

NINE

LOYALTY

HELL IS WAR

So they say war is hell. The metaphor is not new. They've been saying that for as long as there's been both. But then again, war is the elder between them. So maybe, out of respect, we ought to say hell is war. War, I think, should be the privileged metaphor here, because it's real, and it's of this world. War should be the hackneyed word we use to describe all things exhausting and cruel. How was your day? It was *war* man. What about that boss of yours? To *war* with him. The Grateful Dead could sing, *"I may be going to war in a bucket babe, but at least I'm enjoyin' the ride."* And when someone asks me how it's been coming home, I could say, "It's been *war*." And that would capture it just fine, I think. It's been war.

The battle doesn't begin until you're dumped back into civilization. That's where everything turns upside down. That's when it becomes so hellish. So when you see a kid go trailing off to Iraq for the third and fourth time, like he just can't get enough, and you find yourself scratching your head wondering why, you can tell yourself this: Normal is war and war ain't hell. War is the foyer to hell.

THE NINTH CIRCLE OF HELL

Dante's ninth circle of Hell is the circle of traitors, traitors to kindred, to country, and to lords. With Iraq, at the heart of the war, the issue was very much the same. It all came down to loyalty. Who are you going to be loyal to? That was the question. I saw a million angry eyes outside me and inside me and shouting all the while: *Where do you stand? Are you with us or against us? Do you support the troops?* And some of those who were shouting were in favor of the war and some were opposed to it. "Support the troops" became as trite a saying for one side as the other. The troops were reduced to mere commodities in the debate.

In the beginning, I said I'd stick, whether I believed in the cause or not. I said I'd stay loyal to the troops to the end. I said I'd fight to win, if for no other reason than to get more of the troops back home alive. I said that was my cause. It sounded good. But it was an untenable position. *What do you stand for now?* I ask myself. *Where do your loyalties lie?* I am perpetually torn. There is so much about my former comrades that I trust and love, but at the same time there is so much about them that I do not.

When I see a car drive by with a Marine Corps sticker in the window or on the bumper, or a man walk past me with an Eagle, Globe and Anchor embroidered on his shirt or tattooed on his arm, I want to yell out, "Semper Fi, brother. You and I were in the same suck!" (That's what we called it—The Suck.) But then I always stop short when a voice inside me says, *You're not brothers anymore. And you damn sure ain't on the same page of music now. So don't stand there speaking out, speaking ill of his spilled blood, and then tell folks you're supporting the troops. Because you ain't. You broke ranks mother-fucker. You broke the faith.*

I think there is a common impression among outsiders that life in the military is a detached experience and that soldiers are deliberately segregated from their emotions. I disagree. Emotions are an integral part of the soldier's existence and more vital to success in battle than any weaponry or equipment could ever be. The soldiers' bond with each other, and what is often referred to as "the faith" is their strength; it's what keeps them fighting, and on the battlefield it's really all they've got.

But "the faith" is not pure; it is woven into the insensate fabric of the institution, its progenitor. Human and inhuman are blended into one consciousness. "The faith" and the institution live symbiotically. Without one, the other dissolves, and the bond is broken. And without the bond, the war is lost. Small wonder "the faith" is guarded with such vigor. Support for the troops can never be exclusively support for the human beings inside the uniforms; it must be, to some extent, support for the institution inside them as well. Real severance of those two can only be effected by the soldiers themselves. And that can be a lonesome proposition.

In my case, I sensed disparity in the war before it ever got going. Yet I went right along anyway, and there were a lot of reasons for that, but at least one of them was my fellow Marines, my people. I looked around, and even though the war seemed askew, it was my people going off to fight it. So I had two choices. I could either hang back with someone else's people, and live, or I could head over to Iraq with my own people, and die. So I went to Iraq. And when I got there, I did some pretty terrible things. The problem was, I didn't die. A lot of others did, but I didn't. I lived. I came home. And so I was left standing in front of the mirror, staring into my own eyes, and asking myself, *How many times are you willing to go back, to be with your people? How many more terrible things are you willing to do before you die?* Well the answer was clear to me—not one more. So I turned my back on my brothers-in-arms, and I got out. But then there was a new problem. Suddenly, I had no people.

I've met a lot of folks who support war, not because they know one thing about it, but because they would feel guilty if they didn't. They would feel guilty because they never made the sacrifice themselves. Supporting the troops eases their shame for never having been one of them. So they go along to avoid feeling guilty. But I wonder how guilty they would have felt if they had to send Marines down route Jackson every day, knowing that every day there was a good chance some of those Marines would not come back alive, and knowing, too, that route Jackson would never improve for the lives it cost to travel it.

I wonder how guilty they would have felt directing snipers in the night to kill men armed only with shovels? I wonder how guilty they would have felt congratulating a Marine for having inadvertently torn a child to pieces with his machine gun. Would they be able to ignore the torn body of the child? Would they be able to ignore the torn conscience of the Marine? I wonder how guilty they would have felt if they had dipped their hands in all the blood we spilled in Iraq and if they too would not have found themselves looking for a new way to support the troops.

9/11

On September 11, 2007, at 8:43 a.m. I was strolling down the frozen food aisle of a supermarket. The muzak cut off and a woman's voice, dull and even, came over the PA system. She reminded us of the tragedy that had occurred at exactly that moment six years before. She reminded us of the heroes that died that day. Heroes, she called them. By military standards, merely dying is not enough to be decorated for valor. And I've got a military mind. So the word "heroes," as in figures of great courage, didn't quite sit right with me. Actually the whole announcement seemed a bit affected. In some other context, I'm a hero, too. And it sounds just as disingenuous when they say it about me, because I know what I did, and what I didn't do.

On September 11, 2004, I was in Iraq, on the last leg of the deployment, ready to come home. I wasn't gung-ho anymore. I wasn't on board. The presidential candidates were in the final hours of their mud-slinging, and by then, so much mud had been slung, you couldn't tell one of their faces from the other. They looked the same. They sounded the same. And they both avoided the same tough questions about Iraq. Neither of them would ever talk about the gritty facts of war, because they knew, as every Presidential candidate knows, that they could assume the most powerful political office in the world, and be Commander-in-Chief of the most powerful army, without ever speaking about the war in detail.

On September 11, 2001, I was enraged. There was a lot of rage going around that day. I drove down to the Depot and gave my recruits one hell of a speech. I took my rage and I put it right in their guts so they could feel it, too. Their faces shook with it. Their eyes turned red. I've never seen so much genuine desire to fight. They would have shipped out to war that day if we'd asked them to, and they didn't even know how to shoot their rifles yet. Some of them did go right off to war as soon as their training was complete. Then word came back that some of them died, and it really never occurred to me to mind. Mostly I was jealous because I wasn't in the fight, too. I was still on the Depot, doling out rage.

As I stood in the supermarket six years later, the voice on the PA said, "Please join us in a moment of silence, while we remember." Her voice disappeared and then the muzak came back on. *So much for the silence*, I thought. It wasn't even a patriotic tune. I looked around me. Nobody paused. One woman inspected cuts of meat. Another checked her eggs. A man stuffed shelves with loaves of bread. The muzak played on. But I paused. I did what I was told. I remembered 9/11. I remembered all that patriotism and all those waving flags. I remember being pleased with it at first. Then I was dubious. What is all this? I thought. Is this what patriotism looks like? It wasn't the act of flying a flag that I found suspect. It was the lack of doing anything else and going right along with daily life as if nothing had changed.

Back in the supermarket, the muzak stopped abruptly and the voice said, "Thank you." And then the muzak came right back on again. They were going through the motions of patriotism while not giving a whole lot of thought to what it really meant. The consequence of perfunctory or timorous patriotism is, at the very least, a disengaged citizenry. And that strikes me as a dangerous development for a democracy.

OATH OF OFFICE

The very first thing any member of the armed forces does before stepping into uniform is to swear to support and defend the Constitution of the United States. An officer swears that oath again before every promotion. An enlisted service member swears it, too, before every new tour. That's the soldier's supreme authority. And there's something to that. I was always glad to swear loyalty to the ideal of America rather than to a president, or a monarch, or an emperor, because presidents, monarchs and emperors are human beings, and human beings had proven themselves frail in so many instances in my life.

By the time I joined the Marines, I no longer believed in titles. I did not believe in "mother" or "father" or "counselor" or "teacher" or "priest" or "elder" or anyone else with a title, because as a child they had failed me. I spotted a certain ugliness in humanity, and so I went searching for a higher ideal. I became loyal to loyalty itself. I became loyal to the ideals. I went on to believe in honor, and courage, and commitment, and *esprit de corps*. I believed in the Constitution. That's what I put my heart into. That's what I swore to give my life for, because that's what I could trust. There is no human frailty, no greed or desire, no ulterior motives in an ideal.

Since those days I've learned a few things, and one of them is that I don't know much about the Constitution. Kind of strange to swear to defend that which you don't understand. Now I'm not a complete bumpkin. I knew I wasn't signing up to guard an old piece of paper. I knew that much. I knew it was the ideal of America that I was preparing to give my life for. But nobody ever sat me down and said, "Look kid, this is what America is. And so this is what a threat to America looks like. That's what you're going to have to defend against." I didn't know. I didn't care to know. I just wanted to be muddy, and glamorous, and follow orders. I was content with that.

But then I went to Iraq, and all those ideals that saturated my leaders' rhetoric, and saturated my mind, went rotten. We were fighting for freedom. That's what they told us. But I could tell almost immediately that we were not. Either that, or freedom had assumed a new definition. With all the abuses and torture and killing that went on under my county's name and flag, by me, my unit, and every other soldier in my uniform, under the pretense of fighting for freedom, I knew my ideals had slipped away.

So I was cut loose. Abandoned. There was nothing to believe in or be loyal to anymore. Who are the bad guys now? Who are the motherfuckers? I swore an oath to support and defend the ideals of America. Even now I wouldn't stand up in a room and try to articulate exactly what those ideals are or should be, but my working definition has always come up from the gut. My gut told me it was about equality, and decency, and creativity, and cooperation, and freedom—real freedom.

I get angry when I try to describe what I want America to be, because I can't do it without stumbling on all those damned platitudes. They're like landmines. They're everywhere. I'm angry at all the people who turned my ideals into platitudes. I'm angry at the people who turned "fighting for freedom" into a hollow slogan. I'm angry at the people who took those ideals of mine and hung them upside down like a slain animal, and let the blood drain out into the sand. If the Constitution or the ideals of America are our greatest authority, then I think those people who seek to damage them must be our greatest traitors.

THE TROOP TO MISSION RATIO

As a commander, you can't look too closely into your own heart, because you might find things that you don't want to, things that could make those hard decisions of battle impossible. In thinking about war, there's something I call a troop-to-mission ratio. It's not a doctrinal term. I made it up myself to explain the conflict that I experienced as the commander of a rifle company and what every commander must contend with.

To be successful, a commander must believe in both his troops and the mission. He must love them both. He must love his troops, truly, dearly, or they will not follow him. But ultimately, no matter how much he loves them, he must love the mission a little more. He must be prepared to sacrifice his men for the success of the mission. He's got to be willing to spend their lives like cash. Human bodies are the currency of the battlefield commander. How many bodies is that hill going to cost? How many bodies is that beach going to cost? How many bodies is that patrol down Jackson going to cost? He's got to be willing to pay.

But what if the commander looks into his heart and finds that that ratio has somehow reversed itself? What if he begins to love the troops more than the mission? What does he do? What can he do? That was my dilemma. An ambivalence about the war formed inside me and began to grow geometrically until I was utterly consumed by it. Suddenly I looked into the eyes of my Marines, the men I'd served with in Iraq, the men I'd come to truly admire, and I realized my reverence for them had overwhelmed my reverence for the mission. By definition, then, I was ineligible to command. So I resigned my commission. After nearly thirteen years of active service, I left the Marine Corps. For an officer, love of the mission is not merely a good quality, it is an imperative. Love of the troops is secondary.

SAVING LIVES BY SUBTERFUGE

I was once handed a book called, *Patriots: The Vietnam War Remembered From All Sides* by Christian Appy. As I flipped through it, I stumbled upon an account by Lieutenant General Bernard Trainor, USMC retired. His name leapt from the page at me because I'd met him once in 1999, on the day he swore in the graduating officers of my wife's NROTC class at the College of the Holy Cross. General Trainor's account came from his days as a Battalion Commander in Vietnam, and as I read it, I found his story fascinating in the ways it ran parallel to my own story. But I found it contrary to my story as well.

It was 1970. Since his first tour in 1965, he'd become disillusioned. He seemed to have arrived at a place in his conscience where he no longer saw the use of the war or the sense in sending his Marines in to fight it. Once he settled on that conclusion, he began operating in such a manner that minimized the exposure of his Marines to danger. He felt that, as a commander in a failing war, saving the lives of his troops was the only moral or professional thing to do. Of all the stories he must have had, from all those years of service, and all those battles, he chose to share this particular story in a published work. I felt that revealed a definite pride in what he'd done, despite the fact that it was certainly not in keeping with his mission.

In Iraq, I faced a similar situation. I observed the futility of the war and on route Jackson, and it frustrated me deeply. The Jackson Patrol never prevented IEDs; it was their reason for being; the patrol itself perpetuated the danger. Every patrol I dispatched down that road was a gamble of human lives, a gamble with no chance of payoff. We either broke even to bet another day, or we lost. And it wasn't my life being gambled day in and day out; it was the lives of the Marines I deployed. Of course, I wasn't the last word on these missions, and I wasn't the commander signing the orders, or the death warrants, but I played my part. The Jackson Patrol was my baby, mine to run, and that was enough to make me feel responsible. But I knew, just as General Trainor surely would have known, that too much open criticism can be costly. We would both have likely lost our jobs and thrown away our careers on the spot. At that point, neither of us was ready to do that. Yet we saw the lives of our deeply-valued Marines being tossed fruitlessly away and we couldn't bear it. We could have resigned in protest, but neither of us did. We opted for subterfuge instead.

The Jackson Patrol was to be run twice per day, once in the daytime, and once at night. The only times I was permitted to make an exception was when there was some other vital task that needed to get accomplished that day. So, for example, if we had to send a detainee to another base, or if there was a package of some kind, a piece of equipment, a spare part, or a particular weapon system that needed to be picked up or delivered, one of our mounted patrols would have to go. The problem was that we were so short on vehicles and Marines, there just weren't enough to go around. We couldn't do it all. So on the days we had one of these kinds of errands, we would cancel the far more dangerous Jackson Patrol. And that became my tactic.

I'd tell the CO and the staff that we couldn't run the Jackson Patrol because of some other requirement. Nobody would bat an eyelash. We were short-handed. Shit had to get done. It was understood. I never lied, really. I never created a task where none existed. I just managed our assets in the least economical way that I could dream up, so that extra trips were always necessary. There were always opportunities to be more efficient; I made sure those opportunities were missed wherever possible. I tried to never, ever, kill two birds with one stone. Better to kill just one. That way, I could cancel the Jackson Patrol. It wasn't much, but it was all I had to give.

The CO may not have known what I was up to, but the Marines going out on patrol did. They saw the subterfuge, and I know they appreciated it because they said so. But in the end, though these short-lived antics served my purpose to get a few more Marines home alive, I knew they were not enough to justify continuing my career in the Marine Corps. No matter how many patrols I managed to divert, I could never stop them all. I could never save every life. And for every life I did save, I would have had to participate in the killing of another. The only way to save them all would be to stop the war entirely. So I resigned.

Bernard Trainor did not resign. He pressed on with his subterfuge as long as he could get away with it, but he was soon found out. The brass got wise to his half-step tactics. He was ordered to report to the Commanding General, who made it clear to him that if he even uttered the wrong words, he would lose his command, which would effectively end his career. That's when he was taught what I eventually learned, about the troop-to-mission ratio. The General interrogated Trainor about his lack of aggressiveness. The phrase "lack of aggressiveness" doesn't sound like such a big deal out in the civilian world, but in the Marine Corps, it's tantamount to cowardice, and that's a very big deal. To be called that by your own Commanding General is surely the kiss of death if there ever was one.

You cannot survive in the Marine Corps if you don't put the mission ahead of the welfare of your troops. General Trainor tested that theory in war, and he learned fast and hard, it's an absolute. *Don't give the man the wrong answer,* they counseled him. *Don't even utter the wrong words, or you're going to lose your job.* That's all it takes to destroy a military officer's career: *the wrong words.* And yet, for all his undermining of the mission, he did not lose his job. He attributed that to the happenstance discovery of a Viet Cong tunnel system and a great deal of intelligence inside. It was a big find. That's what saved his career. That's what he said. But he didn't just hold on to his job and his rank for a little while longer and then quietly slip off into retirement. He made it all the way to three-star general. That is an incredibly rare accomplishment, not likely achieved on the strength of a single intelligence find, and particularly impressive for an officer who was, at one time, singled out by the Commanding General as an ineffective leader. It seems to me, the only way that could have happened was if the counseling worked.

PERSEVERANCE

WHERE THE CONSCIENCE LIES

Everyone in Iraq witnessed what I witnessed. Everyone knew what I knew. And everyone cared how I cared. I have no doubt about that. We all loved the troops and saw the troubles, so why did I have to break ranks to talk about it? There are probably a lot of reasons for that, including some genuine belief in our cause, but I really do think the most likely was our conditioning to never accept anything short of mission accomplishment. We trained ourselves hard, first to follow orders, and second never to fail, never to quit. We trained ourselves to fight through adversity, to overcome any obstacle, no matter how treacherous, no matter how remote the odds were for success, to press on, always press on.

In his book, *A Marine Tells It To You*, Colonel Frederic Wise writes about his days as a lieutenant in China during the Boxer rebellion and his enthusiastic solution to the "shirkers" who collapsed on the side of the road and could no longer march into battle. "I fixed them," he proclaims. "I took the bolts out of their rifles." He then proudly describes his sergeant's explanation to the other men. "The lieutenant doesn't care what Chinese son-of-a-bitch cuts your throat. But he ain't going to let you make any of those yellow bastards a present of a high powered rifle that works."

I used to like that story quite a lot, and I approved of the tactic. Hell, I admired it. As an officer in the Recruit Training Regiment, I told that very story to every recruit who fell out of a training hike. I said to them very dramatically, "You pull this shit in war and we're going to take your bolt and leave you for dead." Then I taught all the others to step over their bodies like they were rotting carcasses. "Leave 'em," I said. Because the objective always takes precedence over casualties. The other officers on the Depot may not have been citing Colonel Wise, but they were all teaching the same lesson.

It was much the same when I was a rifle platoon commander. One late night, after five days of continuous day-and-night patrols, I took my platoon out on a fifteen-mile hike with full gear. It was a tough movement, no doubt about it. It was tough for me, though I wouldn't admit it at the time. Instead I announced, "We got a truck big enough to carry every last one of you, so you can all quit if you want to. But tonight we're going to find out who's got the heart to finish." In the end, there was only a handful of Marines still standing. We were ragged and red-faced, all of us. Our feet were blistered. Our shoulders were cramped. Everyone was exhausted (everyone, that is, except the kid from Kentucky who never lost the spring in his step and never stopped his infernal impressions of R. Lee Ermey in the film *Full Metal Jacket*). But beaten down as we were, we held our heads high with undeniable pride and looked upon those who'd crawled meekly onto the truck with unmistakable scorn. So that's how we trained ourselves to think and to act: never stop moving forward, never quit. That kind of perseverance can be awe-inspiring under certain circumstances. But it can perpetuate the problems as well.

I think it was understood from the outset that the War in Iraq was suffering from mismanagement. People knew it back home. They were talking about it in the media. They were writing newspaper and magazine articles, even books.

Even in the trenches, among Marines, a quiet grumbling could be heard, but always a quiet grumbling, never out loud. And at first that seemed normal to me, that typical code of silence I'd seen throughout my career, but when the casualties starting pouring in, and when the problems didn't wane, then it didn't seem so normal anymore. It seemed troubling.

Why weren't more people within the military raising their voices? Why was it just the wayward privates and the rogue generals speaking out? Why wasn't every last Soldier and Marine beating the hell out of Washington? Why wasn't I? When so many troops started getting wounded and killed in vain, why weren't they saying, "Hey! Enough is enough!" Why weren't they saying that? But they never did, not with any volume.

The Marine Corps, as an organization, didn't say it, because it didn't think about it. Organizations don't think; they can't, they don't have brains, but the people within them do. The individual Marine, the human being, that's where the conscience lies. The individual Marine thinks about the problems, but you put him in that formation, and you tell him to move out, and the training is going to kick in, and that conditioning to never quit is going to kick in. He's going to be boxed into that formation, and he's going to move out, and he's never going to quit. And if he does, he'll have to break ranks to do it. Then he winds up adrift, cut off, alone. The individual knows this either consciously or unconsciously. He feels it in his gut. So where the training fails to keep a soldier in line, the fear of exclusion will surely assist.

THE PERSEVERANCE OF CLAUSEWITZ

I could hardly claim the title 'Marine Officer' if I never once quoted Carl Von Clausewitz, history's preeminent military thinker and author of the Marine Corps' most holy text: *On War*. The doctrinal publication *Warfighting*, the essence of our combat philosophy, is based almost entirely on the theories of Clausewitz. And this is what he had to say about dealing with the "fog" and "friction" of war.

"If a man were to yield to these pressures, he would never complete an operation. *Perseverance* in the chosen course is the essential counterweight, provided that no compelling reasons intervene to the contrary. Moreover, there is hardly a worthwhile enterprise in war whose execution does not call for infinite effort, trouble, and privation; and as man under pressure tends to give in to physical and intellectual weakness, only great strength of will can lead to the objective. It is steadfastness that will earn the admiration of the world and of posterity."

Clausewitz off-handedly allows for the intervention of "compelling reasons to the contrary" but seems to view that possibility as remote and therefore gives little attention to how, exactly, that intervention might take place. Who, for example, will provide the reasons? Who will judge them compelling? Who will mandate the intervention? Who will stand before the world and at the feet of all the dead and say, "Oh I'm sorry. It seems we've made a mistake!" Who will say that? In light of the very complexities of war that Clausewitz so painstakingly describes, it seems to me that any "compelling reason" provided by any source, no matter reliable, would invariably be taken for "physical and intellectual weakness" and quickly shrugged off by commanders and presidents who might fear their own steadfastness could be contaminated. But if the reasons are in fact compelling, if the mission is indeed faulty, then Clausewitz' equation must be reversed and his mighty perseverance becomes the source of weakness rather than the counterweight.

THE STRUGGLE ITSELF

Gandhi once said, "Joy lies in the fight, in the attempt, in the suffering involved, not in the victory itself." What if this were true for the warriors in Iraq? Then what? And I've heard people say since I was a private myself that men don't fight for causes or flags, they fight for each other. What if that's true? What if the experience of combat is purely about the love of one's brothers? What if it's all about loyalty and nothing more? Maybe that's why the Marine Corps chose *Always Faithful* for their motto.

The whole scenario suddenly changes in this light. The bitter struggle becomes much less bitter. The struggle becomes the very thing that brings us closest to our fellow man and the deep yearning to stay alive, to protect, to suffer, and to endure...together. The struggle becomes nirvana. War is no longer hell. What if all this is true? What if the love of battle has absolutely nothing to do with victory or causes, and has everything to do with the "attempt and the suffering involved"? Then what do we do? All my talk of doctrine, and tactics, and mission statements will not be of much use then, and our perseverance will transform from the means to an end, to the end itself.

I learned a little something about my own perseverance as a Second Lieutenant at the Infantry Officer Course, better known in Corps as IOC. I don't want to belabor the challenges of this period of instruction, but in the interest of setting the scene, I will say that IOC was a tough course. I did it in the winter of '98. We saw a lot of snow and freezing rain that year. We were not allowed coats, or sweaters, or sleeping bags. We ate only one meal a day. And we moved all the time, in light and in darkness, miles and miles, through the gullies and dense woods of Quantico, Virginia.

When we could walk no further, we'd bundle our bodies together on the snow-covered ground for a few minutes sleep until the shivering became too much to bear; then we'd get up and start moving again. That's what we did in IOC. We moved. And there were always deadlines to make. If ever the squad failed to meet a deadline due to the sluggishness of one Marine, the entire squad would be called back on one of those scarce and very precious days off to do it all over again. So staying with the crowd had a particular significance.

My problem was that I had a bad case of bursitis in the knees. The pain was constant and excruciating. In IOC, you could quit for the pain if you wanted to. You were allowed. And you could go find some other job. Or, you could press on, if you wanted to lead Marines. Seldom did one find a lieutenant in that course that did not want to lead Marines, badly, as badly as he ever wanted anything in his life. The longing went to his gut. It went to mine. So I pressed on.

An eight-mile run with all our gear came on a day when my knees were being particularly cantankerous. We ran the event with our squads. If one man failed, the whole squad failed. This was just the kind of training that built a relentless sense of camaraderie in Marines. I wasn't going to be the guy who failed, no matter what. But my knees thought differently on the matter.

To shut them up, I popped 2,400 milligrams of ibuprofen, on top of the few thousand I'd already ingested throughout the day. I'd say by any standard, that's a lot. But I was used to them by then. I was popping them like candy corn all the time. I didn't think you could overdose. Turns out, you can. I did. My mouth went dry. My head spun in circles. My legs wobbled and shook. And all the while the clock was ticking. I never stopped running, though. I staggered along and sucked my canteens dry. Then I stopped sweating. Heat exhaustion was setting in; I could feel it, or maybe worse: heat stroke. I just prayed it wouldn't take me down before I crossed that finish line.

My friend Brian helped me out along the way. He shuffled along by my side and talked to me. He shared his own water. He kept me focused. He was a hard runner, but he hung back with me all the same. He wasn't even in my squad. Finally, when time was running low, Brian had to take off. I was left to make that last leg on my own. And I did make it. I made it all the way. I crossed the finish line with just a few minutes to spare. I'm not sure that I can recall a moment in my military experience when I was prouder. The world was woozy and slow in my head. I nearly blacked out, but I forced down enough water and sugar to stave it off. With quivering hands, I shoved a half dozen candy bars down my throat and poured water over my head to cool my skin. Then I lay down and waited for the spots and the spins to pass. When I finally recovered, and pulled myself clumsily and breathlessly to my feet, the other guys broke the bad news to me.

The squad failed. We were going to have to come back in and do it again on a Saturday. We all turned our heads and stared with deep contempt—*deep contempt*—at the last man trudging in. He was walking. He wasn't carrying his weapon. He wasn't carrying his gear. He wasn't even wearing his blouse. He quit. And we would all pay dearly for it. But I didn't give a damn. All I could think of at that moment was how happy I was that it wasn't I who'd quit and let down the squad.

Think of it! I didn't care about the mission, not one bit. I didn't care that we had failed. I didn't care that we'd have to go through the pain all over again. And I didn't care about my knees or my body swimming in ibuprofen, either. I didn't even care if I died. All I cared about was my squad. I was learning at that very moment, learning, as we were all learning, the greatest lesson of war: our brothers on the battlefield are everything, and all else, including our own lives, is nothing.

PERSEVERANCE TO A MAN

This is a story of real perseverance. Part of the curriculum at the Marine Corps Recruit Depot was swim training. Because it was an inherently dangerous environment, the staff made a concerted effort to closely monitor the recruits in the water, particularly those who were swimming for the first time. This training was not the typical high-stress, boot camp environment. The instructors, I must say, were exceptional at working with new swimmers.

One morning I watched as a young recruit struggled to master the backstroke. He was the last one in the pool that day. The rest of the recruits had finished their training and left. The recruit's head was resting in the hands of his instructor, who walked patiently backwards in the water behind him as he progressed, keeping his face from submerging and offering him words of encouragement. The recruit had been having a hard time all week, but he'd shown some amazing heart that morning. We were impressed. He never asked to quit, no matter how exhausted he got. And we could tell he was surely exhausted. But he never stopped trying.

When he finished his lap, he jumped out of the water, like he was told, and sat at the edge of the pool catching his breath while the instructor critiqued him briefly and told him about the things they'd work on in the days to come. The recruit nodded several times and said finally, "Yes sir." Those were the last coherent words that ever came out of his mouth. He collapsed onto the floor and stopped breathing. He'd been drowning in front of our eyes and we didn't even know it.

His lungs were filled with water, filled with water yet he pressed on without stopping, without a single complaint. I watched as the medics tried to resuscitate him at the poolside for seventeen minutes to no avail. I followed him into the Emergency Room, then later to the Intensive Care Unit. He was intubated for three days. His parents waited beside me, wretched with grief and anger. When their son finally woke up and the tube came out of this throat, we discovered he had brain damage—permanently. His speech was reduced to a stream of incomprehensible slurs.

He rested his life in the hands of the Marine Corps, literally. We let him down and we didn't even realize we were doing it. We followed our procedures to the letter. The recruit's perseverance combined with our unawareness of a flawed program led him to his fate. And that is very much how I came to view the war in Iraq. I think we were blinded by our perseverance, unable to see beyond the trenches in which we fought. We didn't associate the increasing instability and the corresponding increase in casualties with our actions on the ground. We didn't want to. I didn't.

To the fully committed and the faithful, to the believers in country and Corps, whether officer or enlisted, failure to accomplish the mission, whatever it may be, is always the result of a particular commander, a particular operation a particular decision within the framework of the mission, an instance of improper planning or inadequate support. But the mission can never be faulty. There is no procedure in the military to deal with that, no protocol, and there is no room in the military mind for it, either. As long as the orders stand and they come across as noble pursuits (like fighting for freedom), the military will persevere, and the damage being done all the while won't be recognized until it is too late. Of course there is some difference between the physical, intellectual, and moral struggles we, as individuals, face, but I believe that ultimately they all converge into one battle that wages within our essential selves.

T.E. Lawrence (of Arabia) was fighting for freedom in his day, too, and on the same turf. The notoriety of his work has been refreshed among the officers of today, it being so relevant to our own struggles in Iraq. He observed famously, "War upon rebellion [is] messy and slow, like eating soup with a knife." But Lawrence was not wholly enthusiastic about this fight for freedom:

"We were a self-centered army without parade or gesture, devoted to freedom, the second of man's creeds, a purpose so ravenous that it devoured all our strength, a hope so transcendent that our earlier ambitions faded in its glare. As time went by our need to fight for the ideal increased to an unquestioning possession, riding with spur and rein over our doubts. Willy-nilly it became a faith. We had sold ourselves into its slavery, manacled ourselves together in its chain-gang, bowed ourselves to serve its holiness with all our good and ill content. The mentality of ordinary human slaves is terrible—they have lost the world—and we had surrendered, not body alone, but soul to the overmastering greed of victory. By our own act we were drained of morality, of volition, of responsibility, like dead leaves in the wind."

GOING TO GROUND

There's a phrase we used back in the Marine Corps, "Going to ground," and it had a variety of uses. Most literally, it meant to bed down for a period, "bed" being generally the ground we walked on. But it had a humorous use too—cynical but humorous. If a man were to basically fail to function under pressure and, either literally or figuratively, were to curl up into himself and cease thinking or acting, we would say he'd "gone to ground." When a man was just plain sick of the shit, he'd say comically, as though he were throwing in the towel, "I'm going to ground" or "Let's just go to ground." Or more seriously, when he reached a point where courage was no longer available to him, where behaving according to his conscience was no longer possible, he'd go to ground. Courage was moving forward, staying in the fight. Going to ground was sitting still. And that was cowardly.

Toward the end of the deployment, after I'd seen a good deal of the callous regard for life eat up the men around me, I began to know what the courageous thing to do was. But I didn't do it. I did my job instead. I kept my mouth shut. I finished my shift, sat by myself and smoked cigarettes. I thought the thoughts that were true to me, but then I got back up and went to work, thinking the thoughts of a Captain. When I was done, I'd slip away again to my rack and close my eyes and try to avoid that most troubling notion of all: I'd gone to ground.

VISION

The moment a soldier finds himself critical of the military's mission, he instantly redefines himself in a way that utterly alienates him from the organization. He may keep his dissention under wraps for a while, and maybe nobody will notice right off, but he will be discovered eventually. That is a certainty. His new opinions will ultimately translate into his actions, his tone of voice, his shifting eyes, and even into his body language. He'll be found out. And then slowly, he'll be edged out.

I never spoke out while I was in uniform, not publicly anyway. I made my opinions known among friends, but never to the boss. If I had, I probably would have been fired on the spot. But I didn't have to say anything at all. I think my skepticism was apparent. He may not have known the particulars of my politics, but he almost certainly saw it in my eyes. Now you can't fire an officer for having the wrong look in his eyes, but you can be suspicious of him, and you can dislike him. And you can write mediocre reports about him. And you can hinder his future promotions and assignments. And you can deny him awards and decorations. You can always find reasons to mark a man down. You can always justify edging him out.

The truth is that the Marine Corps didn't ruin the career of a bright young officer when they edged me out—I wasn't that good. I wasn't that fast, or strong, or tactically savvy. The best that I brought to the Corps was that I cared deeply for my Marines, and that is good, but ultimately it is not good enough. So they didn't run me out on a rail. But it may have come to that. I felt the possibility in my bones. I was never a tight fit in the officer corps, and for the longest time I could not figure out why. I had the deep-seated military values of any other officer. I was as patriotic as the next man. But there's an indistinct club, a vague inner-circle; it exists, you just can't see it. Why does one man get in and another not? I really don't know. I guess that's why I couldn't get in. I do know it goes beyond the obvious criteria like race and gender because, after all, I'm a white male. Of course personality and skill are factors, but I also believe one's "vision"—how we see the world—plays a role, and my vision was not theirs.

WHEN IN ROME

It was just a matter of time before I had to leave the Marine Corps or before they asked me to go. Being a soldier, particularly an officer, is not merely wearing the uniform; it is in one's state of mind. An officer must always be prepared to "want" war. It's okay for a General to say he doesn't want war, right up until the President says we're going. Then he'd better want war, or he'll be eliminated or passed over. Once an officer finds himself in conflict with his orders, he ceases to function as intended, and so he must go.

There is no such thing as a dissenting commander. Every General who has criticized the war has done so from retirement. Every officer—including me—who has spoken out publicly, has either done so once they got out, or they were alienated, fired, or sent to jail for disobedience. You don't get to command troops and dissent at the same time. It just doesn't work.

There is not quite the same extreme demand for ideological compliance on the part of our junior enlisted troops, nor are there as many incentives. A rifleman need not fully believe. He need only obey. But for an officer, obedience is not enough. He must believe. There is no exception to this rule. When in Rome you do as the Romans, and it's not because you're being polite. It's because you're in Rome. And that's where they've got you, because you don't have a choice.

CONSTRUCTION AND DESTRUCTION OF MYTH

Why do soldiers, such as myself, go to ground at all? Why, once they become aware of the problems and the disparities of war, are they so reluctant to make them known? Why don't they just kick in the boss' door and say, "Take this job and shove it!" Why don't people do that? Why didn't I? I've mentioned a few possibilities already. There was the financial security and the feeling of belonging that I would forfeit; there was the power, the sense of self-importance, and the esteem of my countrymen. There was the fear of reprisal, legal or professional, that hung over my head. All those things were real enough factors, certainly, but I think there is one more that might just have outweighed them all.

The Marine Corps is chock-filled with idealism, but some latch onto the myths more vigorously than others. I was among those. In the sixteen years before Iraq that I spent either in the military or NROTC, I was, in essence, pretending to be at war. I was playing the role. That's what we do in peace-time: we simulate the real thing, so when it finally comes around, we'll be ready. We call it training. But it is still make-believe. We tried, I think, to make our training environment realistic, and in many respects it was, and it grew steadily more so as technology improved.

However, there was always one piece missing. The human piece. Since the enemy was always a fabrication, we could simply ignore the fact that, in a real war, they would be real people, with real emotions and real blood that spilled. Since the killing was always faked, we could skip past the part where we sometimes kill people who perhaps ought not to be killed. Since the seizing of objectives was always temporary, in temporarily reserved training areas, we could omit from our thoughts the unattractive demands of a more permanent occupation. And we did.

For an idealist, this is a hazardous practice. People like me clutch so desperately to the nobility of their existence that in training we fill in those blanks with the most fantastic details, and in doing so construct a myth of unwieldy proportion. The emotional bond we develop with these artificial frameworks is extreme—truly extreme—to the extent that in war the disparity between that which we've come to expect of war (that which we've contrived), and that which crashes down upon us in war can be devastating.

Our ideals are far more fragile and more easily undercut than perhaps we ever imagined and so really demand more robust mental ramparts to defend their existence. We can become so deeply entrenched in the myth that destruction of it is hardly an option. Destruction of the myth is destruction of ourselves. And that, I think, has a great deal to do with why so many soldiers, having grown unsettled about the war, chose to say or do little about it.

SCHIZOPHRENIA

The effort to reconcile the virtues of war with the virtues of humanity produces a state of mind that I would liken to schizophrenia. I want to call war a bad thing; I want to end all the violence, and the killing, and the horrors that it engenders, and yet at the same time I am keenly aware that my lifestyle, in many ways, depends on, and has been made possible by war. My survival is pit squarely against my sense of morality. I cannot serve either one in good faith, and so I am forced to serve both half-heartedly, sporadically leaping from one set of values to the other and utterly blocking out their obvious incongruity. This is the divided conscience that begets all the voices whispering in my ears and multiple personalities skulking around in the back of my mind.

Repudiation of their inconsistencies is so tenuous that the most practical defense is sheer avoidance. But then recognizing the conflict does not make the conflict go away, either. I think it just makes it more painful to bear. Acknowledgment of those inconsistencies and the contrary voices that go with them is the very thing that wrenches our guts. And conversely, to fear them, to dodge them, to sweep them under the rug, is to live in denial. Really, neither option sounds attractive to me. So I remain equivocal—schizophrenic.

I'd say it's kind of like the situation with our chicken. Today's industrial chicken farmer must never reach a point where he believes that the maltreatment inherent in the mass production of chicken meat is immoral or inhumane. The moment he does, he will absolutely be overwhelmed by the competition—the competition who does not. The competition, for example, feels no compunction using growth hormones that plump the birds' bodies faster than their legs can develop, leaving millions of them crippled and unable to walk to water, and so lie down in their own shit and die of thirst. That can't bother the chicken farmer. He has to laugh or shrug it off, or he too will soon be lying in his own shit.

And all the people who eat that chicken (including me) have to laugh or shrug it off as well, or just plain ignore it. We have to rationalize it. We have to justify it. It is for our nourishment, we say. It is for our protein. It is for our survival. That's what we say. That's what we have to say, to let the tragedy go on and on—and it will go on until enough people become willing to sacrifice the benefits of this process and say, "Stop!" Meanwhile, we eat on with schizophrenia. And so war is much the same way. The process of aggression is our provider. It is our sustenance. We are all beneficiaries of war to some degree. To give up war would be to give up those benefits, and that would be a much greater sacrifice than a juicy breast of chicken.

I once heard a lecture given by a retired Army officer, an expert in international affairs, a man to whom people listened . He struck me right off as frightfully schizophrenic and hopelessly entangled in conflicting views of the war. He said from the start: The war should end. And I think he believed it in his heart. Yet it was not so clear whether or not he believed the war should have ever begun, or if he felt we should be prepared to give up what the war was providing us. Those points were not plainly stated. Perhaps they were not yet plainly contemplated.

He declared the war unwinnable. He asserted that the events in Iraq were no longer being determined by the United States. He said countless lives were being lost for no good reason, including his own son's. He said we needed to get the troops home. He criticized America's behavior toward the Middle East as "imperialistic," yet his prescriptions for future policy included "containing Islam," and holding military forces "over the horizon," and influencing or "nudging" Middle East activities in a manner that benefited American interests and kept the oil flowing our way. He spoke of "us and them." He made the thing sound like a holy war. But then he went on to say that he believed our country to be rife with corruption and that American citizens had all but lost their ability to influence policy.

"What can we do?" a man in the audience asked the retired officer.

He answered, "I may be cynical, but I don't think there's anything we can do."

Why such conflict? I thought. Why did he seem so bound to stumble down these rhetorical dead-ends throughout his talk, where he could only stop, scratch his head, and say, "I don't know why that is," or "I don't know why they think that way." And then he'd turn around and move on as if the answers were innately unobtainable and not at all germane to his conclusions. He just couldn't go the distance. He couldn't, or wouldn't, press on for the answers because I think the answers would have been irreconcilable with his identity and his means, surely difficult things to deny for anyone.

There was another retired officer who was not afraid of the answers. It seems there was little in life that he ever was afraid of. He is long dead now, but in his own day he understood clearly the disparity between the nature of his former profession—war—and the justifications for waging it. He was making his way clear of the schizophrenia. His name was Major General Smedley Butler.

In the Marine Corps, there are few names so deeply revered as his. He is one of only two Marines to have ever won two Medals of Honor. That is an impressive feat, and for that his name is recited ad nauseam throughout the barracks of recruit training. Every Marine, of every rank and age, on every base, in every clime and place, knows his name. Smedley Butler spent a lifetime in battle. He was reputed to have deeply loved his Marines. He knew more intimately of war and spent more years in it than any officer in the Armed Forces of my day. He died in 1940. At the time, he was the most decorated Marine in United States history. And when he was done fighting, this is what he had to say:

"War is a racket! It always has been. It is possibly the oldest, easily the most profitable, surely the most vicious. It is the only one international in scope. It is the only one in which the profits are reckoned in dollars and the losses in lives. I spent 33 years in the Marines, most of my time being a high-class muscle man for big business, for Wall Street and the bankers. In short, I was racketeer for Capitalism. I helped make Mexico and especially Tampico safe for American oil interests in 1914. I helped make Haiti and Cuba a decent place for the National City Bank boys to collect revenues in. I helped in the raping of half a dozen Central American republics for the benefit of Wall Street. I helped purify Nicaragua for the International Banking House of Brown Brothers in 1902-1912. I brought light to the Dominican Republic for the American sugar interests in 1916. I helped make Honduras right for the American fruit companies in 1903. In China in 1927 I helped see to it that Standard Oil went on its way unmolested. Looking back on it, I might have given Al Capone a few hints."

Though Smedley Butler's military achievements were significant, his name has been almost completely forgotten outside of the Marine Corps. Few civilians have ever heard of him. Inside the Marine Corps, few know what he did after he won his Medals of Honor. His name was successfully besmirched by the very same Wall Street group he abhorred after he refused to help them overthrow the U.S. government in 1935 and reported their plot to Congress. Smedley Butler demonstrated that you can never serve enough years, you can never win enough medals, and you can never shed enough blood on your nation's behalf to be permitted to find the truth and to speak it without your nation turning coldly away.

FIGHTING FOR OIL

I have devoted this book mainly to a discussion of war in the consciousness; however, with all this talk of incentives and beneficiaries, I would feel remiss if I didn't mention oil. As most people have come to understand by now, America's economy, our military, and our strength as an industrial power are utterly dependent on oil and will continue to be until alternative energy sources are more ambitiously employed. It seems to me that this unavoidable reality has created a sort of cognitive dissonance in the American consciousness with respect to the future of Iraq. Though the notion of fighting for oil may be broadly opposed, the lifestyle that it affords is broadly demanded. I think that makes all Americans the legatees of war.

The link between war and oil is no longer startling news. In his book *Blood and Oil*, Michael Klare explains with copious detail and documentary evidence what has been mentioned offhandedly, clamored about wildly and felt in the gut by millions since the Gulf War: We are fighting for oil. We are fighting to control it, to get it, to have rights to the last of it, to see it flow unhindered into our economy and away from the economies of our "enemies." He tells us what the oil industry and what the U.S. Department of Energy already understand themselves: It's running out. The production of oil is close to, or maybe even beyond, "peak." The sources of oil are finite. The demand for oil is infinite and ever-increasing. The competition to get it is very literally tantamount to the struggle for survival. We are fighting for oil.

In 1980, President Jimmy Carter publicly deemed the flow of oil to America vital to national security, and declared that we would defend it "by any means necessary, including military force." President George H.W. Bush echoed those sentiments before the Gulf War. And ever since, the U.S. has been aggressively deploying its military to secure the oil fields around the world. This is no conspiracy. This is official policy. As Michael Klare points out, U.S. Central Command (CENTCOM) was established explicitly to protect our oil interests in the Persian Gulf region. Its founding documents make that clear. We are fighting for oil. There is no sense refuting that fact anymore. I don't think many people still are. It has become an indefensible position.

During a discussion at Stanford University in October 2007, retired General John Abizaid conceded, "Of course [the war in Iraq] is about oil, we can't really deny that." He was the Commander of U.S. Central Command for the first three and a half years of the Iraq war. Given his proximity to the matter, I think his perspective is worth weighing. But personally, when I hear him say those words—*Of course it's about oil*—I can't help but get frustrated and wonder: Exactly how long did he know that? Did the White House confide that to him directly when he was CENTCOM? Or did they just wink at him? Or did he have to figure it out for himself?

I wonder, because from the war's inception the Bush administration insisted vehemently to the American people (and to the military) that it was absolutely not about oil. And when General Abizaid so unabashedly declares *of course it's about oil*, as though only a fool could think otherwise, I can't help but further wonder if he ever shared this point of view with his subordinates back when he was commanding troops and issuing orders, back when I was out there in Iraq fighting under him for freedom and democracy. Did he think it was so obviously about oil then? Because if he did, the word didn't make it down to my level. I never got the *of course it's about* oil speech.

Where did the denial or the deception begin? I know my own commander was an educated man, very well-read, indeed. It's difficult for me to imagine that he would be surprised to learn that U.S. foreign policy included the security of oil reserves. But never once in his very long speeches to the troops and officers did he mention it. Furthermore, never once was the word "oil" included in any mission statement I ever read, wrote, or heard about. The mission was always along the same lines: *Reduce insurgent activity*, or *Ensure security of the Main Supply Route*, or *Deny sanctuary to the enemy…in order to provide a stable environment for economic development, public safety, and local governance*. It sounded great on paper, but I never saw any mention of oil.

It is precisely this divided aim that I believe is at the heart of all the ambiguity and disorder in our operations in Iraq, the disparity that I sensed on the battlefield and the disparity I find myself discussing so incessantly now. And, at the same time, it is this divided aim that has left me most confounded. Because I think that, at this stage in our history, oil is a logical concern for America and therefore worth at least considering a military option to secure. And that, to me, makes the deception unfathomable.

Why all the talk of freedom and democracy? Why all the turgid speeches about liberation? Why the great dupe? Why not lay the cards on the table and let people weigh in as they are inclined? I cannot escape the impression that the ignobility of shedding blood for oil would not sit well with the vast majority of Americans. I cannot help but suspect that the greatest beneficiaries of free-flowing oil are not actually the people fighting for it, and that a closer look at this situation and all the more sensible alternatives available might likely dissuade them from pressing on any further. I cannot avoid the conclusion that that's why the great dupe; that's why all the fiery rhetoric about terrorists, and radicals, and extremists.

But the prevarications merely produce hazy mission statements, and discombobulated operations, and needless deaths. The true agenda may be concealed from view for a while, but the concealment can really only lead to a conflicted consciousness in our soldiers and our commanders. That is where the truth will ultimately reveal itself. It will reveal itself in the disarray and the desperation that sweeps across the battlefield, because wanton killing only begets more wanton killing, and that is the only kind of killing which remains when the mission is false.

AFTERMATH

PACKING THE LOAD

Since coming home, I've met more than a few vets hit hard with combat stress. They've all dealt with it in their own ways. But I've noticed that they did not all become opposed to war. In fact, some became even more adamant supporters of it. I thought that was a curious reaction. How could one feel so emotionally harried by war, while at the same time be so ideologically in favor of it? It made no sense to me. However, what I have learned most of all about war is that "sense" is not an attribute that often applies, not on the battlefield and not in the mind. So I can appreciate their struggle. Still, I often wonder about the competing forces in this inner fray.

At least one of them is the mental load a veteran carries in the aftermath. In war, a soldier will witness and partake in a great deal of brutality, and the images and actions will no doubt wreak havoc upon his soul, but as long as the carnage is deemed "just," then whatever deed was done, however gruesome, the weight of it can be placed squarely on the shoulders of the government or the people collectively. The burden will remain off the backs of the individuals as long as they believe in the cause. And that is a great burden to unload. If, however, upon return to his native land, the soldier looks upon his war as *unjust*, if he declares to himself that the whole enterprise is immoral, if he casts off the government and the cause, or if he casts himself off of them, then he will quickly find that burden has been placed back on his own shoulders to bear in full. Every horror that he committed, and saw, and connived at in war will be stuffed down into his own pack, and he will forever after carry it alone.

To say I was duped is not sufficient to lighten the load. To cite the lies and the deceptions and the propaganda and the manipulation—true as it all might be—only makes the pack more ponderous. Because what I know now, I could have known then. All that I have extrapolated now, I could have extrapolated before I shipped out to war. But I didn't. I was raving about Smedley Butler one night to a friend of mine, about how adamantly opposed to war he had become after all that he'd seen in his thirty years of battle, and she said perplexed, "Thirty years? What the hell took him so long?" I can't speak for Smedley Butler, but I know it took me a while, too. For some, the folly of war occurs to them innately, and for those people I have recently discovered in myself a great deal of respect. For others like me, it takes time to sink in. But when it finally did, I said to myself precisely what my friend had said to me. What the hell took you so long?

It is fruitless to blame sophistry for the violence I have participated in. It would amount to little more than denial, denial of a fact that is perfectly plain to me now. I should have known better. Instead, I chose to ignore the facts and to ride blithely through the fantasy without critique. Now, I must pack the load alone. For many veterans, I imagine that's a tough thing to conceive, and so often they never do. They let their conscience and their guilt do quiet battle for years, and while they may not hear the shouting, they can feel the turmoil in their guts. The only way, so far as I can tell, to stop the incessant quarrel is to own the responsibility. If I own it, I can disown it. That is the only way to truly unload my pack.

THE MARLBORO MAN

Iraq tastes like a cigarette to me, and cigarettes taste like Iraq. Before 2004, I never really smoked, nor did I go to war. These were both new experiences for me, and I took them up simultaneously, so each of them reminds me of the other. In many ways they are the same. Both damn fool habits. You drag in hard that baleful essence and let it swim into your body. You gag in the beginning. You jerk back reflexively. Your face turns green. But you fight through that shit—not because you enjoy it, but because everyone else seems to. And after a while it starts to feel normal, to feel good, to feel like something maybe you can't live without. It goes in though your arteries, through your capillaries, and down into the deepest parts of yourself, until you're addicted. And when you breathe it out, you find it doesn't all go away. It never goes away. There's always a little bit lingering behind to inflict its damage.

In Iraq, when I wasn't working, I used to sit in my cell with a cigarette and wrap myself up in music and heavy thoughts. I'd take long drags and transform any doleful lyrics into the ballads of war. Everybody was singing about war as far as I was concerned. I went through a lot of packs of Marlboros down there. Now I smoke whenever I want to get back to the desert. I smoke and I entangle myself in those same songs, those songs that for me now sound as much like the battlefield as the pounding of bombs and the staccato of gunfire.

I've heard them say a man has got to have a vice, to remind him he's human. Smoking was mine, and war was too, I guess. I was surely reminded, and how human I felt with every pull. I tried to drink on occasion, because I've always been a drinking man (I smuggled vodka in a contact lens bottle), but I'll be damned if it wasn't too hot for booze, and I was always too damned tired. So the drink came home untouched, but the smokes, they were smoked, and the battles, they were fought, and the damage, it was done. While there are many moments throughout my days that I avoid those things that trigger the memories of war in me, there are many more when I smoke just to capture it, just to see the war again, just to smell it, just to feel it in my spinning head. I can love the burn drifting through my nostrils and down into my lungs. I can savor the stench. I have that capacity. I'm sort of like the Marlboro Man, the guy who talked the talk, who rode the horse, who looked the look, and walked the walk, until finally his bad habit got the better of him.

COMING HOME

Before my experience in Iraq, I always thought there was a distance between the veterans of older wars and me that I could never close, and that we would never be connected. But I was wrong. When I came home, the gap between us had all but disappeared. I listened one day to two Vietnam veterans present their experiences to a tenth grade American history class and try to convey to a room full of fifteen-year-old kids what it meant to have a friend, at one moment just an arm's reach away, then the next moment gone—blown away. I listened to them talk about the fear when the shooting started, about the indescribable concussion of the impacting explosives, about the helplessness, about the guilt, about the anger, and I knew at that moment that I was not alone after all, that we were truly connected.

I realized there are others like me, dealing with the long nights and rage and the regret. And once we find each other, we can see each other's faces. We can touch each other's skin. We can hear each other's voices and the words make sense. When we share our stories, we can feel each other's pain, but we can lose some of it, too, in the transfer. We can save each other's lives. It is the bond we knew in war, and lost. The aftermath is our common ground. Geography is for the politicians. Experience is for the veterans. There is no Vietnam War. There is no Iraq War. There is no Great War. For veterans, there is only war. One war. One front. And we all fight together for our lives.

POWERLESSNESS

I attended a conference on combat stress at which experts in the field, including those from Walter-Reed and Brooke Army Medical Centers and the Department of Veterans Affairs, were invited to speak. Being close to the subject, I was anxious to listen in as mental health professionals from all over the country, military and civilian, gathered to discuss this growing public-health crisis.

Throughout the conference and in all those attending, I sensed a genuine interest in caring for returning veterans. The term "PTSD," for example, was universally and emphatically rejected for its implication that combat stress is a disorder rather than an injury. Real compassion resounded in every voice. Resources were shared. Suggestions were made about how to improve services and care. Touching accounts were given. Everyone seemed satisfied that the conference was moving along well.

But on the final day of the event, the placidity was momentarily disturbed. A woman in the audience suggested the possibility that the war in Iraq was not just. A ripple of discomfort swept over the room. There were a large number of veterans and service-members present, some of them in uniform. One of them stood up immediately afterward and said, "As a fighter, I think comments like that diminish our accomplishments on the battlefield and make it more difficult for veterans to feel welcome when they come home."

There was instant applause. Then the moderator added that, in her work with veterans, she tried to simply honor their service without judgment and deal strictly with their pain. There was more enthusiastic applause, and then the discussion was closed. What this short exchange highlighted for me was that the issues of morality and ethics were, throughout the conference, largely ignored.

In my view, there are two general categories for the causes of combat stress. The first encompasses all those traumatic events that render the individual powerless. Being shot at, for instance, or bombed, or burned; feeling shrapnel hit one's flesh or sail close by; having friends killed or seriously wounded before one's eyes. These are the types of scenarios that make a soldier feel powerless and cause traumatic psychological injuries. And these were the experiences that were discussed almost exclusively at the conference.

But combat stress is not all about powerlessness. There is a second category of causes, far less fashionable to mention than the first. And this is the hard part. Occasionally our soldiers in war are forced to make others feel powerless through their own use of violence. It seems almost too obvious to utter, and yet it was barely mentioned in three full days of lectures by the country's top experts on the subject. What happens when our own soldiers are doing the shooting, the burning, and the bombing? What happens when our boys kill? No matter how well we desensitize them, no matter how just the cause, the violence they inflict in battle will seep into their souls and cause pain. Even in self-defense, killing hurts the killer, too.

The trouble with this category of combat stress is that it invariably pulls us toward that ever so uncomfortable and divisive question: Is this war just? The polarizing effect of it is so intense that it imposed instant silence on an auditorium filled with mental-health professionals, all deeply concerned for veterans' welfare. And it is that silence that can be so ruthless, because while counselors strive diligently to never ask about the morality of war, there will be a great many veterans who cannot stop asking. For them, the pain they feel is inextricably bound to that ugly question: Is this war just? To suppress the question is to suppress their pain. From a treatment perspective, that is the very worst thing we could do.

So if counselors of veterans dealing with combat stress are unprepared to contend with the morality and ethics of war, if they are unable to face the possibility that our troops are capable of regrettable violence, too, or if they are unwilling to discuss among peers techniques for dealing with it, then they will quickly discover that they've missed the boat on a significant portion of the pain that wells within America's veterans. No matter how divisive the questions of war, counselors must be prepared to hear them. And no matter how compassionately they may work with the feelings of powerlessness, they must also be ready to work with the feelings of guilt.

COMBAT STRESS

I went to a meeting once about "coming home" and the people asked me, "How do you cope?" I said, "I write. And I do this. I talk. I bore the shit out of people for as long as they'll tolerate it, because I won't shut up." That's not every vet's way, but it's my way. I told them a few stories and they said, "Thank you," and I said, "I'm not here for you. I'm here for me. This is my therapy. So thank you." Because my ability to cope depends, not only on assembling my narrative, but on finding people to listen to it, a whole community of people. If a man comes home to a world of deaf ears, he can feel alone in the most crowded of rooms.

So these people, these decent folks, churchgoers, community members and veterans of older wars, asked me with genuine sympathy, "How can we help?" And right there, they put their fingers on the troubling question. It's troubling because we're swimming in the answer everyday. We're living in the answer. We're breathing it. All the evidence sits in the open, on the side of the road, like the carcass of a dog stuffed with an IED. It's ugly. It stinks. And it's waiting to explode. But we drive on by and pretend not to notice. I looked into the eyes of this small handful of people, and I knew in my heart they wanted to help. They really did. But as we talked and talked about the struggle of the returning combat veteran, never once did any one of them approach the real answer. Not even the veterans themselves.

"Don't push too hard," they said. "Give the veterans time. Give them space," they said. "Show them availability. Show them support. Show them you care. Show them respect. Stand in silence before them." All of it, and I'd heard it all before. But meanwhile, the question remained unanswered. How can we help? And I said to them, "Don't you wonder why we can't drum up more than a handful of people to even ask that question? Don't you wonder, with all the damage that wars do to our soldiers' bodies and minds, with all the suicides pouring in, why the Department of Veterans Affairs can't seem to establish any meaningful rapport with veterans, why they are so abysmally underfunded, why their priorities so often appear at odds with veterans' needs, and why they seem so inclined to conceal their problems rather than vigorously publicize and correct them? Doesn't that strike you as a clue?"

Combat Stress is a subject close to my heart. I'm emotionally invested, and so I tend to get rankled in discussions about recovery. I get rankled by all the apparent confusion. "What do you think all this rage is about?" I ask. "Where do you think the stress comes from? It doesn't come from the blistering hot days on the parade deck, or the long deployments away from home, or the tough training, or from shining too many boots, or eating too many MREs. It comes from trauma. It comes from witnessing, and participating in, extreme violence." And these well-intentioned folks nod their heads knowingly, like they've heard it all before, and they think they know what it's all about, but then they just can't seem to answer that question of theirs. How can we help? They can't find the answer for the same reasons a commander must love his mission more than his troops, for the same reason that the old-timer from Charleston says "Fuck 'em" when I tell him about dead Iraqi children, for the same reason a soldier in formation must break ranks to dissent, and for the same reason that Mike and Tony and them couldn't answer their own question—*why the fuck don't these people stop?* They are all the same question, and they all have the same answer.

How well understood combat stress has been in any given time or place would be, I suspect, proportional to how resistant that society was to knowing about it. In WWI, combat stress was called "shell shock." The doctors of the army concluded that it was the manifestation of a flawed character. That's a story most have heard by now, and it passes us by like a patch of foul-smelling air. People wave it away and mutter, "They just didn't know any better back then." But there was at least one woman who knew. She wrote about the fragmented consciousness of a combat veteran with such clarity and understanding, one would hardly believe she wasn't a doctor or a veteran herself. But she was neither. Her name was Virginia Woolf. She was just a writer. That tells me, if nothing else, that the information was there. The capacity to know existed. It wasn't beyond human understanding. They weren't too primitive. If Virginia Woolf knew about combat stress, everybody else could have known, too. They didn't know because they didn't want to know.

Combat stress has broken out from the confines of ludicrous diagnoses. The world understands it a little better now. There are books. There are studies. There are good doctors working. Yet the suspicion lingers on. When I was in NROTC, a WWII vet was invited by our command to speak. He started right off by suggesting that combat stress was a sham or some newfangled ailment of a whiny generation. He bellowed, "In my day, we didn't have flashbacks; we just had bad dreams!" The room erupted in laughter. We liked his attitude. We were already absorbing the preference for war over our fellow human beings.

WWII was "the good" war. It was also an incredibly violent one. Millions of people died across the planet. That's not a good war. And yet few veterans talked about it. When they came home, everyone told them their war was necessary. It was just. It was noble. Everyone. So who were these veterans going to talk to about their "bad dreams," or their rage, or their sleepless nights? Who would want to spoil that image of the "good" war by describing all the terrible sights and sounds that went along with it? Who would want to be alienated or walk away from all that glory? No wonder none of them wanted to talk about it.

It is difficult, even now, even for our own military, to truly believe or acknowledge that combat stress, pervasive though it is, actually exists, or that it is a genuine injury and not merely the result of a dysfunctional brain. They are still calling it a "disorder". I think that goes a long way toward explaining their refusal to recognize combat stress as a legitimate wound meriting the Purple

Heart. When those at the highest level of the military do not acknowledge combat stress, then those at the lowest level, those suffering from it, and those outside the military have trouble doing any different. So it continues to be an enigma to all, and the unanswerable question remains: *How can we help?*

I say they can't help. They can't help as long as they carry the nagging assumption that it is the veteran's consciousness that has become deranged—not their own. I say they can stand in silence acknowledging the veteran and what he's done, but they'll never be able to help him until they acknowledge why he did it. It's not good enough to extend a sympathetic smile and a pat on the head. It's not good enough to give him a slice of pizza, or a shoulder to cry on, or a moment of silence. "Fuck silence!" That's what the veteran is saying. He's saying, "I want you to get to a place where you can believe, really believe, that the troops *are* more important to you than the mission, that the people in your world *are* more important to you than this fucking war and all that it provides you." That's what he's saying.

A truthful understanding of combat stress cannot exclude the questions of morality. For many veterans, these questions are at the very heart of their distress, and so they must be asked and discussed openly without any preconceived notions. But if a person seeking to help veterans, however good-intentioned, is attached to a government, an industry, a faith or a community that inherently privileges war over consequences, then that person can never fully question the morality of war in his or her own mind and therefore can never fully engage the trauma in the veteran's mind. To say to the traumatized veteran, with however much compassion, "You are broken. I will fix you," is to assume that his perspective is incorrect and not worthwhile, and it is to deny him the chance to release some of the guilt he may be harboring. Consequently, the guilt remains bottled up and festering.

The work that is done to support veterans and to understand their experiences is indeed significant, and it does help quite a lot. It has helped me. I have no doubt about that. And I am truly grateful. But I feel in so many instances that they just don't go the distance, or that they can't or they won't. They will get as touchy-feely as a man could ever stomach, but they won't get tough. They won't point their fingers at the most obvious issue and say, "War did this. Now why do we have war?" For most people the answer is too costly to find. There is simply too much to lose. And so they remain, by definition, partial to war. And that is why they can never truly and completely address the veteran's illness. As long as combat stress remains in the category of "tragic necessity," we will never be able to cure it.

EMPATHY

The residual doubt about the validity of combat stress comes almost exclusively from the fact that not every veteran deals with it, and that leads naturally to the question: Why not? What makes one man writhe in guilt, for example, while another man moves on scot-free? Whatever the distinction, clearly it resides in the brain. By eliminating the assumption that war is inevitable or necessary—even if only in theory—we can move past the concomitant assumption that the afflicted warrior is in some way malfunctioning. It frees the analysis from such default classifications as "disorder." Suddenly the veteran's distress can be viewed as the product of a good quality, not a bad one; and I think that would be valuable for wounded veterans to feel: that their distress is a good thing and natural. If a veteran were to be welcomed into a community that told him that, I suspect his transition home would be a whole lot smoother.

Having become keenly interested in the stories of other vets, I have listened to a lot of them. I've listened to WWII, Korean, and Vietnam vets. I've listened to Gulf War vets. I've listened to Iraq and Afghanistan vets, too. And in all the stories, from all those vets, I couldn't help but notice one conspicuous trait that ran faithfully through them all. It was empathy. Riddling their accounts were phrases like, "I think of that man's wife or his girlfriend"; "I think of his kids"; "He was young. He was like me"; "I think of his future" ;"I think of his pain"; "I think of his loss."

The terror in their stories was always, always seen through the eyes of the bloodied. And that is the good quality, the empathy, I think, that shows itself so vividly in every veteran who comes home from war, racked from his or her experiences in battle. I don't feel that my own empathy has ever been quite as pure as those other veterans I've heard speak. I was always mixed up in that craving for war. But there have certainly been times in my life, and even in this book, when the images I've latched on to, while not themselves exaggerated, have been portrayed with exaggerated sympathy. I know it's true, and I'm okay with that. I stretch my feelings in that direction as much as I can now, to compensate, I suppose, for having stretched the other way for so long.

It is these veterans' clear vision of humanity that must be embraced. That's the commodity most precious to society. Not everyone has to face war to gain that vision, but the veterans who have paid a high price for theirs. To dehumanize the enemy, to kill him, as is the business of the military, is to create a major conflict within the essence of such empathetic characters. Their profound sense of empathy in war is their undoing, and it is the very component of their selves that causes their stomachs to wring in the aftermath of the terrible things they saw and did. The more they empathize, the more they are undone.

This creates an especially equivocal situation for veterans of the Iraq War. Empathize is precisely what we attempt to do in a hearts-and-minds campaign (at least ostensibly), so those who do it most passionately are most affected when the time comes to kill. It seems to me that veterans of this brand must be encouraged not only to see the humanity of others with such clarity, but to see the humanity in themselves as well. They must see that empathy, see it as a good thing. Perhaps then their guilt can be expelled, and forgiveness achieved.

THE SIGNIFICANCE OF THE WAR STORY

I grew up listening to a lot of war stories, though I tended not to notice the contexts in which they were told. I didn't notice, for instance, the diverging tempers and attitudes that went with them. I also didn't notice that certain war stories could only be told among certain people, at certain places and times, or that some war stories could never be told at all. I didn't recognize the boundaries around me or even my own preferences. But I recognize them now.

I can see now all the barriers that exist between a veteran returning from war and the community that awaits him. When he gets home, he can tell them all his boot camp stories. He can tell them his liberty stories, and his sea stories, but he may be surprised to find that his war stories are, in so many circumstances, not welcome. And when I say war stories, I don't mean those humorous vignettes that people can chuckle about. I'm not talking about the good stories (I know there are those too); I'm talking about the ugly stories, the ones that lack heroes or happy endings, the ones that are tough to hear and talk about.

So delicate is the subject of war and so inflammatory, a veteran's account of what took place is often blocked wherever he turns. His stories are blocked at the dinner table to keep the conversation polite. They're blocked in the media, which in its headlong pursuit for strict neutrality winds up delivering the impression that war is a more innocuous place than the American cities whose violence they report ad nauseam. They're blocked by candidates who can't afford to offend a single voter. They're blocked at work, in school, in church, and at parades and memorials. Everywhere they're blocked because the stories are too unseemly, too divisive. So they're blocked.

Barriers can crop up in the most unexpected places. The families of those deployed, for instance, can become barriers, because it would be inappropriate to tell those unseemly stories in their presence. It would be inappropriate to tell those unseemly stories to the families of those getting ready to ship out, and those who have already come home, and those who have fallen and those who have been wounded. There is always someone close by who makes telling those unseemly stories inappropriate. There is always a barrier.

Simple things can become barriers, inanimate things. Bumper stickers, t-shirts, campaign slogans. Even a man's Medal of Honor can be a barrier. We can read his citation to find out what he did to earn that medal, but if the things that struck him about that day are not captured in the citation and if his story doesn't quite measure up to the enthusiasm of the people who place so much esteem in that medal, he may find himself reluctant to talk about it. He bears a great responsibility wearing that medal. He has expectations to live up to—his own, the military's, his family's, friends', and everyone else who wants to believe that war is glorious. So if his version of the story is not so glorious, he may start to feel that there is no one he can tell it to.

Ironically, not having a medal can be a barrier too. Because that myth of war is so powerful, a veteran can't help but ask himself, *Did I do enough? Did I see enough? Did I kill enough? Did I suffer enough to have the right to feel the pain I feel right now?* The pressure to measure up is tremendous and so often it can act as a barrier between a veteran's community and his stories. If a veteran says "War is hell" and it turns out he was a truck-driver or a welder, people may say to themselves, "Oh, well he was only a truck-driver or a welder. He didn't see any real action. What does he know of hell?" It's not an uncommon response. And so the veteran will close down and his stories will be lost.

Barriers are everywhere. I've seen them. I've felt them. I've been them myself. As much as denouncing war can create a barrier, justifying it can create one as well. When I was a commander sitting across a desk from those Marines who were tormented by their experiences and I said to them, "You did what you had to do. You did the right thing." I created a barrier. When they requested an appointment with the psychiatrist, when they asked me for help and I responded with skepticism, I made myself a barrier. As much as I cared about them, I refused to hear their pain. I refused their war stories. And that is a tragedy I think, because there is some real value to those stories beyond fulfilling the morbid curiosity of the people back home who have never seen combat.

For a veteran, sharing war stories is part of the process of reintegration into his community. His memories are often fragmented, incomplete, or blocked out. The emotions are not always coherent. They don't always make sense. Sometimes they're extreme, so the attitudes that go with them are extreme too. Pulling all those extremes into a story is how he can begin to organize all that he's seen and felt in war. By branding those stories inappropriate, pushing them away, or throwing up barriers, the community, loving though it might be, inadvertently flings a wrench into that process.

But war stories benefit more than just the veterans. I believe the community gains every bit as much by listening to war stories as the veteran does by telling them. It is their only opportunity to know what war actually is, and how the current war is proceeding, because, really, there is no other source. The media won't show it, and that always astonishes me. From literature and films, people get at least the sense that war, in general, is a violent endeavor, and yet when our own war is covered on the news, with our own loved ones fighting, not a drop of blood is ever shed, not a body ever bagged, or pulled off the plane beneath an American flag.

They offer only passing mention of the casualties and occasional photographs of men with their young faces and dress blues before they were shipped off to war and killed. Even when our own troops are victorious in battle, the torn bodies of those foreign people they killed are seldom shown or even remarked upon, despite the fact that their deaths were integral to our victory. The media will show the parades, but they will rarely acknowledge what those parades cost.

History books aren't much use either in depicting the realities of war, because they have no smells or sounds. They don't bleed, or cuss, or crave the kill, and that in itself is a barrier. They don't mention the souls behind the rifles; they don't show all the faces of war; and that is too bad, because that's where all the stories lie, in the faces—not on the surface, not on the skin, but in the creases, always in the creases, and the pockets, and the shadows.

War stories also have a moral value. They are the healing stones of our society. The ethical problem of war is no small issue and demands the attention of all people, yet so many find themselves ill-equipped or unable to enter the discussion because they have limited access to the true nature of battle. Instead, they remain informed mostly by diluted reports and romantic tales which fill the atmosphere with a false sense of purity.

War is a lot of things I suppose, but it is not pure. And if there are issues of morality to be contended with, I think that veterans' stories are very likely the key. They are our only source of unexpurgated truth, which makes them pretty valuable. Ignoring the trespasses against humanity won't heal any wounds. Forgetting the horrors or stuffing them down really doesn't clear the conscience; it just quietly contaminates the soul. I think the only way that our country can achieve any measure of reconciliation in the wake of wars (even the "just" wars), is to deal with those violent moments honestly and to embrace the notion that whether or not one believes the cause of war is good, the violence will always be bad for the soul. To do that, war stories must be available and heard—all the war stories, not just the glorious ones.

So for me, that's what the war story is all about. It's about pulling down those barriers, bringing out the faces, letting people see those creases, and understand the pain that often goes with them. It's about letting the healing, and the reconciling, and the reintegration occur. The stories will be infinite and diverse. They'll be ambiguous, and that's good. They should be ambiguous because the consciousness of a soldier on the battlefield is ambiguous too. When the war stories are all pulled together, they capture that ambiguity well. They capture the struggle. And that is good.

CASUALTY CALLS

When you want to leave the Corps, you don't get to just turn in your dog-tags and walk out the door. You've got to give notice. I gave the Marine Corps about six months. In return, they gave me a job where I could really think things over. During that time, I was the sole Casualty Assistance Calls Officer (CACO) for 2d Marine Regiment at Camp Lejeune, North Carolina. The regiment itself was in Iraq, and for every casualty they took, it was my job to the call the family back home and let them know. I made a lot of calls. They say war is hell. Whoever coined that phrase was probably never a CACO. That was hell. The thunder of incoming rockets and mortars was like sweet music to my ears compared to the ringing of my own phone.

I got calls night and day from the casualty section to let me know there was another man wounded, another report inbound, another notification to make. Then began the sweat, and the racing heart, the pacing, and the pleading, and the panic. I'd stare at the phone, sometimes for hours, literally, with a casualty report in my hand, trying to build up the nerve to do my job. They said it would get easier after a while. They were wrong.

I used to really struggle before those calls. I'd have to psyche myself up. I talked to myself because really there was no one else. Sometimes I'd shout at my wife for no reason at all if she came around while I was working up to a call. Then I'd shout at the mirror when she stopped coming around. Who, but my reflection, would stand for that? I'd stare numbly at the casualty report and say, "How can they ask me to do this again?" But the casualty report didn't know. It didn't care. It was just a piece of paper. It would stare numbly back as if to say, "They didn't ask." And when dread finally succumbed to that ever-buoyant sense of obligation, I would suck in a deep breath and make the call.

Sometimes, I would only have to say my name: *Captain Boudreau, United States Marine Corps*, and that would be enough. Sometimes, that's as far as it would go before I would hear the voice on the other end of the line breaking down into tears. I didn't have to say a word, but they knew what it was already. They knew what my name meant. It meant that something terrible had happened. And then I'd have to confirm their suspicions and tell them: Yes, something terrible has happened.

It was no easy task to tell mom and dad that their boy was coming home without his arm and his leg, or that his body was burned, or his flesh torn, or his spleen obliterated, or his lungs punctured, or his stomach ruptured, or his femur shattered. The war itself paled in comparison to that. It was no easy task to tell them that he was out there somewhere, somewhere in the world, but most of the time I didn't know where. I'd use my most official sounding voice, to keep things orderly in my head, and out of reach from those intractable emotions of mine.

One night I held the casualty report for a Marine who'd gone into surgery in the Combat Support Hospital (CSH) in Iraq to have both his legs amputated. The report was fourteen hours old. I didn't know his condition or his location. I didn't know if he'd made it through surgery, or if he was alive or dead. I didn't know if he was still in Iraq, or if they'd shipped him to Landstuhl, or if he was already on a plane for Bethesda. I didn't know if he was stable, or intubated, or unconscious. All I knew was that fourteen hours earlier he had been alone in Iraq on an operating table getting his legs cut off. And that is what I had to tell his mother.

She did not receive me well. She screamed, she cried, she cursed me and the Marine Corps. Then she hung up. Then she called me back at midnight looking for updates. But there were no updates. I asked for her patience, but patience was the one thing she was utterly unwilling to give. So she called me back at one, and two, and three in the morning. She was begging me for good news. But I didn't have any good news to give. I wasn't in the good news business. That was life as a CACO.

Not every wound was dire. Actually, most were only concussions and perforated eardrums and such. The wounds were mild, so the calls should have been easy—easy for me. But they were never easy for the people on the other end of the line, so every notification managed to be gut-wrenching, and not easy at all. No matter how slight the injury, there were always the desperate pleas for mercy, no matter how merciful fate had actually been. They would weep hysterically, and sometimes I would want to say: It's not that bad. But often they wouldn't believe me. They'd insist that I was wrong, or I was lying, or I was concealing the facts. Only the voice of their own son would be enough to convince them otherwise, which was not always available for me to provide.

Most common to all these calls were the never-ending questions, the assiduous search for every last little detail. "What was my boy doing when he got hit?" they would ask me. "What was he wearing? What was he carrying? What was he riding? Which seat was he sitting in? Who were his friends? What were their names? Where were they from? Where are his belongings? How do I speak to him? How do I see him?" Then the questions would shift from personal to political. "What was the mission? Why was he there?" It was sometimes difficult to answer, or to know. The casualty reports never mentioned those types of things. I would often try to use my own experience to fill in the blanks, but that proved challenging, too, because suddenly I would be cornered into admitting that there were times in Iraq when even I did not understand exactly what we were doing or why.

Of course, painful though they might have been, not making the notifications was never an option. The families had to know, and I had to call them. There was just no getting around that. So I required a lot of pep talks from myself. "Just tell her what you know," I would say to myself in a stern voice. "Give her the facts, listen to whatever she's got to say—whatever she's got to say—and hang up. It's that simple." I gave myself advice like this because there was no one else around to give it. If there'd been a boss, if there'd been a peer, if there'd been anyone at all in that building of mine, I know for sure that's just what they would have said to me. But the building was essentially deserted. And I was always alone. So I'd try to imagine what their response to my kvetching might be, and in their absence I would relay it to my reflection in the mirror.

It was the institution in me talking, the training, the indoctrination, the military mentality welded inside my brain-housing group. It was the voice of the whole officer corps ringing in my head, telling me just what to think, that strict adherence to procedure would make the job simple. "Simple!" What a line. What a word. *Simple*. The casualty report was simple, too. We called it a PCR, and it was short and sweet, and to the point—exactly how I was supposed to be on the phone. But it just never worked out that way.

I spent a lot of time teasing out the bright side for myself and for the recipients of my bad news. "Your son is going to be all right," I'd say to mom and dad. "He's tough. He's a survivor." In most cases, I hadn't even met the Marine. I told them what I did because I knew that's what they wanted to hear from me, and because I knew they'd believe what I said. They needed to find, take hold of, and really believe in any good thought about their boy. They had more need to believe than they ever had in their whole lives. That's what survival was going to demand of them. And so I would do my best to help them. I would say, "I know you worry about being strong for your son, but don't, because I promise you, he'll be strong for you, because legs or no legs, arms or no arms, that's what Marines do. They're strong in life for everybody else." These words were neither true nor false. They were unconnected to any specific personality. It was the myth of the Marine Corps that I offered, and I offered it hundreds of times.

What I found out years later was that, during the months when I was making all those casualty calls, there was an epidemic quietly spreading throughout the country, an epidemic of suicides among veterans. I mention these suicides often because the numbers really are shocking. They're devastating. And yet strangely, in all those casualty calls that I made to the families, among all those wounds that I reported, never once did I call up mom and dad and say, "Your boy is coming home with a broken heart."

Never once did I say that.

THE BEGINNING AND THE END

In Iraq, part of my job was to extrapolate stories from the bits of data that swirled around my head like fireflies. I would snap them up as quickly as I could and try to shed some light on what had truly occurred outside the walls of the COC. It was steady work for my imagination, and it drew my mind into places my body could not venture. So it became a habit, this mental exploration of the battlefield. I found myself always leaping into stories from a distance.

One early morning in Camp Fallujah, I stepped outside and gazed out across the open desert as the sun peeked over the horizon. All was quiet and still. From beyond a distant dune, I heard the faint popping sound of enemy mortars being fired onto our camp. I looked up into the sky as if I might see them in flight—sometimes you can—and then I looked over my shoulder as a series of louder wumps echoed from afar through the gentle air. I knew nothing of the aggressors or of the casualties they inflicted. I didn't need to know. But there I was, trying to know all the same. Every time I caught a glimpse of a riddled car, or rubbled building, or a bloodied uniform, I'd want to know what happened to the people inside them. Where had they been? Where had they gone?

The blood stains and the body bags summoned some very elaborate and very gloomy images within me. These images were drawn from spotty reports, or casual anecdotes, or low-resolution imagery, or sometimes from nothing at all. Whatever the source, it was never the whole story. My imagination filled in the blanks.

I was so frequently trapped in the COC that my mind did strive to make up for what I could not see with my own eyes. But I think there is some value to that, because so much of our war was impersonal, and so much of the death was meted out from a distance, beyond anyone's eyes. Those who seek to bring the carnage close through their minds make it personal again, and that is good. Indifference might just be the most pernicious ingredient of war.

My time in Iraq was just a slice of the war, very much like that passing mortar—I was present for neither the launch nor the impact. It lives in my memory less as a story than as a series of moments, a pandemonium of discrepant emotions. The conflagration is still ablaze. I've worked hard to sort out my thoughts on the war, but I know the search isn't over, and it may never be. I still get angry, sometimes for stupid things like falling salad-dressing bottles. I still cry over spilt milk. Sometimes I get angry because everyone else isn't as angry as I am. "Why the fuck aren't you angry?" I shout. "There are people dying here—a lot of them. This is worth being angry over." And it is, I think, but it's not worth the blind rage that has consumed so much of me over the years. The space I seek inside myself is somewhere in between. I understand that right now, at this particular moment, while the house is dark and the world is quiet, and while I'm at ease. But I don't always understand it. Life is going to return in a few hours and all the mayhem that goes with it, and when it does I'll probably stop understanding it again.

Sometimes, someone has to grab me by my collar and remind me. They have to remind me that it's not my wife's job to understand the war. It's not her job to understand what goes on inside my head or to keep the kids quiet and happy and the dog out of my way with a juicy bone. It's not her job to know when I want the lights on, or the lights off, or to touch me when I want to be touched, or to leave me alone when I want solitude, or to listen to me when I need listening to, or to talk to me when I need talking to, or to know from one moment to the next which time is which. That's not her job. She can be loving, and caring, and affectionate. She can, and she is, but it's not her responsibility to come up with a solution for me. That's my responsibility, because ultimately it's my struggle. I am packing *Inferno*. But slowly, slowly, day by day, year by year, I am unpacking it.

My Guide and I entered that hidden road
To make our way back up to the bright world.
We never thought of resting while we climbed.

We climbed, he first and I behind, until,
Through a small round opening ahead of us
I saw the lovely things the heavens hold,

And we came out to see once more the stars.

—Dante Alighieri

ACKNOWLEDGMENTS

I must thank, before all, my family—my wife Suzanne, and my sons John and Jake. They have done much more than endure my absence as a writer; in many instances they have endured my most onerous presence as a veteran. The process of documenting my thoughts on war has corresponded greatly with the process of coping with and overcoming them. It has been a long journey. Whatever progress I've made over the past few years, I owe most significantly to my family—my litter bearers I call them—who carry me along through life. Without their gracious support (support I did not always graciously allow), this book would never have been possible.

The writing of *Packing Inferno* dragged on for over four years. Many drafts and iterations of it were conceived and discussed among friends, and written out, and then subsequently scrapped. There were many times when I lost sight of my objective, lost hope, and just turned off my computer and gave up. But then there were also many times that I regained my vision and made a fresh start. I imagine it's the same for all writers, though not all writers must contend simultaneously with their memories from war and the frequently turbulent emotions that accompany them. I would attribute my perseverance at least in part to my realization that the process itself was useful to me. The deeper I contemplated war, the more I understood my own relationship to it. And that went a long way to ease my distress.

The greater part of my perseverance is owed without question to all the people around me who consistently offered their support and attention. All my ranting about war would have been far less productive had they not been there to listen. I should point out that not every last one of them agreed with all that I had to say. But they put their opinions aside to help me and for that they deserve a great deal of thanks. The people who did agree with me deserve thanks too. Many of them contributed their time and advice generously (and sometimes mercilessly), to help me produce the best book that I am capable of.

Because the processes of my writing and of my coming home from war have been so inextricably bound together, I really do consider any support given for one to be inherently support for the other as well. So the people, for which I have to express my appreciation, were not all involved in the actual transcription of my experiences; many of them were simply by my side, sharing a few beers, talking to me, and more importantly listening to me talk to them. Most of these people probably have no idea how precious those moments were to me or how effectively they helped me to understand my own consciousness. I include them here now to make sure they do know.

For all their generosity, wisdom, and assistance, my gratitude goes to: Norma Akamatsu, Michael Albert, Michael Boorstein, Dan Burland, James Carroll, Frances Crowe, Barbara Day and the rest of the Day family, Rick Doblin, Yoav Elinevsky, Barbara Goldin, Ira Helfand, Tom Kovar, Ian Lamont, Stephanie Levin, Blair Maerowitz, Rosie McMahan, Bob Meagher, Matthew Mitchell, Michael and Annie Mithoefer, Chris Moffatt and his family, Marty Nathan, Stephen O'Brien and his family, Ilario Pantano and his family, Scott Ritter, Joel Thomas-Adams, Lisa Tripp, Jonathan Shay, Andrew Wimmer, David Wood, and the entire Boudreau family. This list is not all-inclusive; so I apologize to those who I have neglected to mention by name. I thank you all.

In particular, I would like to acknowledge all the members of the Veterans Education Project (VEP), who have been so kind and helpful in drawing out my stories. It was their compassion and encouragement that kept me writing and thinking about my experiences in war rather than burying them away. Among the superb group at VEP, special thanks must go to Rob Wilson and Susan Leary, and the Vietnam veterans Al Miller, Gordon Fletcher-Howell, Don Chevannes, George Williams, Bob Schmid, and Jim Munroe, who have really offered me tremendous personal support. I am deeply grateful to them all.

The material in this book and the issues with which I contend can be, at moments, extremely sensitive and often controversial to the extent that is has become, in so many circles, taboo to even mention them, much less publish a book about them. Where so many people have been inclined to resist the conversation completely, Adam Parfrey and Feral House never hesitated for a moment. For their steadfast confidence in me and my writing I owe them great thanks.

Finally, I must acknowledge the U.S. Marine Corps, without which, of course, there would be no book. For better or worse, the man I am today is in no small part owed to them, and I do think there is a great deal that is better. I grew up in the Corps. I loved the Corps. Certainly there is much about the Corps I've grown not to love so much, but it is, nonetheless, a central component of my identity. To the Marines I served with, I am grateful and honored. I entered war of my own accord—I was not forced—and it was they who brought me through alive and without a scratch. For that alone, I am indebted to them.